P. 52

W9-AMX-052

WITHDRAWN

FIRE AND ICE

FIRE AND ICE

THE ART AND THOUGHT OF ROBERT FROST

BY LAWRANCE THOMPSON

Some say the world will end with fire
Some say in ice.
From what I've tasted of desire
I hold with those who favor fire.
But if it had to perish twice,
I think I know enough of hate
To say that for destruction ice
Is also great
And would suffice.

NEW YORK / RUSSELL & RUSSELL

SALEM COLLEGE LIBRARY
WINSTON-SALEM, N. C.

PS
3511
R94
Z93
1961
c.2

COPYRIGHT, 1942, BY HENRY HOLT AND COMPANY

REISSUED, 1961, BY RUSSELL & RUSSELL

A DIVISION OF ATHENEUM PUBLISHERS, INC.

BY ARRANGEMENT WITH LAWRANCE THOMPSON

L. C. CATALOG CARD NO: 61-15326

PRINTED IN THE UNITED STATES OF AMERICA

To Jeannette and Wilbert Snow

89407

TABLE OF CONTENTS

CONTENTS

TO THE READER

Robert Frost has always looked on the writing of poetry as a pleasurable game. He delights to play with words until they take nicely varied patterns of sound and shape and thought. Always caring most for the performance, he has managed to reconcile the old rules of poetry with his new idiom. Like a versatile athlete who can do his best with a minimum of wasted effort, he moves gracefully through form to his intended goals. And the success of his seemingly casual accomplishment may be judged in part by the widespread response of those who have shared his pleasure in poetic action.

Poetry which offers genuine delight even to the accidental reader can make its way successfully without revealing all the secrets of its subtle grace and meaning. Such is the test of any good poem. But Robert Frost's achievement deserves more than indifferent perusal. The closer examination, in the following essays, has grown out of frequent returns to his poetry over a period of many years. The purpose and method, here, is to suggest and analyze some of those less obvious levels by considering separate aspects of his performance.

With no illusions as to the regrettable limitations of my own critical experience, I was led to the writing of this book because I was disappointed in the attempts of others to examine the poetry of Robert Frost. Excellent indeed are many separate reviews which have appeared in various periodicals since the publication of *A Boy's Will* and *North of Boston*. Nevertheless, those restricted evaluations have been general, and inevitably superficial. I believe that *Fire and Ice* is the first published attempt to offer a detailed consideration of those various aims and accomplishments which find integrated expression within the poetry of Robert Frost. My own specific approach might be described as a leisurely stroll among the poems, in order to discover numerous distinct perspectives for particular scrutiny. The careful progression of my method, within a threefold arrangement, may not become apparent to the reader, at first glance. In fair warning, I may say that my iterations are deliberate. Certain chapters included under the section on theory have their complementary chapters within the section on poetic practice. For example, my consideration of Robert Frost's theory concerning "The Function of Metaphor" is designed to prepare the reader for a better appreciation of the poet's practice, as it is analyzed in "The Metaphor in Action." Again, "The Yankee Manner" finds specific elaboration in the four related chapters which begin with "The Sense of Humor."

I can wish for the reader no greater excitement than that which I have derived from the surprise of recognition and discovery. Poems which seemed at first glance so very lucid and direct have often proved to possess facets and surfaces which catch the light in its purity and break it into myriad gradations of color. Beneath the intricate structure of Robert Frost's poems may be found not only wide technical range of intent and extent but also a spiritual depth of sight and insight.

Perhaps Frost's sly manner of playing hide-and-seek with metaphorical mischief places on him some blame for the limited appreciation given by so many of us for so many years. Allow him his reticence, for he will not come out boldly to gratify the near-sighted. Grant him also his patience, for he believes he has shown himself well enough to be understood by the discerning. Only such a faith could have kept him from explanations and defenses.

Occasionally, in offhand and oblique prefaces to other people's books or in remarks during his public readings, he has offered hints as to his own rules of the game, his own theory of poetry. I have tried to combine these with his poems to suggest the background of his writing. I have also related his own rules to those laid down independently by others, from the Greeks and Romans to the English and American poets past and present. Unlike so many contemporary poets who seem to pride themselves on parading their scholarly erudition in verse and prose, Frost has quite thoroughly assimilated his own knowledge garnered in wide traveling through literature. Such deliberate and thorough assimilation is one sign of his dominant interest in performance as contrasted with theory.

Many critics have warned us that all theories are merely arguments after the fact, attempts to justify what has happened. First the poet, then the poetry, and finally the poetic theory. I have no quarrel with that. After all is said by creator or critic, the poetry survives only if it manages to establish a successful blend of many diverse components. A good poem has never been hurt, a bad poem has never been helped, by that which has been said of it before or after publication. Nevertheless, many a good poem has been permitted to pass current at less than face value because it has suffered from the shortcomings of the reader. We frequently fail to bring to a poem the awareness required for accurate recognition. If, then, poet or critic is able to awaken in the reader a more penetrating method of understanding and appreciation, such a service may help the reader to evaluate poetry in terms of that worth genuinely created by the poet. If my essays increase the reader's pleasure in recognizing the depth and range of Robert Frost's thought and art, I am satisfied.

LAWRANCE THOMPSON

Princeton University
April 3, 1942

POETRY IN THEORY

More than once I should have lost my soul to radicalism if it had been the originality it was mistaken for by its young converts.[1]

A BACKGROUND
OF POETIC THEORIES

LIKE a splendid river, the stream of English and American poetry has absorbed innumerable and varied tributaries during many hundreds of years. The larger tributaries, possessing distinct characteristics and forces, have often modified the direction, and have always enriched the quality, of the main stream; the smaller ones have been assimilated without effort or effect. As a tributary expressing a force and idiom of its own, the poetry of Robert Frost has enriched the main stream without trying to modify the direction, because his poetry has been content with the old ways to be new. Yet his poetry may eventually prove to have been the most important American tributary during the first half of the twentieth century. By contrast, much of the so-called experimental poetry has poured against the main current in nervous cataracts and waterfalls which, had they been as strong as they were noisy, would have broken the banks and redirected the course of the main stream. That course certainly will be modified again, as in the past. We have become increasingly aware, however, that most of the violent experimentalists succeeded merely in stirring up muddy waters which briefly obscured the serenity of an ever-varying and ever-fresh tradition.

In poetic theory, much of the past is always offensive to the future, and this is by no means deplorable. Each generation finds its own forms of expression, its new poetry, and time makes its choices of the best. Whenever the established forms have hardened into conventions and dogmas, fresh intuitions have discovered ways of inducing a renewal of vitality and meaning. These

---

[1] Reference for this and subsequent notes will be found following the last chapter.

changes have naturally called forth defenses of the new and protests against the old. No better guide to the varying course of the main stream of poetry may be found at first hand than carefully selected utterances of poets and critics who have defined the differences.

Here as elsewhere we need to be reminded that we are in the midst of a process; that beginning and end are out of sight. The common reader, who finds himself floundering in a welter of modern definitions, theories, opinions, and prejudices concerning the poetry of today, may be inclined to forgive me if I begin my consideration of Robert Frost's accomplishment by presenting a background sketch of certain arbitrarily restricted viewpoints and problems which have concerned poets and critics past and present. Such a reader, being the one for whom this book is written, may indulge my desire for extreme simplification, even if it is at odds with the current critical jargon of highly specialized and technical terminology.

Roughly, there are two general considerations examined anew in scores of defenses and protests: first, the source of poetic inspiration and, second, the nature of the poet's intent or means of gaining that intent through his artistry. After innumerable attempts to resolve the first consideration and to explain poetic inspiration in generalized terms, we have found no simple explanation for, or key to, the creative impulse, the "divine madness," the "fine frenzy." More profitable satisfaction has come from considerations of the poet's conscious intent, and the means of achieving that intent. This second consideration is our immediate concern, generally, in this essay, and specifically as it relates to Robert Frost in the chapter which follows.

Again by arbitrary simplification, it may be said that conflicting opinions concerning the purpose, or the desired and fitting effect, of the poet may be resolved into three opposed theories. At one extreme, defenders maintain that the dominant aim of poetry is to delight. At the other extreme, the opponents claim that the dominant aim of poetry is to instruct. Between these two extremes, another group asserts that the aim of poetry is both to instruct and to delight. This basic conflict, forcing critical factions to take sides today, was also apparent to the Greeks and Latins. When Plato described the beginnings of poetry at the solemn feasts called Panegyrica, he emphasized the virtuous intent of the gifted singers whose verses were calculated to instruct and to delight. Plato was reiterating the traditional Greek belief that poetry had primarily a direct moral purpose when he grudgingly admitted poetry to his ideal commonwealth only in so far as it might serve as handmaiden to moral and political education. On the other hand, Aristotle abandoned the didactic point of view by considering first, in his *Poetics*, the different forms of poetry, their origin, their growth, the apparent laws of their structure, and their effect on the emotions and thoughts of an audience. Thus Aristotle, indirectly protesting against Plato's viewpoint, was the first to isolate aesthetic standards from moral standards. To him, the first aim of poetry was a refined pleasure. But his analysis led him to ethical and moral considerations. Obviously, he did not wish to liberate himself completely from his heritage of Greek thought on the purpose of poetry.

English poets such as Sidney and Dryden, seeking aid from the Greeks and Latins on matters of poetic theory, did not always reflect any consciousness of difference between Plato and Aristotle on this point. When Sidney reiterated that the aim of poetry was "delightful teaching," he echoed the Greek and Roman viewpoint. In apparent opposition, Dryden wrote: "I am satisfied if it [poetry] cause delight; for delight is the chief if not the only end of poesy: instruction can be admitted but in the second place, for poesy only instructs as it delights." Dryden's claim is not so much a cleavage as a gradation, for he acknowledged elsewhere that he believed the aim of poetry in general was "to instruct and to delight." These two brief samplings indicate the deliberate tendency of English poets to favor a reconciliation between the two extremes of delight and instruction, in poetic theory and in practice.

If we turn to American poetry, the opposed theories of Emerson and Poe may be taken as starting points for a general understanding of problems much debated among contemporary critics. Sharing tenets firmly rooted in idealism, they arrived at diametrically extreme conclusions. Poe insisted that the end of art is pleasure, not truth; that in order to effect intensity of pleasure, the work of art must have unity and brevity; that in poetry the fitting means of arousing pleasure is the rhythmical creation of beauty. His slight acquaintance with Platonic doctrine led him to insist that, since ideal beauty exists only in a realm beyond the immediate perception of man, the poet is obliged to create moods which are somehow reflections of heavenly beauty. Effect, and contrivance for effect, dominated Poe's theory of means to the end of pleasure. To him, sadness over the death of a beautiful woman seemed the highest possible subject matter for achieving that effect which afforded a profound sense of the beautiful, tinged with melancholy. And he took the trouble to show how perfectly "The Raven" had been constructed by a calculated and artificial cunning to produce a preconceived effect.

Emerson seemed to share Poe's major premise when he began by defining art as the creation of beauty by man. Using things as symbols, he continued, the artist combines them in new forms to express his intuition of eternal beauty. Then Emerson parted company with Poe by asserting that all great art is organic in a double sense. First, from the organism, or the intuition, proceeds the appropriate form which expresses it. Second, the intuition, or the thought expressed, proceeds from a reality beyond the author's understanding. Thus, when the artist aims to express ideal beauty, he merely permits it to express itself through him. To Emerson, ideal beauty is ideal truth and goodness, these three being inseparable. And through poetry man is assisted to realize his complete potentialities. Thus Emerson, in his relating of the Platonic concepts of goodness, truth and beauty, considered poetry an instrument for instruction as well as for delight. At times he seemed to go so far as to indicate that poetry is a means to an end rather than an end in itself, and his inconsistencies on this point are troublesome.

These brief summaries may be sufficient to indicate that Poe's theory is essentially art-for-pleasure's sake, while Emerson's theory is ultimately art-for-wisdom's sake. In so far as Poe finds poetry an end in itself, his position is the more defensible. But Emerson's theory that art is organic seems far superior to Poe's insistence on achieving an effect through merely calculated contrivance. Neither of these quite describes what we find in great art, which reconciles the organic and the artificial. Emerson's position is given corroboration by such tendencies as the functional design of modern architecture, which requires that there be a fitness of means to end. In quoting Michelangelo's definition of art as "the purgation of superfluities," Emerson holds that not a particle may be spared in artistic structure—and this sounds extremely modern. There is yet another side of Emerson's theory which satisfies me. He criticizes that aspect of romanticism which is forever yearning for the unattainable, the not-here and the not-now. Poe, like Shelley, reiterates his desire to make poetry express aspirations akin to the desire of the moth for the star. But Emerson, in commenting on Greek drama, observed that the Greeks "found the genius of tragedy in the conflict between Destiny and the strong *should*, and not like the moderns, in the weak *would*." In this respect, Emerson reiterates his concern for that kind of moral necessity which Aristotle emphasized in the conclusion of the *Poetics*. Poe seems to find a closer kinship with the wishful thinking of Neo-Platonic romanticism.

The opposed positions of Emerson and Poe did not result in any immediate taking of sides. Their contemporaries such as Longfellow, Lowell, Holmes and Whittier had not shown the same concern for defining their independent positions; to the contrary, they had patterned their verses largely after the established forms popular in English poetry during the late eighteenth century and the early nineteenth. Many poets who came after them were so imitative that they failed to make any important impression on the main stream of poetry. Exceptions such as Walt Whitman and Emily Dickinson asserted their individuality as nonconformists whose poetic abilities were strong enough to exert fresh influence on many who followed them—and their alignment was plainly on the side of Emerson, not of Poe. Furthermore, they succeeded better than Emerson in practicing his principles of organic structure in poetry. Each of them fulfilled Emerson's dicta that all men live by truth and stand in need of expression; that the experience of each new age requires a new confession so that the world seems always waiting for its poet.

The faded conventionalism and vague repetitiousness of so much imitative verse which filled out the end of the nineteenth century in America brought occasional protests in the Emersonian tradition. Lizette Woodworth Reese's lines "To a Town Poet," corroborating the best advice of Emerson and Whitman, called for the expression of

> Faith in the time, faith in our common blood,
> Faith in the least of good;
> Song cannot fail if these its spirit fill!
>
> .   .   .   .
>
> Let trick of words be past;
> Strict with the thought, unfearful of the form,
> So shall you find the way and hold it fast,
> The world hear, at the last,
> The horns of morning sound above the storm.

And in 1896, Edwin Arlington Robinson called more impatiently for a poet,

> . . . for a beacon bright
> To rift this changeless glimmer of dead gray,
> To put these little sonnet men to flight
> Who fashion in a shrewd mechanic way
> Songs without souls, that flicker for a day,
> To vanish in irrevocable night.

Twenty years after these isolated protests, poets and critics organized themselves as crusaders who, finding poetry out of joint, were not timid about setting it right through violent correctives and new panaceas. They seemed to forget that a sufficiently intense inner necessity for self-expression had always enabled competent poets to shoulder their ways out of hard shells and dead conventions. In their stormy reaction against what they considered to be the inherited iniquities of threadbare formulas, many of these crusaders held up as their great liberator and guide that intrepid individualist, Walt Whitman. This was in some ways a strange choice. Whitman's virtues as an experimental poet should not have blinded his admirers to his weaknesses and shortcomings as the archromantic of nineteenth century America. Only a new brood of romantics could ever have rallied around Walt as a prophet of that new idealism which came into vogue among the new revolutionaries in poetry and criticism. With kaleidoscopic speed, the more active experimentalists arranged themselves into different and wonderful patterns before they settled down to be themselves.

There were lessons to be learned from a consideration of the old ways in which poetry had managed to keep its vitality, but the past was pretty much a bucket of ashes. While Sandburg preached and practiced a banjo version of Whitman's majestic free verse, Lindsay sauntered over the country singing lyrics which were sufficient evidence that "the rhythmical creation of beauty" was not enough. In more vehement self-assertiveness, the cult of Imagism, making strange bedfellows of Ezra Pound, Amy Lowell, Hilda Doolittle, John Gould Fletcher and others, tried to correct the corruption of poetic diction by giving more importance to jewel-hard words than to ideas. A flurry of manifestoes and protests, defenses and explanations, began to appear rapidly as introductions to those new books of poetry or as articles to those new magazines of poetry which crowded hard on each other's heels soon after the militant beginning of 1912. We were told that a new day had dawned for poetry, that the feudalism of the past had been wiped away.

Unfortunately, the potentialities of the new programs were not so great as their limitations. Younger poets came along to formulate younger theories; reactions overwhelmed the reactionaries. And the internecine battle is still being waged in desultory fashion, although the initial furor subsided long ago.

When the first smoke of battle began to lift, it appeared that the opposed theories of Poe and Emerson had suffered intricate elaboration and deliberate modification without changing the basic tenets of art-for-pleasure's sake and art-for-wisdom's sake. These two positions are still being defended by opposed groups today, and may be discovered in critical and poetic theory, much obscured by erudite logic-chopping. Certain aspects of the Emersonian position proved to be closely akin to the poetic theory and practice of Robert Frost. But Emerson's aesthetic utterances were elucidated and modified into a somewhat extreme aesthetic by the "new humanists," whose dogmatic claims were much too rigid to attract Frost. Poe's theory, greatly modified, found new representation in those divided cliques of poet-critics who quarreled in the wake of leaders so different as T. S. Eliot and Ezra Pound. For our purpose, however, it is important to examine the twentieth century modifications of the opposed theories.

In aesthetics, the new humanists reasserted a belief that beauty could be considered with reference to quantity and quality; that in matter of quantity, or degree, there should be an adequate artistic sense of conscious selection, design, form, by means of which any art or human form-giving is differentiated from the turbid flux of nature. Thus, according to their creed, the major concern of the artist is to translate subjective impressions and perceptions into objectively formulated statement. They further differentiated between degrees of beauty and kinds of beauty. Like Emerson, they evaluated the kind of beauty in a given work of art by asking what truth or goodness is implicit in the beauty, which may help to determine its relative worth. Perfection of form is only one aspect of a work of art; the relative value of goodness and beauty in its content is another aspect which must be considered in the total evaluation. What is it that has this perfection we talk about, and how does it compare with other works of art which likewise have it? Again, in considering the possible kinds of matter which the artist may select (sense impressions, natural feelings, emotions, reason, ethical imagination), the new humanists placed highest value on reason and ethical insight. To positions of secondary importance they subordinated natural impressions and emotions. In this way they proposed to establish a balance and reconciliation between *being* and *meaning* as component elements in a poem. During this very sensible procedure, however, the defendants too frequently seemed to rest a not altogether casual hand on the meaning side of the scales, and thus they often vitiated their intended impartiality. This error, indeed, was one major point of criticism leveled against the aesthetic theories of the new humanists by their opponents.

[10]

But the opponents were by no means content with mere fault-finding. They had their own creeds and principles, largely formulated after theories which the French Symbolists had laid down in the last half of the nineteenth century. The way had been prepared for the Symbolists by Baudelaire, who called particular attention to the poetry and critical writings of Edgar Allan Poe because it seemed that Poe offered rational correctives for the looseness and extravagance of romantic poetry. Mallarmé assisted the movement by urging the need for a strict overhauling of the language of poetry to gain purer meaning for ordinary words. This, he proposed, was another means of controlling, through intellectual and rational discipline, the subjective, impressionistic, sensuous and emotional perceptions of the poet. In the process of correcting the artificial trappings of poetry, the Symbolists felt that the most exact arrangement of words was the natural phrase into which a cadenced poem fell when spoken; that the classical Alexandrine was a tyrant from which French verse needed to be set free. Hence the Symbolists made a fetish of their *vers libre* because it seemed an added gain to the achievement of individuality and precision in poetry. From this tenet came the obvious admission that there was no hard and fast dividing line between poetry and prose; that the intensity of perception and the discovery of accurate expression must establish the difference. Each poet should be permitted to choose symbols which seemed best to represent his own unique and complicated personal and subjective experience. Poe, for example, had indicated one particular kind of symbolism derived from a transference between the perceptions of the different senses. He spoke of feeling the heaviness of night and of hearing a melodious sound issuing from the flame of a lamp. This recording of interrelated sensations led the Symbolists to develop their own usages, which were novel variants of the mixed metaphor.

This French cult of individualism and liberation naturally permitted each poet to make up his own rules, his own aesthetic, as he went along. Ostensibly a protest against romanticism, it proved to be merely another aspect of romanticism in danger of becoming so much a private concern of the poet that he might lose a com-

SALEM COLLEGE LIBRARY
WINSTON-SALEM, N. C.

mon ground of communication with the reader. A complicated association of ideas, expressed in an illogical patchwork of seemingly unrelated metaphors and symbols, might satisfy the poet as a record of his unique personal perceptions, but might need elaborate footnotes to become intelligible to the uninitiated. Nevertheless, such an effect satisfied the Symbolists because they believed that to be good a poem must be difficult.

When T. S. Eliot turned to the Symbolists for guidance and inspiration, he drew most heavily from the critical utterances of Remy de Gourmont and the poetic accomplishments of Corbière and Laforgue. But Eliot also inherited from Poe, indirectly through Remy de Gourmont and Paul Valéry, the creed that a work of art is an object constructed deliberately to produce a certain effect; that since the effect is the only important goal, the work of art can have no relation to any practical human uses which may be achieved through the instruction of prose. In *Axel's Castle*, Edmund Wilson points out that one cannot possibly isolate aesthetic values from all other values as the early Eliot wished to do; that such theories lead ultimately "into pedantry and into a futile aestheticism."

Unfortunately, Eliot has had strong influence on younger poets who have come after him. And Poe, exported first to France and thence to England, has come into his own among many American poets who are reasserting the doctrine of art-for-art's sake and are denouncing the opposed creed of art-for-wisdom's sake. Wallace Stevens, for instance, has maintained with much consistency that poetry has nothing to do with practical or moral ideas. And at one point in his various career the self-styled "irresponsible" MacLeish concluded one of his verses with this line: "A poem should not mean but be." How strangely inconsistent of Mr. MacLeish to put such a bald statement of his *meaning* into the *being* of a poem!

On this subject of meaning or content as opposed to being or structure, these two arbitrarily divided schools quarreled openly and sharply with each other. It is necessary to digress briefly if we are to understand this important aspect of their differences. We may easily find plenty of meaning in the poems of those moderns who have owed something to the French Symbolists, directly or indirectly. And the dominant tone of that meaning is frustration and disillusionment. Outside their poems, many of these writers have explained themselves. Hating the false optimism of Wordsworth and of Emerson, who described nature as benevolent and man as potentially divine, the reactionaries adopted a pessimism equally false: nature was a tyrant and man the slave to animal instinct or to brutal circumstance.

This new fad of meaning, related to the "scientific" doctrines of Zola, seemed to be a part of that revolt against the false idealism expressed in the Platonic dilutions of the romantics. How could man be expected to control his own destiny when he was dominated by animal instincts and desires or by the accumulated and organized products of these forces as they expressed themselves in a hostile social and economic environment? The transcendentalists and intuitive idealists like Emerson had challenged the religious dogma of the Calvinists by considering man potentially divine; the "naturalists" challenged religious dogma by considering man essentially animal. Supporting the latter group came the Freudians with their doctrine that the first motivation for all action was a primitive sexual urge or animal desire which could be blamed for almost all human shortcomings. Thus the world seemed too sad and life too uncontrollable for anything but the wistfulness of hope and the stoicism of despair. Such pretenses and aspirations as existed in mankind offered splendid subject matter for ironic portrayal—and this ironic portrayal became the favorite theme of meaning (willy-nilly) which colored much of the post-Symbolist poetry.

Obviously, the optimistic interpretation of life in terms of man's godliness is no more faulty than the pessimistic concept of man's bestiality. It would seem apparent that what we have in mankind is an inextricable mixture of godliness and devilishness; forces constructive and destructive, loving and hating. This middle position, recognizing the apparent dualism in man's nature, was adopted by the new humanists, who built upon it their own interpretations. To them, it seemed that absolute skepticism was as impossible as absolute idealism; that man can live by the practical expedient of accepting the relativity of things as more healthy than the disease of negation; that certain working standards may be derived from the history of human experience; that within certain limits man has freedom of the will to conform to these values which have, roughly, zones. So long as these beliefs may be considered without any dogmatic definition of boundaries, Robert Frost has found himself in agreement. At least, his cautious agreement has shown itself through his impatience with the opposed beliefs.

Much of contemporary poetry and criticism has attempted to reconcile these opposed positions, particularly as they have influenced poetic theory. The tendency seems to aim toward the reconciliation of being and meaning in poetry. T. S. Eliot's essays in criticism, frequently quite at odds with his own poetry, brought precision and freshness to the established forms of historical criticism. His emphasis on technical and aesthetic considerations was specifically intended to be not only a corrective for the biographical and deterministic approaches of Taine and Sainte-Beuve but also a militant protest against the ethical and moral bias of much new humanist criticism. Nevertheless, his plea for dialectic discipline which might help to establish the terminology and analytical methods of literary study was more closely related to the aesthetic (however faulty) of the new humanists than to the aesthetic of the Symbolists.

Humanistic criticism needed the corrections urged and practiced by Eliot and his followers. But the need for standards in literary criticism, urged by both sides in the controversy, became even more apparent as the experimentalists continued to carry their individualism into realms of aesthetic anarchy. Unfortunately the proposed methods of arriving at those standards seemed to be involved and futile, as different camps of critics fell into habits of contradiction, raillery, and name-calling.

The appeal for correctives brought many different answers. For example, I. A. Richards and C. K. Ogden quite glibly proposed, in *The Meaning of Meaning*, to clarify the critical atmosphere in very scientific fashion by exploring the fundamental nature of speech. This contribution helped and hindered by attracting an interested but highly grudging set of followers too deeply concerned with that restricted aspect of poetry: semantics. And the atmosphere was further complicated by Richards's fondness for a critical terminology employed by psychoanalysts. In the consequent preoccupation with the nature of correspondence between word and fact, the search for new precision in critical definition and analysis led many new critics to evolve their own obtuse terminology. And the reader who tries to find help by exploring the criticism of this school is often more thoroughly baffled by the new criticism than by the new poetry.

As leaders in the new criticism, two poets, John Crowe Ransom and Allen Tate, turned critics to accentuate their reactionary position against the humanists by insisting primarily on poetic analysis in so far as it involves form and technique. In his recent book of essays entitled *Reason in Madness,* Mr. Tate (with whom Mr. Ransom finds himself in general agreement) makes his position clear by reiterating that "poetry solves no problem but its own." Again, he says, "There is probably nothing wrong with 'Art for Art's sake,' if we take the phrase seriously, and not take it to mean the kind of poetry written in England forty years ago." In his poetry, however, Mr. Tate sometimes makes the reader more conscious of his thoughts than of his artistry. In reading his poetry, one is inclined to believe that he, like Poe, finds this world almost unbearably hopeless, and yearns backward and forward out of it all. He asserts that confusion is everywhere, even in criticism, and urges the search for a "moral unity as the highest good that men can seek." Curiously, such an assertion takes Mr. Tate from the subjective individualism of the post-Symbolists (with whom he has some apparent sympathies) swiftly through the middle-ground position of the humanists (for whom he has little use) and on into the camp of the absolutists whose idealism is based on unity. One of Mr. Tate's reviewers pointed out that in such a totalitarian Utopia, moral unity is attained by liquidating the dissenters so that all activities may be geared to the one central idea in art—as well as in science, government, and economics. The reviewer concluded: "Mr. Tate may be right: mankind has always craved such a unity. Let a few of us, in protest, nail to the mast of our sinking craft the banner, 'Moral disunity is desirable, because it is the condition and the result of freedom.'" And Robert Frost would prefer to be numbered among the few who sail on in that not too decrepit craft.

An attempt to reconcile the opposed positions has been made by another poet, Yvor Winters, in his *Primitivism and Decadence: A Study of American Experimental Poetry*. It is enlightening to notice that he acknowledges his indebtedness not only to Allen Tate but also to the late leader of the new humanists, Irving Babbitt. In taking to task the experimentalists, Winters points out that the confusion and inadequateness of much modern poetry arises from its willful attempt to stumble along without subject matter. But he goes much further than this by reasserting the traditional convictions of major poets since Sidney: that poetry should enrich one's awareness of human experience, increase the intelligence, and strengthen the moral temper already sensitized by ethical thinking and feeling. Winters, whose technical sympathies and practices in poetry are strongly attached to free verse, could never be called a conservative or a traditionalist in either his poetic practice or his prose criticism. Yet his critical viewpoint includes an appreciation of certain general principles and standards which may be deduced from a study of successful experiment and growth in any period of English and American poetry.

Modern poetry, then, may be seen to be no frightening hodgepodge of confusion and chaos. In principle, it is closely related to the same problems which have always concerned poets and serious readers of poetry. The impatience with the past and the search for correctives have led our contemporaries into numerous bypaths of experimentation—and eventually we shall be better able to discover which bypaths did not come out to dead ends. Or to return again, these many radical and distinct fountainheads of originality have sent streams of poetry onward to the splendid river. Which of these separate streams have sufficient merit to add body and quality to the great tradition, anyone is permitted to guess. I happen to believe that the poetry of Robert Frost has that idiom of originality, that richness of quality, that significance of shape and weight which will be considered worthy and permanent addition in the years to come. In poetic theory his relation to his contemporaries is sufficiently distinct to invalidate neat classification. It is given separate treatment in the chapter which follows.

A poem begins with a lump in the throat; a home-sickness or a love-sickness. It is a reaching-out toward expression; an effort to find fulfilment. A complete poem is one where an emotion has found its thought and the thought has found the words. . . . My definition of poetry (if I were forced to give one) would be this: words that have become deeds.[2]

ROBERT FROST'S
THEORY OF POETRY

I<small>N</small> a literary age made nervous by the tugging conflicts of factions, Robert Frost has been able to win the admiration and respect of opposed individuals even while he has stoutly refused to take sides in the controversies. Almost miraculously he has moved about in the conflagration unscathed—like one of those figures in the fiery furnace. A glance at his sojourn among poets will reveal the paradox of his friendships. Before the turn of the century his early verse was praised by Richard Hovey; before the first World War, he had earned and returned the warm affections of such English poets as Edward Thomas, W. W. Gibson, and Lascelles Abercrombie. In 1913 that American renegade in London, Ezra Pound, had sent to his countrymen an enthusiastic review of *North of Boston*—and Harriet Monroe printed it in *Poetry*. Returning home, Frost found that he had been praised warmly in an early issue of the *New Republic* by Amy Lowell, leader of the free-verse Imagists. More understandably, Edwin Arlington Robinson sent a letter of rich praise in 1917. Poets so diverse in method as Ransom, MacLeish, and Hillyer revealed their obligation to Frost's poetry in their early work. And in 1936 an English edition of his *Selected Poems* was issued with introductory essays by a curious foursome: W. H. Auden, C. Day Lewis, Paul Engle, and Edwin Muir. The secret of Frost's wide appeal seems to have been that his poetry, from the beginning, caught fresh vitality without recourse to the fads and limitations of modern experimental techniques.

The problem of the experimentalists was to determine how free poetry should be if it were to escape the threadbare conventionalism of an outworn tradition. Naturally the emphasis was on new forms, in this declaration of poetic independence, for freedom of the poet's material has always existed, together with certain abiding limitations of the poet's method. Frost carried on his own distinct experiments, emphasizing speech rhythms and "the sound of sense." He has called attention to "those dramatic tones of voice which had hitherto constituted the better half of poetry." In Frost's theory of poetry, the self-imposed restrictions of meter in form and of coherence in content stand not halfway down the scale of grace. He has made many casual references to the general quality of those limitations which work to the advantage, not to the disadvantage, of new and lively poetry.

The restrictions of the experimentalists, ironically seeking liberation, have amused Frost. With pleasant banter he has teased his contemporaries by jesting about their desperate "quest for new ways to be new." Behold the fantastic variety of restrictions in their freedom, he said: "Poetry, for example, was tried without punctuation. It was tried without capital letters. It was tried without any image but those to the eye. . . . It was tried without content under the trade name of poesie pure. It was tried without phrase, epigram, coherence, logic and consistency. It was tried without ability. . . . It was tried premature like the delicacy of unborn calf in Asia. It was tried without feeling or sentiment like murder for small pay in the underworld. These many things was it tried without, and what had we left? Still something."[3]

There were other kinds of restrictions which amused Frost, such as those of overemphasis. Perhaps poetry could be used to purge the world of wickedness and bring heaven down to earth in the form of an international brotherhood. This was a shift of emphasis from one type of pure poetry to another type of pure poetry! Frost offered his own anecdote for comment:

"I had it from one of the youngest lately: 'Whereas we once thought literature should be without content, we now know it should be charged full of propaganda.' Wrong twice, I told him. Wrong twice and of theory prepense. But he returned to his position after a moment out for reassembly: 'Surely art can be considered good only as it prompts to action.' How soon? I asked him. But there is danger of undue levity in teasing the young. . . . We must be very tender of our dreamers. They may seem like picketers, or members of the committee on rules, for the moment. We shan't mind what they seem, if only they produce real poems."[4]

The restrictions which Frost accepts in his theory of poetry save him from the dangers of two extremes: nothing of content (pure art) and nothing except content (pure preaching). He is also unsympathetic with those who think they may set up as goals of perfection the expression of thought or emotion in the form of abstractions: sound merely for the sake of sound, or inner agitation which becomes wildness with nothing important enough to be wild about. The danger of this last experiment, he says, is that "we bring up as aberrationists, giving way to undirected associations and kicking ourselves from one chance suggestion to another in all directions as of a hot afternoon in the life of a grasshopper."[5] So much for those who have imitated that beauty of free association in thought or emotion which the impressionistic Symbolists established as a fad in poetry. Furthermore, Frost hates to see poets use their medium as a vehicle for shrieking frustration and disgust. Grievances he would willingly restrict to prose, so that poetry might concentrate on griefs, on "woes, woes immedicable"; might be permitted to go its way in tears.

These, then, are some of the restrictions which Frost considers to be of false value in poetry, popular as they may have been among the straining experimentalists. But this process of paring away at the nonessentials does not bring us in to any kernel, any simple answer which Frost has as to the nature of poetry. To him the mystery, the wonder, the virtue, the magic of poetry is its heterogeneity of elements somehow blended to a single autonomous unit. The problem of the poet is to achieve this integration, this fusion. The difficulty of calling on a poet to explain is that we call on him to reverse the process and resort to deliberate analysis, disintegration, diffusion. Such a task, repugnant to Frost and to many poets, is left to the analysis of the critics. But the gulf between integration and analysis is one which criticism has never succeeded in bridging, nor is there much hope that even our specialized scientific approaches through the terms of psychology, philology, and metaphysics will bridge the gulf. Fortunately, the hints and observations thrown off by the poets themselves help us to reach across the gulf until the distance is at least reduced.

Form

Refusing to arrange his observations into any kind of systematic theory, Frost has mentioned several specifics and factors which seem to him important. Rejecting the hard and fast boundaries of definition as too dangerous, he has indicated certain elastic principles which seem not only sensible and salutary but also deeply rooted in the experience of poets in any age. Cautiously, he begins by finding the initial impetus of the poet to rise out of intensely perceived experiences which are given expression because of the hunger, the need for expression, in the Emersonian sense of the word. But he qualifies his use of the word "expression" with some care. How dangerous it might be to suppose that the response to the desire for expression should inevitably produce an artistic utterance. There have been some inartistic screams in modern poetry. But to "gape in agony," he says, and to write "huge gobs of raw sincerity bellowing with pain" are obviously kinds of expression which, be they ever so heartfelt, are too formless to be considered as anything other than mere expression. They lack shape.

Form, then, may be said to be the most important characteristic which Frost finds essential to poetry in any age. But the spread of meaning in that very elastic word must be suggested before such a simple statement is understood. For example, we may start with the great variety of stanzaic forms and then break any of them down to the rich formal relationships of rhyme to rhyme, of line to line, of sentence to sentence, of words which talk back and forth to each other in the poem. When we recall that another characteristic of form is balance and equilibrium, or controlled unbalance, we open up entirely new vistas. Furthermore, form in poetry is modulated also by the relation, the balance, of emotion and emotion, of thought and thought, of emotion and thought, of the image and the metaphor, of the specific and the general, of the trivial and the significant, of the transient and the permanent. All these facets appear to Frost as related aspects of that terse but by no means simple word "form."

To give form in poetry is also to employ that intricate method of conveying organization, shapeliness, fitness, to the matter or substance or context or meaning of the poem. Before meaning finds its place in a poem it must become subordinated to its proper balance with structure. And Frost goes further to assert quite bluntly that another requirement of poetry is that this formal fusion of distinct elements shall achieve the personal idiom of the poet's expression without sacrificing that happy correspondence which must exist between his own experience and the experience of those who come after to read or hear the poem.

Such fundamentals are even more complicated than they seem to be. But it is the duty of the lover of poetry to perceive at least the outer aspects of these fundamentals. And those who have tried to explain have sought different ways of getting at the problem. For example, it may be appreciated that modern critics have with good reason rejected the conventional division of poetry into two simple components: form and content. A peculiar interrelationship is disregarded in such arbitrary separation. Out of the fusion grows a quality which is neither form nor content, but somehow a by-product of the fusion. John Crowe Ransom has described this extra quality as "texture" and is willing to call the fusion which produces it "structure." But this new combination of terms helps only slightly to increase our awareness of the complexity in a good poem. For example, none will claim that meaning or content or context has disappeared because it has become integrated as structure. To the contrary, the process should have increased our acuteness in perceiving the overtones of meaning enriched by the position of meaning in the structure of the poem. Now it happens that many modern poets and critics are willing to assume that meaning, having undergone a peculiar metamorphosis in a poem, is no longer meaning; that it has been translated into something rich and strange. Granted, Frost says, that it has been enriched; still it is meaning. And he is willing to go so far as to say that meaning is the ingredient best able to save poetry from effeteness. He finds variety in poetry more closely allied to the many-sidedness of content than to the many-sidedness of form, difficult as it may be to extricate the one from the other in a poem. To me, the odds seem to favor neither the one nor the other. And I believe that Frost's own poetry is at its best when the two elements have become so completely reconciled that they are happily joined in a holy marriage and defy any attempted separation.

The Poetic Impulse

But how does this complicated relationship first begin to take shape? Frost has told us something of his own personal experience as it concerns the genesis, the working out of a poem. Again and again he has said that there is a striking analogy between the course of a true poem and of a true love. Each begins as an impulse, a disturbing excitement to which the individual surrenders himself. "No one can really hold that the ecstasy should be static and stand still in one place. It begins in delight, it inclines to the impulse, it assumes direction with the first line laid down, it runs a course of lucky events, and ends in a clarification of life—not necessarily a great clarification, such as sects and cults are founded on, but in a momentary stay against confusion. It has denouement. It has an outcome that though unforeseen was predestined from the first image of the original mood—and indeed from the very mood. . . . It finds its own name as it goes and discovers the best waiting for it in some final phrase at once wise and sad—the happy-sad blend of the drinking song."[6]

In this aspect of the poet's intent, Frost implies that he finds himself impelled forward as if by faith, so that the poem is somehow believed into existence. "The beauty, the something, the little charm of the thing to be, is more felt than known." As for the source of that initial impetus, he finds it growing out of a flash of recognition; a fresh perception. But there is another kind of recognition which might be called a correlation. Somehow it amounts to a new awareness of self. The present moment serves as a fulminating agent which fires experience lost in the dark of memory and causes that experience to burst into flame. This accident, producing an emotional intensity, might be described as an act which projects the past into the future. Frost has his own striking analogy:

"For me the initial delight is in the surprise of remembering something I didn't know I knew. I am in a place, in a situation, as if I had materialized from a cloud or risen out of the ground. There is a glad recognition of the long lost and the rest follows. Step by step the wonder of unexpected supply keeps growing. The impressions most useful to my purpose seem always those I was unaware of and so made no note of at the time when taken, and the conclusion is come to that like giants we are always hurling experience ahead of us to pave the future with against the day when we may want to strike a line of purpose across it for somewhere."[7]

This kind of inspiration is in no way related to what Wordsworth had in mind when he referred to "emotion recollected in tranquillity." It is more closely related to the recognition-scene, so long a source of surprise and emotional tension in dramatic narratives. In a peculiar sense, the poet's fresh recognition creates an emotional crisis. He is impelled to find release from that crisis—and the resolution of it is the poem.

Frost implies that there are two kinds of recognition which he has experienced as one part of the poetic impulse; two different ways in which this sense of interplay between the past and the present is first motivated and finally resolved in the form of a poem. The first way occurs when some experience in the present inspires an emotional recognition that is more a matter of sense impression than of clear mental perception. The emotional tension—the lump in the throat—which is established through such a recognition, impels the poet into the physical act of recording in poetry the details of the immediate moment; the details of that immediate experience which happens to the poet in the physical world, or which is happened upon by the poet in the nonphysical world of his own reverie. Uncertain as to the precise nature of this sudden meeting between past experience and present experience, the poet ventures into the recording of the moment, the capturing of the incident. He proceeds with this recording as an act of faith, without foreseeing the outcome. And as this emotional tension finds its gradual resolution in the poem, the emotion finds its thought. In other words, the mental recognition of meaning in this emotional experience gradually asserts itself on a new plane of metaphorical reference. It may find its expression in a stated simile or it may find its expression merely through that which is implied or suggested.

This first kind of recognition which Frost suggests, as a part of his poetic impulse, may be demonstrated by examining a single poem. The more easily understood the poem may be, the better are the chances of making it serve as an illustration here. For that reason I choose the graceful and familiar "Stopping by Woods on a Snowy Evening." In fair warning, I must confess that I do not know the story as to how Robert Frost happened to write this poem. But my guess, even if it should prove wrong in specific details, may still have validity as a general illustration of that process which I am trying to clarify. The poem is a dramatic lyric which breaks into the middle of an incident, so that there is a drama-in-miniature revealed with setting and lighting and actors and properties complete. At the beginning, the reader finds the curtain going up on a little action which approaches the climax of an experience, real or imagined; that is, an experience which happened to the poet or one which came to the mind of the poet as possible. A rural traveler is the actor whose brief soliloquy describes the circumstances under which he has stopped his horse-drawn sleigh to enjoy, in spite of cold and loneliness, the strange beauty of white snowflakes falling against a background of dark trees. There are many reasons why he should not stop; common-sense reasons which seem to occur even to the traveler's little horse. But the spell of the moment is so strong that the traveler is reluctant to leave, regardless of the winter night and the cold storm. He is impelled to move on by the realization of duties and distances; those "promises" which he must keep and the "miles to go" before he completes his journey. Thus the poem ends, and the images which crowd the statements are direct and unmistakable. Where, in such lines, does the emotional tension resolve itself into the mental focus of a metaphor? If this simple little poem is to be considered as one in which the resolution suggests two planes of reference, the reader must be made aware of words and images which face two ways at once. Considered from the viewpoint of the poetic impulse, it is quite probable that the poet, impelled emotionally to record this real or imagined experience, did not immediately see in it any metaphorical correspondence between the sight of the moment and the insight of the past-in-the-present. Yet a correspondence appears with dramatic clarity in the final stanza. The reader is aware of more than one possible meaning for such words as "promises" and "miles" and "sleep." And it is probable that the poet also came upon these words with a conscious perception and recognition of a rational focus which grew out of this moment first felt vaguely and emotionally in the form of an inner tension. Almost with a sense of surprise the poet may have found a second plane of reference which gave deeper importance to the little incident which became the poem. But Frost's characteristic reticence and shyness, a part of his New England heritage, led him to be satisfied with those three words which suggest, without explanation or elaboration, the rationally perceived focus of this correspondence.

Each reader has no difficulty in making an elaboration from this implied metaphor. In the poem, the specific incident has completely displaced the general analogy. If a reader is satisfied to settle for the specific as satisfactory in itself, there is nothing to hinder him from so doing. On the other hand, if he wishes to continue with the extensions of the metaphor, there is nothing to hinder him from that added pleasure. The most obvious correspondence would suggest the analogy between the specific experience of the rural traveler and the general experience of any individual whose life is so frequently described as a journey; a journey including pleasures and hardships, duties and distances. In the light of such analogies, the other images offer correspondences which are valid. There is even a slightly tragic implication suggested by "the coldest evening of the year." Yet within this bitter cold occurs an elementary revelation of beauty which lays claim on us as existing nowhere else. Regardless of the dark and cold, we are prone to tarry quite irrationally because of this paradoxically somber excitement and recompense. The reluctance to leave becomes an expression of the endless hunger for holding and making permanent a dark moment of pleasurable discovery in a transient experience. But we are impelled forward and away by other and inevitable commitments. There are the "promises" which we have made to ourselves and to others, or which others have made for us. And there are the "miles" we must travel through other kinds of experience before we yield to that final and inevitable commitment: sleep in death.

I am well aware that this kind of metaphorical extension is distasteful to some, and is frequently branded by others as impressionistic nonsense. I am equally sure that any poet who uses metaphors with the deliberate purpose of suggesting more than is stated offers his readers, through the very nature of his method, the freedom to read the poem on as many different planes of reference as may be discovered. The only restriction is that such induced correspondences must not be made if they invalidate the initial relationship of the specifics to each other. The rules of the game are as old as poetry. Children derive much pleasure from playing with those square boxes of different sizes which may be put together, one inside another, until they are contained within a single block. They may be treated without imagination as a single block, but the pleasure begins when they are telescoped outward. In a restricted sense, the pleasure derived from opening up a metaphor may be compared to the pleasure derived from opening up that single block which has so many proportionate identities hidden within it.

I have said that Frost implies a second kind of recognition which he has experienced in the poetic impulse. The second occurs when the emotional pleasure is derived from the sudden mental perception of a thought which comes into sharp focus through the discovery and recognition of a particularly apt correspondence or analogy. The difference between these two approaches to the writing of a poem should be clear. The first begins as an emotional response which gradually finds its resolution in a thought metaphorically expressed; the second begins with the perception of the metaphor, and the rational focus is so pleasurable in its sudden discovery that it produces an emotional afterglow. The first leads the poet to venture into the writing of the poem as an act of faith, without foreseeing the outcome; the second leads the poet to give shape and weight to a rational correspondence which has been perceived clearly before he begins the writing of the poem. Nevertheless, Frost is fond of handling each of these by letting the specific displace the general until the analogy is implied or stated as a kind of climax to the poem.

In selecting an illustration for this second process, I again venture a guess. For reasons which may become clear before I finish, I am willing to suppose that one poem written in this second manner is that entitled "For Once, Then, Something." Here also is a dramatic lyric, with its single actor unfolding, through his brief monologue, a setting which builds directly to a climactic moment. At the beginning, there is an implied reference to other actors who may be considered collectively as the antagonist. Before we go further, let us imagine the manner in which the poet's thoughts may have led him to recognize in the action of this moment the apt incident or metaphor which brought a sense of pleasurable response and emotional tension. Those who have examined Frost's poetry with care are familiar with his increasing fondness for metaphors which make use (or fun) of concepts and problems in systematic philosophy. His own middle-ground position permits him to control an ingrained skepticism in such a manner as to deal playfully with the extremes of affirmation and denial. He has frequently suggested that he is particularly wary of hydra-headed Platonic idealism and of all those glorious risks taken by any who boldly arrive at transcendental definitions. Pleasantly scornful of those who assume too much as to the extent and validity of human knowledge, Frost tells us, he has often shared the longing which inspires philosophers to project their systems beyond the realms of the known and the knowable. He has never grown tired in his own cautious search for truth, yet he has never been tempted to believe that absolute truth could be defined satisfactorily even by the most profound philosophic systems. As he says in his poem entitled "Neither Out Far Nor In Deep," we all will continue forever to watch and hope, "wherever the truth may be." In *A Witness Tree*, he sums up the persistent attempt to resolve the inscrutable, thus:

> We dance round in a ring and suppose,
> But the Secret sits in the middle and knows.

"For Once, Then, Something" is the record of an incident which pleased Frost, apparently, as a happy analogy which might serve to state the paradox between his own watchfulness and his own skepticism. Obviously, the poem is so nicely constructed that the reader may enjoy it on a single plane of reference, without any concern for the epistemological implications. But my supposition is that Frost's experience happened to bring the analogy into sharp focus with his lifelong accumulation of prejudices concerning the extent and validity of knowledge; that he deliberately prepared the incident for interpretation on an epistemological plane of reference, by using one word which is so obviously placed that it stands out like a sore thumb. Here is the poem, complete:

> Others taunt me with having knelt at well-curbs
> Always wrong to the light, so never seeing
> Deeper down in the well than where the water
> Gives me back in a shining surface picture
> Me myself in the summer heaven godlike
> Looking out of a wreath of fern and cloud puffs.
> *Once*, when trying with chin against a well-curb,
> I discerned, as I thought, beyond the picture,
> Through the picture, a something white, uncertain,
> Something more of the depths—and then I lost it.
> Water came to rebuke the too clear water.
> One drop fell from a fern, and lo, a ripple
> Shook whatever it was lay there at bottom,
> Blurred it, blotted it out. What was that whiteness?
> Truth? A pebble of quartz? For once, then, something.

As soon as that naked word "Truth?" asserts itself with whimsical and teasing boldness at the beginning of the final line, the reader is made aware of a new kind of game. One may enjoy trying to examine the bottom of a well through water, but only a poet would look there for truth. So the reader turns back to the beginning of the poem to examine the images and phrases in the

light of that single word. Do the images corroborate the implication of such a brazen hint? The first line immediately becomes
an oblique reference to the long-standing quarrel between the
speaker as a skeptical relativist and his antagonists as believing
absolutists. Next we come to the nature of the taunt: the speaker
has been ridiculed as an egocentric who can do no better than
perceive the absolute being as the reflection of his own not-too-
pathetic human image. Then a further correspondence is suggested between the specific search below the surface of the well-
water and the general search below the surface of human
experience for some meaning which will satisfy human yearnings
for certainty. Having perceived this general connotation, the
reader finds an easy addition in the description of the speaker
who is also taunted by his more idealistic, possibly religious,
friends because he has hindered his own search by taking his
position "always wrong to the light"—and suddenly the religious
extensions of the word "light" fall naturally into the pattern of
this second plane. Once, however, the poet humorously suggests
that his endeavor seemed to permit a passing glimpse of something. Perhaps he had caught sight of the hidden mystery itself.
But too soon the spell was broken by a seemingly deliberate accident and a rebuke. It seemed as though there might be some
intelligence which intended that this human being and others
should never have more than a glimpse.

Thus the incident of the traveler in the snowy woods and of
the spectator peering down into a well are two examples which
help to explain Frost's remarks concerning his own experience in
analyzing that mysterious process which has to do with the poetic
impulse. Wordsworth took pleasure in turning from the present
to find an emotional excitement and inspiration in happy memo-
ries of the past. Paradoxically, Wordsworth's pursuit of ultimate
reality in the impulses from a vernal wood became a form of
escape from the unpleasantness of the momentary and transient
actuality. Frost's method is diametrically opposed. He takes
pleasure in ignoring the ultimate reality of the philosophic and
religious absolute; takes pleasure even in turning his back on the
past, until a momentary experience is illuminated with richer

value by that which his past experience accidentally brings to the present. And Frost's quest of the present moment as the greatest reality becomes a pursuit in the Emersonian sense; it becomes implicit with newly perceived aspects of an evident design in the universe. Always, the past cuts across the present moment to reveal and illuminate the moment by transforming it into a metaphor which has for him beauty and meaning. It may be valuable to reconsider his own statement here:

"For me the initial delight is in the surprise of remembering something I didn't know I knew. I am in a place, in a situation, as if I had materialized from a cloud or risen out of the ground. There is a glad recognition of the long lost and the rest follows. Step by step the wonder of unexpected supply keeps growing. The impressions most useful to my purpose seem always those I was unaware of and so made no note of at the time when taken, and the conclusion is come to that like giants we are always hurling experience ahead of us to pave the future with against the day when we may want to strike a line of purpose across it for somewhere."

But in the process of that resolution from the moment of poetic impulse to the final completion of the poem, there arises the persistent need for cunning and artistry. Frost does not imply that the poem writes itself. The poet must establish a careful balance between the personal intimacy of the experience and the separation of the experience through statement which gains perspective without loss of intensity. The thoughtful statement of the relationship between the present experience and the remembered experience balances the emotion. Equilibrium is truly a large part of what is meant by artistry. "Keeping the thing in motion," Frost has said, "is sometimes like walking a rolling barrel." Again he feels it analogous to riding an untamed horse: "The great pleasure in writing poetry is in having been carried off. It is as if you stood astride of the subject that lay on the ground, and they cut the cord, and the subject gets up under you and you ride it. You adjust yourself to the motion of the thing itself. That is the poem."[8]

Accidentally, a poet may lose one kind of equilibrium, fall off, and continue his journey to the end of the poem in a truly pedestrian fashion. Then the critical reader becomes painfully aware of the accident and is able to point out the place: "This is where he fell off." To Frost this loss of balance was a part of what Poe meant when he said that there was no such thing as a long poem; that he could show any reader of a long poem where the rider fell, and how far he limped before he again managed to climb astride his Pegasus.

There is a pertinent paradox in the poet's craving for the intimacy of experience which gives insight and, at the same time, his longing for separation which permits objectivity and perspective. As a part of the poet's preparation, Frost has often hinted at this problem. The dark woods seem to become a symbol of that withdrawal from life for the sake of clarification. The first poem in his first book, "Into My Own," sang the yearning for lostness in "dark trees" that "stretched away unto the edge of doom," because such lostness would lead to self-discovery. One might not do violence to "Birches" by discovering in the final passage a reflection of the poetic hunger for withdrawal which might permit swift and exciting return, with grace and without effort, to a new sense of life:

> I'd like to get away from earth awhile
>
> . . . .
>
> And climb black branches up a snow-white trunk
> *Toward* heaven, till the tree could bear no more,
> But dipped its top and set me down again.
> That would be good both going and coming back.

In the response to poetic materials and poetic insight the deliberate and conscious craftsmanship must be combined with a sense of surrender to the material which has been possessed. "You adjust yourself to the motion of the thing itself." The muscular assertiveness of the will defeats its own purpose. The poet as rider finds his curious animal to be tender-mouthed. Or it might be said that the poem which succeeds has the casual grace of the dancer completely responsive to the rhythm of the music and concerned only with an almost reflexive expression of the emotion thus inspired. The shrewdness of the poet is to remain true to the mood and true to the material at the same time. We may not like Plato's metaphor of the perfect image concealed in the untouched block of marble. But in the nature of poetic response to a moment and situation in time and space, the poet is responsible in a strange way to elements which he may distort only at the peril of destruction and loss. I find a happy analogy, regardless of the original intent, tucked away at the heart of Frost's poem, "The Axe-Helve":

> He showed me that the lines of a good helve
> Were native to the grain before the knife
> Expressed them, and its curves were no false curves
> Put on it from without. And there its strength lay. . . .

So the perfection of the poem arises out of the poet's pleasure in discovering words, images, metaphors, phrases, "native to the grain" of the emotion, the thought, the situation.

There is a peculiar satisfaction which Frost finds from the ultimate resolution, release, or completion of a poem. Out of the chaotic confusion of daily impressions and thoughts the poet captures a moment with his words and achieves a kind of crystallization which gives to his chaotic raw materials not only shape but weight. And this metamorphosis creates that sense of stability which Frost refers to when he speaks of "a momentary stay against confusion." His poem "West-running Brook," which furnished the title for his fifth book, is built around an elaborate metaphor which has a particularly happy connotation if one interprets it in the light of the poet's intent. The metaphor is built around the image of one wave which rides forever above a sunken rock: permanence in transience. "The stream of everything that runs away" is able to create the illusion, but only the illusion, of "not gaining but not losing" because of the black water "flung backward on itself in one white wave." It suggests to the poet the analogy of existence:

> And it is time, strength, tone, light, life and love—
> And even substance lapsing unsubstantial;
> The universal cataract of death
> That spends to nothingness—and unresisted,

Save by some strange resistance in itself,
Not just a swerving, but a throwing back,
As if regret were in it and were sacred.
It has this throwing backward on itself
So that the fall of most of it is always
Raising a little, sending up a little.

We may go on to play the age-old game of analogies and say that
the poet's hunger for creating a sense of stability and of crystallization from the flux of things has in it a sacred regret of its own
—and a sense of triumph in his accomplishment, for this very
reason. From the viewpoint of the artist, Frost hints that we all
know that sense of comfort and pleasure because it is also derived
even from the most humble achievement of form in our lives.

Meaning

If we may return a bit, Frost's image of experience hurled into
the future, as if by intuitive foreknowledge of the eventual need,
is very closely related in spirit to Emerson's theory of poetry. The
flash of recognition is a happy response to that union of impressions present and past. But the gradual elaboration of the thing
felt with delight leads naturally to a statement of the larger understanding, the half-sad, half-happy wisdom of the conclusion. In
quite a different context of associations, Emerson once spoke of
the way in which the thoughts of the present gave to the thoughts
of the past a new arrangement in the mind of the perceptive
individual, so that the utterance was fresh. He continued: "It
came into him life; it went out from him truth. It came to him
short-lived actions; it went out from him immortal thoughts. It
came to him business; it went from him poetry. It was dead fact;
now, it is quick thought. It can stand, and it can go. It now
endures, it now flies, it now inspires. Precisely in proportion to
the depth of mind from which it issued, so high does it soar, so
long does it sing."[9]

We may recognize a further relationship between the theories
of Emerson and Frost. One speaks of dead fact becoming quick
thought; the other speaks of a "clarification of life" which grows
out of poetry. We are back to the problem of meaning, and of its

importance to the poem. Is meaning in a poem a means to an end
or is it an end in itself? Each would say that there is no pat
answer to such a question. There are several different planes of
thought on which the question may be considered. On the first
plane, each would say that beauty is its own excuse for being;
that the delight is the goal. On a higher plane, there is a new
by-product analogous to that which is created when the material
merges with the shape the poem gives it. There is a difference
between making poetry a means to an end and in finding, at the
conclusion of a poem, that something more than pleasurable
emotion has been created. I am convinced that both Frost and
Emerson have sometimes confused these differences in their own
poems, but I am sure that in theory their awareness of the difference is demonstrable. On this higher plane of reference, there is a
pleasure which arises from a deeper understanding. Let the poem
start and finish ever so playfully; it will touch and illuminate
experience. Robinson put it thus:

> The games we play
> To fill the frittered minutes of a day
> Good glasses are to read the spirit through.

The little game, the poem, is in no sense a picture of life as it
actually exists. It is not a key to the poet's philosophy of life. It is
more closely akin to a momentary glimpse which is at once a
distillation and an elaboration of a moment. Yet somehow in the
preservation of that transience the poet touches on the permanent.
Relationships are the essence of metaphor and of poetry to Frost.
And Emerson calls the poet "the Sayer" not only because he is
namer of beauty but also because he is "a perceiver and dear lover
of the harmonies that are in the soul and in matter—and specially
of the correspondences between these and those."

The first concern of the poet is with that substance which he
wishes to express. And he must have enough drive in an emotional
sense to encompass and relate the parts. If he is able to possess his
material with an intensity which gives artistic validity to the
material, he may then take pleasure in the shapeliness of the
poem, the autonomousness of the creation. In that shapeliness is

its excuse for being. But this does not inhibit either artist or reader from finding another kind of pleasure in the meaning.

Because a poem subordinates meaning to its proper balance in structure, one is not able to test the validity of a poem's morality by the standards either of religious creeds or of scientific fact. What may be true for a poem may be false when tested by the average rules of good conduct. For example, Eliot's ironic poem "The Hollow Men" may outlast all his other poems. It is an excellent poetic epitome of pessimism and disillusionment. As such, it has its own validity, its own truth, its own morality, even though its meaning is plainly opposed to the idealism of Christian morality or to the facts of human nobility and heroism in the face of a tragic world. Quite obviously a poem is able to succeed and have its entity without recourse to these standards. Yet, because the material of poetry is so deeply rooted in life and living, that material inevitably relates itself to, and is colored by, the larger affirmations of human morality. And it would seem to be one characteristic of lasting poetry in any language, in any age, to reaffirm in its independent fashion the various aspects of strength in human courage, human love, human aspiration. Because fear, hatred, despair, and negation are equally aspects of human experience, these also demand their place as materials for poetry.

It is the poet's virtue to develop that insight and wisdom which enable him to recognize and represent the apparent conflict between the constructive and destructive elements, the good and the bad, in nature and in human experience. Those elements, so inextricably related to each other, furnished the basis for dramatic conflict in Greek tragedy. Again, the all-inclusiveness of Shakespeare's insight, with its recognition of the good in the bad, the bad in the good, and triumph of constructive forces only at great cost and waste of good, tallies with our own experience after more than three hundred years, and helps to give his poetry permanence. Obviously, the possession of insight and wisdom in perceiving these spiritual relationships is not enough to create poetry; but it seems to be one of the essentials of lasting poetry. And at the risk of being called didactic in his affirmations, Robert

Frost has subscribed to such a general rule, such a limitation if you wish, in the writing of his poetry.

It has been said that "in the high artist, ethics and aesthetics are one." How true—and how dangerous. The test is a familiar one: does the artist handle his ethical and moral observations in such a way as to make them implicit? If he does not, he has failed in a very serious way. Robert Frost's poetry frequently takes that risk, and does not always succeed in keeping the thoughts implicit. When the ethical or the moral content becomes explicit, it threatens to destroy the artistic structure, which may not be strong enough to contain it. Such an accident does not invalidate the ideas or concepts, but it does invalidate the position of these ideas or concepts in a poetic frame. No matter how noble or profound the thought, it fails to justify the shortcomings of intended artistry. There have been few poets who could set out bluntly, like Milton, "to justify the ways of God to man"—and proceed to subordinate, or to keep implicit within the structure of the poem, such an overpowering goal. Most of the Puritans were more bold than talented in their attempts to prove that art is concerned with directing the individual to apprehension; that art is therefore a means to knowledge and truth. It would seem to me that any aesthetic theory which begins by reducing art to a means is doomed to failure; but the double handicap of Puritan theory was that the end, in their eyes, was redemption from human depravity. And such an end was so important to them that the intended balance was often sacrificed almost eagerly!

Robert Frost's poetic theory, quite at odds with Puritan aesthetics, is nevertheless colored by his Yankee heritage of Puritan teaching. His own belief in poetry as "a clarification of life" seems to have close relation to the ideas of that other New England individualist who was not ashamed to find certain virtues in Puritan concepts, provided they could be inspired with flexible vitality. Emerson said that the poet's creative power was derived from his passionate craving to express the existence of harmonies and correspondences which are discovered between the present and the past, the seen and the unseen, the material and the spiritual. And Frost's personal description of his poetic intent seems closely related to this explicit statement from Emerson:

"For it is not metres, but a metre-making argument that makes a poem,—a thought so passionate and alive that like the spirit of a plant or an animal it has an architecture of its own, and adorns nature with a new thing. The thought and the form are equal in the order of time, but in the order of genesis the thought is prior to the form. The poet has a new thought; he has a whole new experience to unfold; he will tell us how it is with him, and all men will be the richer in his fortune."

But there are nice differences between the Puritan desire to redeem the individual from his human depravity, the Emersonian desire to interpret "harmonies" as proofs of human divinity, and the Frostian desire to make poetry "a clarification of life." The Puritan argument is as debatable as the Emersonian argument. Frost prefers to leave to prose those questions suitable for debate; he finds poetry at its best when its statements and observations touch realms of spiritual values where there is no room for argument: sorrow, aspiration, loneliness, love. Songs are built around everlastingly perceived values which are true for us all. It is not the poet's function to argue that "in Adam's fall we sinnèd all" or that in Christ's death we were all saved. There are still a few of us who consider these as subjects for controversy. And Frost points out that we don't join together in singing an argument. But in human nature there are certain enduring qualities and everlasting truths which permit us to join in hymns of joy or threnodies of sorrow. Let a poem be written on these themes and it will last, says Frost, for "it will forever keep its freshness as a metal keeps its fragrance." So he has generally avoided venturing into poetic argument. Poetry deals with a meaning and truth which may clarify the mingled goodness and badness of life without growing too optimistic over the existence of the one or too pessimistic over the existence of the other. And these overtones of significance, implicit in the poem, are permissible as subject matter for connotation on that higher plane of poetry. This is Frost's answer to those who ask how poetry can become a "clarification of life" without making meaning an end in itself.

The Poem and the Reader

We are now in a better position to consider that aspect of a poem which faces outward to find response from the reader. The poet's aim and purpose represents one plane of the poem; but when he has achieved release from the need which prompted his utterance, the test of the poem has just begun. For the poem, "twice blest," faces not only toward the poet and his intent but also toward the reader and the understanding which the reader brings to it. And the difference between these two planes of reference is obviously the difference between the poet's experience and that artfully limited expression of the poet's experience which is projected in the content of the poem so that it may be shared by the reader. Thus the content must risk the danger of being further restricted by the reader's experience and perceptivity. These determine the degree to which the poem's inherent merit and meaning may be appreciated. Thus considered, the poem is something more than a mere expression of release for the poet; its function is not fulfilled as an autonomous unit if it has merely satisfied the poet. For the poem must be able to establish a basic correspondence between writer and reader. If it fails to contain statement intelligible at least to the intelligent, and intelligible to the degree that there is a common ground in experience for general agreement as to its denotation, then it does not succeed as a poem, no matter how certain the poet may be that his intent is stated. A good example of such failure is Eliot's most famous poem, "The Waste Land," and Eliot acknowledged its failure on this score when he felt obliged to supplement it with his erudite and esoteric footnotes. Such a solution of the problem through the trappings of explanation invalidates the required autonomy of the poem and delivers it immediately into the arms of the snobbish or the academic readers who may keep it limping about on flimsy crutches of praise and elucidation. The simple fact remains: the poem, as such, fails to satisfy the initial requirement of autonomy, regardless of its curiously ingenious pastiche craftsmanship.

But the reader's recognition of correspondence between himself and the poet in that denotation which is essential to autonomy may readily be seen to constitute only the first step in appreciation. It might be called the foundation on which are built higher levels of perception. For it is the nature of poetry to convey or suggest moods and meanings apart from the explicit and recognized meanings. And this difference between that suggested and that stated is the difference between connotation and denotation. Although connotation may be made in several different ways, Robert Frost has concentrated in theory and practice on his two particular favorites: on the tone or sound of words themselves or in their relation to each other—and on the symbolic meaning of words and phrases. To him these seem to be the basic elements in the poetry of any age and remain today the most fecund of the "old ways to be new." The first of these he has elaborated as "the sound of sense," as opposed to the more limited poetic theory concerning the musical sounds. To Frost, as we shall see in the following chapter, this phrase of his tends to deprecate the *merely* musical: the sensuously titillating, at one extreme, or the spiritually moving, at the other extreme. And it will be seen that his theory of "the sound of sense" is quietly antipathetic to that particular attitude toward sound in poetry which was the preoccupation of Poe or to Lanier's theory of musical notation in verse.

The connotation of words and phrases in their double meaning is, of course, related to the age-old poetic use of comparisons, implied or stated. But Frost has developed his theory of the metaphor in a manner peculiar to his poetry. And this development will also be considered at length in a subsequent chapter.

It is essential to remember that these different aspects of poetry which have been considered separately in this analysis of Frost's theory are completely merged in the artistic expression so that they become inseparable parts of the whole. On consideration, the reader may be conscious of the manner in which the content of the poem faces inward toward the poet's experience and outward toward the experience of the reader. And our enjoyment may be heightened by the hints at experiences greater than those which find their way into the poem. This is part of the charm of poetry. But no reader is fair to the poem if he insists on crowding the poet with questions as to what is "back of it." Frost is willing to laugh at anyone "who stands at the end of a poem ready in waiting to catch you by both hands with enthusiasm and drag you off your balance over the last punctuation mark into more than you meant to say." His answer is always ready: "If I had wanted you to know, I should have told you in the poem."

*A dramatic necessity goes deep into the nature of the sen-
tence. Sentences are not different enough to hold the attention
unless they are dramatic. No ingenuity of varying structure
will do. All that can save them is the speaking tone of voice
somehow entangled in the words and fastened to the page for
the ear of the imagination. That is all that can save poetry
from sing-song, all that can save prose from itself.*[10]

THE SOUND OF SENSE

Before we may understand Robert Frost's theory concerning
the sound of sense, it is necessary to glance back at those earlier
attitudes toward poetic diction which were in part so distasteful
to him that they called forth his reaction. The recognized importance of sound in poetry is as old as poetry itself. But our present
search need take us back only to Coleridge, whose gospel of poetic
sound was based on "the sense of musical delight." This doctrine
was a distinct innovation quite at odds with the theories of Dryden
and the Augustans, who were interested in smooth numbers and
not in exalted musical poetry. Nevertheless, Coleridge's theory
quickly rose to such popularity that it dominated the poetry of the
nineteenth century. Quite obviously, it was the source of Edgar
Allan Poe's principle, implied in his famous definition of poetry
as "the rhythmical creation of beauty." It was also the inspiration
for much in Swinburne, whose passion for wonderful images and
musical sound carried to its extreme the nineteenth century pleasure in delicious auditory sensations. This preoccupation also led
Swinburne to espouse the cause of pure poetry which might glorify
the manner and minimize the matter of verse. In America,
Lanier's "musical notation of verse" carried Coleridge's theory to
a different extreme, in so far as it attempted to superimpose
scientific principles as guides to an end falsely desired.

In their best poetry, Coleridge, Poe, Swinburne, and many others
demonstrated their theories with convincing success. One need not
go beyond the magic of verbal music in "Kubla Khan" or
"Christabel" to recognize immortal accomplishment and proof.

But the principle became a dogma and the dogma became a curse as its imitators carried it to extremes or wore it threadbare in England and America. Even the major proponents themselves demonstrated how poetry intended as music might become merely artificial jingle. No better example of such failure may be found than in the majority of Poe's poems. Long before the reactionary protests of the "new poetry" movement, there had been isolated attacks on mere prettiness of sound.

The modern experimentalists, proposing to correct the sonorous artificialities of such popular models as Tennyson and Longfellow, found their inspirations for correctives in curiously different places. Exploring the possibilities of such fundamentals as speech rhythms, the Imagists turned back to the free-verse Symbolists in France and discarded the old metrical forms in order to liberate the more natural cadences and rhythms of sentences. And this was but one of many protests.

Working independently, Robert Frost turned back to the utterances of Wordsworth and Emerson, who had stressed the inherent poetic quality of those speech rhythms heard from the lips of the people who lived close to the soil. But there is a striking difference between Wordsworth's insistence on "plainer and more emphatic language" and Frost's theory of the sound of sense. Each poet set out in revolt against entirely different traditions of the past. The artificiality of poetic diction which Wordsworth deplored was that of monotonous eighteenth century restraint, while the artificiality of poetic diction which Frost deplored was the lush exuberance of nineteenth century artifice. Each sought to find correctives in a poetic language more intensely emotional because its roots were fixed in direct and natural expression.

Frost does not wish merely to reflect in poetry the elemental passions in the speech of common men, as Wordsworth did. He is aware of Wordsworth's subservience to this language as an end in itself. Coleridge had quarreled with Wordsworth on this score and had protested that the poet is the master of words and phrases, not the slave. And Frost's position here is more closely related to Coleridge's assertion that "the best part of human language, properly so called, is derived from reflections on the acts of the mind itself." Thus the poet's concern with words is the concern of an understanding master who knows how to arrange and control words and phrases to produce the desired result.

Here Frost parts company with Coleridge, who thus excused himself from paying close attention to the sort and order of words heard in the market, wake, highroad or plowfield. The poet as master, Frost seems to say, may still sharpen his understanding by giving ear to the elemental power of homely and passionate speech, of terse rational statement, of hard and flat epigrams so frequently heard among rural people. Such listening does not require slavish copying in the Wordsworthian sense; but it may offer correctives to that kind of artificiality which grew out of Coleridge's own preoccupation with musical sound.

Both Coleridge and Wordsworth were agreed that poetry must be judged by the test of psychology; that a preoccupation with sound in poetry was one important means to one important end: the pleasure of the reader. Frost's development of his own theory concerning sound in poetry also has this psychological basis; but the end which he seeks is a nicer gradation of meanings conveyed to the reader through sound. He is interested in the *sense*, or the meaning, that is communicated by the sound. He begins by exploring the psychology of sound in words and points out that a spoken word has two planes of meaning even in prose. On one plane there is the restricted meaning of denotation, regardless of whether the word is written or spoken. On the second plane there is an additional meaning of connotation which is given by the tone of the voice.

The simple word "oh" may be recognized on the first plane as an exclamation. But the tone of the voice is necessary to determine the nature of that exclamation. It may be spoken to convey scorn, amusement, surprise, doubt. And it is possible to convey meanings through tones of voice even when the words themselves are not understood. Frost has used as an example the conversation of two people talking in a closed room so that their voices can be heard although their words cannot be distinguished. The listener, hearing only the sounds but not catching the words themselves, is still able to understand certain definite aspects of meaning in such a conversation. "This is because every meaning has a particular sound-posture," says Frost, "or to put it another way, the sense of every meaning has a particular sound which each individual is instinctively familiar with, and, without being conscious of the exact words that are being used, is able to understand the thought, idea, or emotion that is being conveyed. What I am most interested in emphasizing in the application of this belief to art, is the sentence of sound, because to me a sentence is not interesting merely in conveying a meaning of words; it must do something more; it must convey a meaning by sound."[11]

When Frost first elaborated this theory, in 1915, he pointed out that there was nothing new about it. At that time Robert Bridges was emphasizing his own interest in "speech rhythms" as an essential aspect of poetry and poetic diction. Earlier, and nearer home, Emerson had singled out the speech rhythms of New Hampshire natives as praiseworthy guides to poetry. And Frost called particular attention to one passage in Emerson's poem "Monadnoc," which summed up the matter:

> Now in sordid weeds they sleep,
> In dullness now their secret keep;
> Yet, will you learn our ancient speech,
> These, the masters who can teach.
> Four-score or a hundred words
> All their vocal muse affords;
> But they turn them in a fashion
> Past'clerks' or statesmen's art or passion.
> I can spare the college bell,
> And the learned lecture well;
> Spare the clergy and libraries,
> Institutes and dictionaries,
> For that hearty English root
> Thrives here, unvalued, underfoot.
> Rude poets of the tavern hearth,
> Squandering your unquoted mirth,
> Which keeps the ground and never soars,
> While Dick retorts and Reuben roars;

Scoff of yeoman strong and stark,
Goes like bullet to its mark;
While the solid curse and jeer
Never balk the waiting ear.

This, then, was Emerson's statement of that principle of sound-posturing or of getting the sound of sense which Frost sought to bring into his poetry. And Frost found further corroboration when he examined those intense and crisp dialogues in Shakespeare's plays; dialogues built, as Frost said, of "lean sharp sentences, with the give and take, the thread of thought and action quick, not lost in a maze of metaphor and adjective." Furthermore, Shakespeare makes gesture and movement and tone of voice implicit in the spoken sentence: "by his way of writing he has given or indicated his own directions. There is only one way to read each word" in these dialogues.

Such an approach to poetic construction led Frost quite obviously into the realm of dramatic monologue and dialogue, where the give-and-take of conversation permitted a natural and appropriate use of carefully selected phrases and sentences possessing the rich and homely idiom of speech rhythms. Later we shall consider the working out of his theory of the sound of sense in actual practice. But it should be noted that Frost, like Browning, carried the dramatic quality into his lyrics—even into those which appeared in his first book, *A Boy's Will*. That his second book, *North of Boston,* was primarily devoted to dramatic narrative and dialogue indicates that period in his career when he became most deeply preoccupied with the development of those poetic principles which we have been considering.

His objective characterizations of those rural New Hampshire men and women, whom he had learned to know and love during years of living among them, quite naturally grew out of his search for the most satisfactory subject matter which might enable him to practice his principles concerning the posture and the sound of sense. How could he better apply those theories than by giving poetic form to the epigrammatic and idiomatic thoughts and emotions of those down-to-earth and unaffected country folk whom Emerson had referred to as "rude poets of the tavern hearth."

Here, in the overtones of words and meanings, was the very stuff of poetry as it had been exemplified in the great tradition of English literature. Years later, when Frost had completed his initial experiments with poems which were miniature one-act plays in verse, he applied his principles in the direct form of drama. This was done, he said, "without (as I should like to believe) having gone very far from where I have spent my life."

Unlike the Symbolists and the Imagists, Frost found no trouble in correlating the speech rhythms with metrical regularity. There are to him two rival sound-factors in poetry: the cadence of the spoken sentence, and the regular beat of the meter. Although separate in analysis, these two became one in poetic creation. Having equal rights, neither should become subordinate to the other. But such a reconciliation is not particularly difficult in English poetry because, as many have pointed out, the rhythms of conversation fall quite naturally into iambic patterns. Thus, if the poetic line is iambic pentameter and the speech rhythm of the sentence is fitted to such lines, any slight departure from the strict iambic does not need to be condoned or explained, because the rhythm will return to it. And many poets who have not intended to glorify speech rhythms have nevertheless gained variety and richness in the iambic line through deliberate and conversational variations of accents.

But there are further reasons why Frost followed Emerson and Wordsworth in his particular consideration of folk speech. This language has intrinsically two elements in common with poetry: proverbial or epigrammatic turns of phrase, and a natural musical cadence. The very limitations of a small vocabulary and of expressiveness in folk speech force the speaker into direct statements shaded by those tones of voice which convey the peculiar intensity of emotion and thought. Carlyle pointed out that if you "think deep enough you think musically." And from the beginning, all art has been an amplification and sophistication of those deeply felt expressions. Poetry thus finds revitalization when the creative imagination summons up experience fresh from life, and experience which has not been evoked in quite the same way before. And Frost in turning back to this perennial source of inspiration, was eager to break away from the threadbare subjects and tones of poetry: from the wonderful, the beautiful, the heroic, the eternally sublime. The quest for new subject matter and for new treatment of it led him to listen to all the tones of life with a new consciousness that any aspect of life could be a fit subject for poetic treatment if its vitality could be re-created in poetic form.

Such a goal might have taken him into the arms of the "local color" enthusiasts who were having their little day when *North of Boston* was first published. But his characterizations were not concerned with the quaint, the picturesque, the peculiar. Instead, they disclosed and elaborated in subtle and indirect fashion new aspects of the ageless verities: the sorrowful conflicts between good and good, the persistence of loneliness even in love, the power or the failure of love to make recompense for the difference between man and woman. These are but a few of the themes which are unfolded and clarified anew in the homely scenes of his dramatic narratives and characterizations. With them may be found occasional delineation of emotions and thoughts which have been psychologically twisted by fear, hate, pride, jealousy, fatigue. And always there is the subtle indirection of Frost's dramatic method. So much more is suggested than is stated. Somehow the thoughts and emotions are embodied in a context of words which suggest not only a physical setting—a room, a road, a garden, a farm, a grove, a hill—but also a psychological setting.

Any reader whose appreciation of poetry is grounded in the heightened emotional tension of nineteenth century poetry may find Frost's poetry, at first reading, too flat and proselike, because it "keeps the ground and never soars." But his tones of voice are deliberately restrained and relaxed, carefully held down to the natural looseness of conversational rhythms. This is a part of his revolt against the outworn mannerisms of sublimity and prettiness in nineteenth century poetry. He is willing to depend on the compensatory strength of emotional thought implicit in those two planes of meaning, those two planes of sound, which his words and phrases contain. Yet he will not agree with Wordsworth, at one extreme, or with the Imagists, at the other extreme, in their identical contention that there can be no basic difference between the language of prose and the language of poetry. For Frost there must always be in poetry the reconciliation between the cadence, the rhythm, of the spoken sentence and the cadence, the rhythm, of the meter. Lacking this reconciliation of these two elements in sound, the intended poem, as such, has failed. Achieving it, the poem combines manner and matter with its own subtle music which is as natural as it is unmistakable.

*Enthusiasm is taken through the prism of the intellect and
spread on the screen in color, all the way from hyperbole or
overstatement, at one end to understatement at the other end.
It is a long strip of dark lines and many colors. I would be
willing to throw away everything but that: enthusiasm
tamed by metaphors.*[12]

THE FUNCTION OF METAPHOR

PARTICIPATING in the revolt against strain and rage in poetry,
Robert Frost continued to revolt against the revolutionaries, as
strain and rage came back into fashion. Meaningless howls of
despair were just as distasteful to him as meaningless howls of
rapture. There had always been a favorite method for bringing
emotional extremes under control in poetry: enthusiasm tamed by
metaphor.

But the general reader is confused by the discovery that there
are so many approaches to metaphor, so many uses of metaphor
in poetry. Exactly what is the essential function of metaphor?
Many poets, in their attempts to define their tastes, prejudices, and
differences, have been willing to set bounds and to assert correct
usage. There is no simple answer. Some have said that the function
of metaphor in poetry is merely decorative and extraneous. Others
have said that metaphor cannot be justified even on such modest
grounds. If we define metaphor as the use of a word or phrase
(literally denoting one kind of object or idea) in such a way that
it suggests an analogy or a comparison, then we may understand
that the simplest metaphors are words themselves. Each word is a
symbol which *carries over* to our minds an image or an idea.
Obviously, words are makeshift devices which are not satisfactory
because they cannot carry over to our minds exact identities. They
are implements of clarification, and we use them because they
progress toward clarification, not because they ideally accomplish
their intended purpose. We apologize for the inadequacy of words
by finding other words to modify them and assist them; we

develop adjectives and adverbs to help us clarify the intended meanings of nouns and verbs. The process continues and the supply of words is always increasing. Consider, for instance, the way in which "red" seemed good enough to denote a particular color. But if the "red" were still faint as in the morning sky? Probably before Homer somebody had noticed the analogy between the pale red of morning and the pale red of a rose petal— and the analogy became a convenient metaphor which was reduced to a word, an adjective: rosy. But the search for correspondences and analogies continued until the cherry-red gave us another shade of red; and the flesh-color of a fish was a convenient clarification for still another shade. The list of words to define merely that one color, red, has been growing rapidly during the last hundred years.

Always the goal of these sound-metaphors, words, was clarification and definition. It could not be said that the metaphor helped the word; the metaphor was the word and is the word. So, when Frost considers the function of poetry, he thinks of metaphor as that rational act of comparison which brings into focus some analogy to sharpen and clarify the apprehension. At its best, he says, the metaphor is more than a help to the poem; it *is* the poem. The two are inseparable. Leaving the specific metaphor and considering the metaphor in a general sense, in its relation to thought which is so essential to the taming of emotion in prose or in poetry, Frost finds a comparison for the process: the metaphor (as a means to an end) is like a prism, in that it refracts the blinding white light of emotion into its components, breaks it up into colors and shades of colors. Such a means of discrimination leads the poet quite intelligibly to define poetry as a clarification of life.

This organic function of the metaphor in poetry does not restrict the metaphor solely to the realm of identity with the total context of the poem itself. The uses of metaphor are numerous enough in poetry to be fanned out. On the lowest plane the metaphor in poetry is accidental, trivial, or merely ornamental and decorative. Even those who have been willing to restrict it to a single limitation in their poetry have never succeeded in preserving that single limitation whenever they began to apply it. Refusing the limitations of various schools of taste and prejudice in the use of metaphor, Frost has run the gamut of usages in his poetry. In the process he has managed to avoid many of the prejudices, old and new, which may be considered briefly in order to establish his position.

His first rebellion against the inherited usages of the romantics and of many Victorian poets was inspired by his refusal to believe that there were images and ideas which were essentially poetical and others which were not poetical. The roots of this strong prejudice in favor of poetical materials may be traced back through Tennyson, Coleridge, Wordsworth, and back of them even to Addison in the early eighteenth century. But the consistent practice of such a theory had been the strongest proof of its specious and invalid nature. Poets since Chaucer had proved that the only true test of poetic materials was the use made of them in metaphor by the poet. So Frost set out to find images and experiences common in human life but uncommon in poetry, and out of these he began to fashion his metaphors. A botanist, he was willing to gather into his poems flowers so common as bluets and weeds, or so rare as orchises and rose pogonias. Loving the ways and voices of birds, he was content to build into his metaphors such sober creatures as night hawks, crows, and oven birds; or if he wished he was still willing to make use of the more familiar in poetry: the swallows, bluebirds, hummingbirds. His only concern was to give a poetic significance to the images, regardless of the tastes of others for supposedly poetical images. And when he turned to people in his dramatic narratives, he broke away from the familiar treatments of the heroic, the lovelorn, the ostensibly joyous and mournful. Instead, he built metaphors around the virtues and shortcomings of prosaic farmers, tramps, housekeepers, bill collectors, census takers, and hired men. Familiar with rural scenes, he brought into his metaphors stone walls, cellar holes, abandoned houses, kitchen chimneys, lockless doors, grindstones, and axe helves. From the beginning, he used the images of rural country life in New England because he knew them and loved them best. And these have furnished metaphors for general and universal thoughts and emotions.

Other reactionaries who set out to prove that metaphors should
be more than ornaments turned back to the metaphysical poets
for their inspiration. Nurtured in the French Symbolist tradition,
which had given rise to theories that poems were best when they
were most difficult, the twentieth century reactionaries fell down
and worshiped the elaborate and frequently abstruse subtleties of
thought and expression which they found in such metaphysical
poets as Donne, Cowley, and Herbert—but highest hymns of
praise were lifted up for Donne. Many of the moderns seemed
willing to say that they found sanction in the metaphysical poets
for all metaphors and all conceits. Unfortunately the more fantastic metaphors of the metaphysicals were as bad in their way as
were the "intrinsically poetic" and nonrational metaphors and
decorations of the romantics. Like the worst of the metaphysicals,
some of the moderns developed a new kind of strain and rage in
metaphor until they left their readers so far behind that even
persistent study failed to reveal that which the metaphors supposedly intended to clarify. Apologetically, and with a touch of
diffidence, some poets turned critics and tried to explain. Frost
refused to be interested in those intricacies of metaphor which
imperiled the common ground between the poet and his reader.
He preferred to develop metaphors which were quite simple in
denotation, so that the reader might find his pleasure in exploring
the less simple connotations and extensions in subsequent readings.

In the matter of poetic diction, so essential to the construction
of the metaphor, Frost refused to be interested in abstruse words
and esoteric phrases. Again he was willing to live in the fear of
losing that common ground between poet and reader. Communication remained more important to him than unique expression.
He knew that words had never been accurate conveyors of images
and ideas. And he was amused to watch the preoccupation with
semantics which began with the amazingly pretentious discovery
that words failed to convey ideas with enough precision. True
enough, the daily usage establishes rigid connotations which
destroy the intended flexibility of words. Emerson had called

words petrified poetry. To Frost, each poet who perceives his function correctly tries to give new life to the metaphorical quality of words by stretching them out of their old meanings through establishing new tensions in different contexts. When he says that poetry is the constant renewal of words he is thinking of that stretching process which takes them briefly out of drab homeliness and honors them in such a fine relation with other words that they flash proudly for a moment with new vitality before they die back into the common everyday usage.

Another danger has remained with Frost as a warning in his use of metaphor: the testing of analogies and comparisons to be sure that they are apt to convey the intended relationships. Again the rational process comes in to counterbalance the emotional element in poetry. If the comparison is not apt, if it is made without discrimination and precision, the analogy which has been established becomes mere words, words, words. In *Hamlet* there is a striking juxtaposition of good usage and deliberately bad usage in this matter of comparisons. Choosing his image nicely, Hamlet gives a recorder to Guildenstern and asks him to play a tune. Guildenstern says that he does not know how to control the stops on the pipe in such a way as to make it play a tune. Hamlet is ready to press home the analogy: does Guildenstern, with his clumsy and prying ways, suppose that Hamlet is easier to be played on than a recorder? The clarification is quite successful. Then comes "that great baby" Polonius, and Hamlet bitterly indulges in a brief game of bad comparisons. Does Polonius see yonder cloud that seems to have the shape of a camel? Indeed, says Polonius, it does look like a camel. But, suggests Hamlet, perhaps it would be more discriminating to say that it is really more like a weasel? Yes, Polonius decides that it is backed like a weasel. These two premises should lead us to suppose that there might be some similarity in appearance between a camel and a weasel! But Hamlet carried his play one step further: perhaps this camel-weasel shape of the cloud is more like the shape of a whale. Now we have it, and Polonius exclaims that it really does look *very* like a whale. Who is fooling whom? Hamlet wonders. In disgust he changes the subject.

[54]

In one of his playfully serious poems, Frost tells a fable about a hornet which sets out to hunt as usual for flies, but makes a mistake and attacks first a nail and then a huckleberry. Before the poet moves on to his analogy he jests at the Poloniuslike hornet:

> But for the fly he might have made me think
> He had been at his poetry, comparing
> Nailhead with fly and fly with huckleberry:
> How like a fly, how very like a fly.

The implication is that something more than instinct is needed if poet or reader or hornet is to venture into this game of comparisons with a high average of success. Cautious and discriminate testing is required. And humorous as Frost may be in his poem, he is serious in his theory of metaphor correctly used. His own observations on the subject make fitting introduction to any study of his practice:

"I do not think anybody ever knows the discreet use of metaphor, his own and other people's, the discreet handling of metaphor, unless he has been properly educated in poetry. Poetry begins in trivial metaphors, pretty metaphors, 'grace metaphors,' and goes on to the profoundest thinking that we have. Poetry provides the one permissible way of saying one thing and meaning another. People say, 'Why don't you say what you mean?' We never do that, do we, being all of us too much poets. We like to talk in parables and in hints and in indirections—whether from diffidence or from some other instinct. . . .

"What I am pointing out is that unless you are at home in the metaphor, you are not safe anywhere, because you are not at ease in figurative values. You don't know the metaphor in its strength and its weakness. . . . All metaphor breaks down somewhere. That is the beauty of it. It is touch and go with the metaphor, and until you have lived with it long enough you don't know when it is going. You don't know how much you can get out of it and when it will cease to yield. It is a very living thing. It is as life itself. . . .

"But it is the heights of poetry, the height of all thinking, the height of all poetic thinking, that attempt to say matter in terms of spirit and spirit in terms of matter. It is wrong to call anybody a materialist simply because he tries to say spirit in terms of matter—as if that were a sin. The only materialist—be he poet, teacher, scientist, politician, or statesman—is the man who gets lost in his material without a gathering metaphor to throw it into shape or order. He is the lost soul."[13]

If, as they say, some dust thrown in my eyes
Will keep my talk from getting overwise,
I'm not the one for putting off the proof.
Let it be overwhelming, off a roof
And round a corner, blizzard snow for dust,
And blind me to a standstill if it must.[14]

THE YANKEE MANNER

ROBERT FROST's ingrained Yankee manner pervades his art as thoroughly as it pervades his personality and his attitude toward life. From the viewpoint of his artistry, this manner asserts itself in a fine blend of caution, critical detachment, shrewd appraisal of self and others, diffidence, dry terseness, and laconic indirection. In the poems, these diverse elements act as pigments which permit endless combinations and shades of color when mixed with words, phrases, sentences, and symbols. One may easily recognize the most obvious aspects of Frost's all-suffusing Yankee manner; but the reader must realize that these aspects, often deliberately isolated, are related manifestations which have a common source in the very core of the poet's being. And the elements which have been listed are those which are most responsible for that original idiom which is the poet's crowning difference from any other poet, English or American.

We must recognize these elements separately and then we must recognize them as they combine to play on each other. Even as a poem, once analyzed, comes to life again only through a more clearly perceived fusion of the parts, so the poet when considered piecemeal may be understood in all his vitality and consistency only when the diverse and apparently contradictory elements of his personality are reconciled and unified in artistic action. Validity, in a poet or in a man, does not require that the individual shall be consistent; it happens, however, that Frost's integrity has in it a consistency which heightens, invigorates, and dignifies it.

In the artistic process, the Yankee manner may prove to develop virtues and vices; with Frost it has done both, as he well knows. Successfully employed in his highly complicated poems which appear at first glance so simple, these motivating habits of detachment, terseness, and indirection have enabled him to achieve qualities of objectivity, insight, compression, and rich symbolism. Unsuccessfully employed, these have been responsible for a cold flatness, prosaic lines, extrinsic moralizings, faulty ellipsis, and obscurity. Frost understands himself well enough to live in the fear of these poetic vices. He confessed to a part of that fear in his first book when he wrote:

> We make ourselves a place apart
> Behind light words that tease and flout,
> But oh, the agitated heart
> Till someone find us really out.

In the same poem, "Revelation," he asserted his desire to speak with sufficient clarity to keep his poems from developing into hide-and-seek games. Yet there has always remained in him the conflict between his instinctively reticent indirection and his sophisticated craving for clarity and directness of statement. In his successful reconciliations he has chosen words and phrases which may be considered metaphorically and yet may also be considered as blunt statements, flat and final as the showdown in a poker game.

This conflict between Yankee instinct and artistry may be resolved in terms of Frost's literary alignment with poets past and present. Seeking freedom from extravagant poetic mannerisms which might give too much coldness or (less likely) too much heat to his verse, Frost developed his own natural response to a sense of proportion and structural beauty, to a sense of lucidity which might be achieved through restraint and concision. The growing sense of balance in his thought and his art predisposed him to the discovery of a kinship with classical poets and their poetry: the precise compression of songs and epigrams in the *Greek Anthology*, the happy-sad blend of feeling and thought in the odes of Anacreon, and the stoical restraint in the lyrics of Horace and Catullus. In English poetry, Frost was predisposed to lack any lasting sympathy with the careless extravagances of the romantics, the painfully laborious conceits of the metaphysical poets, and the indiscriminate adorations of the Petrarchian school. If necessary, he knew where he would find more congenial companions. So far as English lyrics were concerned, Ben Jonson and Herrick represented in theory and practice that return to the classical spirit which he has admired and sought to master without loss of originality. Obviously, these prejudices in the period of his poetic development were colored to a large extent by his Yankee heritage.

A sympathy for classical restraint in art and thought is only one motivation which seems to find its source in the Yankee manner. Frost's critical detachment is responsible for that rare degree of objectivity which asserts itself even in his most personal and autobiographical lyrics, particularly in those strong love lyrics where love is seldom mentioned. Furthermore, this same detachment, enabling the poet to consider both sides of an attitude, a character, or a situation, helps to create his persistent smile at the humorous, the amusing, the ludicrous. Carried one step more, this same detachment explains quite naturally Frost's highly developed sense of life's ironies, small and large. Although irony will be examined later, in specific forms of poetic expression, it may be considered here, briefly, as indispensable to the poetic theory. At first, Frost's irony seems to grow out of his reticence and his pleasure in understatement. With the poems, ironic understatement often becomes a means of enriching the extensions by implying more than (or even the opposite of) that which is stated. Such usage frequently creates a soft echo of teasing laughter between the lines themselves, so that the reader who is caught off his guard is prompted to look again more carefully because he wonders whether the poet is serious or playful. Perhaps he is both at once!

This pleasure in teasing the reader seems always a part of Frost's ironic detachment and indirection. He likes to point out that it is the manner of the poet to say one thing and mean another. But such is also the manner of the ironist. In his poems, then, metaphor and irony frequently join hands and dance gaily together. Such deliberately ironic equivocation implies a willingness to sacrifice the understanding of certain readers who may not be able to tell, even on second reading, whether they are to believe what they read. But the game of ironic argument, since the days of Socrates himself, has always been played on the supposition that there were two sides who played: the understanding ones and the naïve ones. The poet's intended meaning can be enjoyed to the full only by a reader who is not so naïve as to accept every statement at face value. And this must inevitably leave some readers outside the pale. So be it. There would be no fun in the game if both sides won.

Closely related is Frost's crafty manner of putting himself in a seeming position of censure or misunderstanding. He loves to start out by making fun of himself, then conclude indirectly by making fun of others. The jests and banter have in them an undertone of kindliness and affection which save them from wounding. Direct or indirect, the ironic statement becomes a criticism which is so gentle that it would seem as if the poet had first tried out the sting on himself before inflicting it on others. Even Frost's most sadly serious laments over sorrows induced by the loss of cherished ones, and things, are restrained by objective detachment. He seems to turn his griefs over carefully and gently until he finds at least some reasons for sad smiling. Quite naturally he came to appreciate the ironic secret so nicely expressed by Plato: "Serious things cannot be understood without laughable things, nor opposites at all without opposites, if a man is really to have intelligence of either."

On a different plane, the Yankee manner seems to express itself by revealing the dramatic irony of situation, as in the *North of Boston* poems. The poet shares with the reader his own perception of illusions, while he permits characters to reveal themselves in actions and situations which would have been different if the characters had been aware of the illusions as such. The Greek dramatists seem to have developed dramatic irony because they were using familiar legends and thus were not able to count on the dramatic element of surprise, as the plot unfolded. Although Frost uses the element of surprise, in his miniature dramas, he seems to take pleasure in permitting the reader to know the ending before he starts, as in "The Death of the Hired Man," so that the attention is brought to focus more clearly on the manner in which the actors respond to situations which bring them to an ironic position, whether or not they perceive it. Frost's dramatic irony, thus used, asserts itself through creating a conflict between people and people, between people and circumstances, so that the actors are led to suppose a situation which is directly the opposite of that which exists.

On a third plane, the Yankee manner seems to be largely responsible for a more direct use of irony in Frost's later poems which are openly satirical. Out of his critical detachment and objectivity has grown a natural middle-ground stoicism and acceptance which permits him to view with a kind of cosmic irony the extremes of optimism or pessimism, of blind agnosticism or of blind faith. We have already seen his use of such irony in a poem, "For Once, Then, Something." The later fashion in which Frost turns such discernment to poetic uses will be considered in a complete chapter.

These various manifestations have been sketched and hinted here merely to suggest that the reader needs to be on his guard. There will be sufficient elaboration in the following pages to demonstrate that many modulations in tone and texture have been derived from Frost's inherent and thoroughly mischievous Yankee manner; modulations which have been of great value to his artistry.

POETRY IN PRACTICE

All that can be done with words is soon told. So also with meters—particularly in our language where there are virtually but two, strict iambic and loose iambic. The ancients with many were still poor if they depended on meters for all tune. . . . The possibilities for tune from the dramatic tones of meaning struck across the rigidity of limited meter are endless.[15]

METER, RHYTHM, AND RHYME

THE practical working out of Robert Frost's theory concerning "the sound of sense" or "sound-posturing" can be appreciated only through a direct and technical analysis of his prosodic accomplishment. In brief, the goal which he set for himself was the reconciliation and unification of three separate planes of sound. The first of these is the basic and theoretically rigid meter, which Frost is willing to reduce "virtually" to "strict iambic" and "loose iambic." These basic accents, fitted to the variable structure of the line and of the stanza, offer an underlying foundation for words and phrases. The second plane of sound is derived from the words and phrases as they might be pronounced without regard to meaning, without regard to context. The third plane of sound is derived from the tones of voice which give particularly intended shades of meaning to the words when they are spoken as units in their contexts of phrases and sentences.

These three planes of sound may best be understood if we consider a brief example. Let us form two iambic feet out of four identical words, so that we are conscious only of the metrical accents: "No, no, no, no." The iambic stress falls on the second and fourth of these words and establishes a basic rhythm. Turning to the second plane of sound value, the words themselves have an auditory meaning of nasal consonants and long vowels. Even when the accent of the iambics is combined with the sound of the words themselves, we do not know how the phrase is intended, how it is to be understood. The third plane of sound is needed. Obviously, these four words could be varied with extraordinary range by placing them in different contexts. The third plane of sound is derived from the meaning—triumphant, reproving, scornful, sad—given to these words through the tone of voice when the words are spoken in an intelligible context. Suppose, then, that we substitute the word "life" for the last "no" and let the newly created phrase take its place in the context of King Lear's tragic lament, spoken while he leans over his daughter Cordelia and is suddenly overwhelmed by the fearful thought that she is dead:

> No, no, no life!
> Why should a dog, a horse, a rat, have life,
> And thou no breath at all? Thou'lt come no more,
> Never, never, never, never, never!

Immediately, in such a familiar and painful context, the sound of the sense is the sound of heart-rending anguish and hysteria. The basic meter of this blank verse is the five-stress iambic, and this basic meter constantly asserts itself throughout the passage, in spite of modifications in accent produced by the meaning of the spoken words. The richness of connotation in these phrases and sentences depends primarily on the tone of King Lear's voice as that tone has been established in terms of the cumulative context: his strong love for Cordelia, the estrangement and its tragic implications, then the joyful reconciliation shortly before her violent death. Such a context gives an agonized posture of meaning to the sound of these words as King Lear speaks them. Nevertheless, the total effect depends on a threefold integration of sound values here: metrical accent, word sounds, sense sounds. These three planes of sound, separate in analysis, are blended in performance. As Frost has pointed out, there is nothing new in his theory, for it is always demonstrated as an essentially dramatic quality in all good poetry, regardless of form. From his own remarks, however, it is evident that Frost became particularly aware of this important quality through his protracted and technically conscious reading of Shakespeare's plays.

The same passage from *King Lear* may be used to illustrate a further development of these ideas. If we should examine the history of English and American prosody, we could find periods when poetic theory moved to the extreme assertion that metrical smoothness was of paramount importance to poetry. The school of Alexander Pope fastened such convictions firmly on the eighteenth century. We could also find another school, represented by the exponents of free verse, which moves to the extreme assertion that the irregularity of speech rhythms is of paramount importance to poetry, and that metrical monotony is a vice from which poetry needs complete liberation. Robert Frost maintains that in almost all great poetry there is a reconciliation and balance between these two possible extremes. Neither one can be permitted with safety to dominate the other persistently. If we look again at King Lear's speech, we may see that such a reconciliation is apparent. After the four strong accents of the famous phrase "No, no, no life!" the second line is almost perfectly regular in its five iambics, and even corroborates the proper emphasis of meaning for "should." The third line may be interpreted variously without violating the iambic pattern too severely. Then comes a deliberate reversal of meter in the cumulative and hysterical anguish of "Never, never, never, never, never!" This introduction of trochaic feet in such a nervous crescendo is a powerful corroboration of Lear's unbalanced grief, conveyed by the contextual meaning of the words themselves. The effect is a heightening of the sound of sense. Moreover, the line is the more powerful for the very reason that the iambic rhythm has been maintained hitherto, beneath and through the speech rhythms in the earlier lines. The two extremes of meter have contributed their own peculiar characteristics.

Now let us examine Robert Frost's use of these three sound values which are unified in creation and in re-creation, although they may be separated in theory. A few examples must suffice; then the reader may continue independently with further analysis—or ignore it, if it seems to interfere with the pleasure of his reading. There may be justification for beginning with blank verse, and with a thoroughly familiar passage:

> Something there is that doesn't love a wall,
> That sends the frozen-ground-swell under it,

> And spills the upper boulders in the sun;
> And makes gaps even two can pass abreast.

Taken thus, these four lines have no context of sense to support and amplify them; they must serve also as introduction, in "Mending Wall," and must help not only to establish a setting of images but also to prepare for the exploratory and quizzical tone of voice which finds an outcome in the brief conflict of opinions between the wall menders. The regular iambic pentameter of the first line is modified by the substitution of a trochee in the first foot, and the modification seems to carry the reader into the poem with an almost impulsive sense of ease. In the second line, the undulating sense of thought and meaning is corroborated and heightened by the substitution of a spondee, which makes the rhythm of the line buckle upward when four almost equally strong accents are brought into close proximity with each other: "That sends the *frozen-ground-swell und*er it." In the third line there is another integration of sense and sound. Although the line might be considered metrically regular, the very light accent required by the short vowels in "upper" accelerates the tempo momentarily and gives an appropriately jostling juxtaposition to the plosive consonants in "upper boulders." Then comes another effective variation in the fourth line, where the gap-sense is heightened by the dactylic substitution in the second foot, so that three accents crowd together and slow down the basic rhythm: "And *makes gaps eve*n two can pass abreast." Nevertheless, the enriching of the lines in this manner depends largely on the first two planes of sound. Later, the meaning of the context establishes the characteristic tone of the speaker. After the game starts, and the mischievous narrator begins to tease his neighbor with quizzical demands as to why they should bother to repair unnecessary fences, a nice example of sound-posturing occurs. Who wants the wall down so much as to keep taking it down every time after it is mended?

> I could say "Elves" to him,
> But it's not elves exactly, and I'd rather
> He said it for himself.

In context, the two accented words, "could" and the first " 'Elves' "
earn an almost equal stress; then the sentence turns the corner
of the line, and the next two words are unimportant because of
the meaning beyond them. If we should try to let the iambic
pattern have predominance in this second line, we should know
immediately that we have violated the sense of the words. Furthermore, we have been prepared to enjoy the teasings. So the playfully ironic weighing of such a whimsical suggestion requires us
to read the line in such a way as to build to a crescendo on the
"l" in "elves" and then follow through with the diminishing
irony of the word "exactly" before the pause: "But it's *not elves*
exactly." In keeping with this deliberate aside, the line moves on
after the comma-pause, or caesura, to an extrametrical syllable
perfectly in keeping with the seemingly bemused character of
the Yankee drawl. This kind of reading, in order to taste the
subtle nature of the lines, requires a mental sympathy and alert-
ness which is by no means greater than the sympathy and alert-
ness given by that "fit audience though few" which enjoys the
subtle irony of any good poem. And only in this way can the
reader enjoy the interplay of the three planes of sound which
combine to heighten the total effect.

To appreciate the variety and range which Frost achieves in
blank verse, we must be aware of the fine modulation required
by different situations and characters in the dramatic narratives
and dialogues. Again, familiar passages may help the reader to
follow the analysis without trouble:

> Mary sat musing on the lamp-flame at the table
> Waiting for Warren. When she heard his step,
> She ran on tip-toe down the darkened passage
> To meet him in the doorway with the news
> And put him on his guard. "Silas is back."

On the first two planes of sound values, the reconciliation may
seem quite ordinary. Notice, however, that the first line has
thirteen syllables instead of ten; that no kind of elision will reduce
these to ten; that none is supposed to do so. Yet there are only
five accents required or permitted by the line. The crowding in

of unaccented syllables through anapaestic substitutions is a means of slowing down the line. Furthermore, the technical success in creating a deliberate progression in the first line depends in part on the trochaic substitution in the first foot and on the accumulation of repeated vowel sounds. It is also possible that the line is slowed down, so that it accentuates the sense of waiting and musing, by the second trochaic substitution which brings two accents together and makes the voice linger in pronouncing "lamp-flame." In the second line, the position of the word "waiting," together with its trochaic accent, brings the reader to the caesura at the end of the sentence, with a compressed sense of time slowly passing. The beginning of the second sentence runs out the iambics in the second line, then leads to a third line which is accelerated nicely, as it starts, so that it heightens the meaning of the words: "She ran on tip-toe." Although the short vowels and the monosyllabic words help to give this effect, the line is almost strictly iambic, with the exception of the extrametrical syllable at the end. The iambic rhythm returns in the fourth line and continues in the fifth, although the caesura following the sentence-end is nicely used before the abrupt trochaic accent of the revelation: "Silas . . ." In this short passage, the basic metrical pattern and the rhythm of the conversational words are nicely integrated.

Two snatches of conversation from "The Death of the Hired Man" may help to show another technical accomplishment in blending sound values. The meaning of Warren's impatient refusal to "have the fellow back" is clearly established before the husband begins an imaginary conversation in which he argues with himself and then answers himself. Actually, he seems to be using the arguments he has heard before, under similar circumstances, from his tenderhearted wife:

> " 'He thinks he ought to earn a little pay,
> Enough at least to buy tobacco with,
> So he won't have to beg and be beholden.'
> 'All right,' I say, 'I can't afford to pay
> Any fixed wages, though I wish I could.'
> 'Someone else can.' 'Then someone else will have to.' "

But these arguments are deliberate caricatures of those which might have been spoken by Warren's wife. The predominance of monosyllabic words, and the implied clipping of the t's and the impatient explosive tones implied by the b's, create in the reader's ear the sound-posture which tells how the sentences should be read if they are to convey Warren's impulsive annoyance and disgust over the news that Silas is back. When the rhythm of the meter is violated by the substitution of the trochee at the beginning of the fifth line, the correct stress is given to "*Any* fixed wages." Again, the substituted pair of trochaic feet at the beginning of the next line gives the effect of interruption, as the next argument in favor of Silas is introduced; then the extrametrical syllable, at the end of the line, gives the intended value to "have" before it.

Contrast Warren's tone with the tone of Mary's answer, given as soon as she is permitted to begin. Knowing better than to irritate her husband with any arguments when he is in such a mood for answering them, she develops an indirect method of soothing him and of playing on his sympathy by describing the poor old fellow:

> "He's worn out. He's asleep beside the stove.
> When I came up from Rowe's I found him here,
> Huddled against the barn-door fast asleep.
> A miserable sight, and frightening, too—
> You needn't smile—I didn't recognise him—
> I wasn't looking for him—and he's changed.
> Wait till you see."

The meaning of the sentences, by themselves, conveys Mary's solicitude. But the quality of that solicitude, as it is given in the tone of her voice, is amplified by the interplay of speech rhythms and metrical rhythm. So much of pity is crowded into the first variation from the iambic pattern: three accented syllables, "He's worn out." Then the metrical rhythm returns appropriately in the brief reference to his sleeping. Again it is broken deliberately with a trochaic foot at the beginning of a line, and the off-accent in "Huddled" hints at the sudden surprise of her discovery. Although an elision could be made if the context permitted the next line to read, "A sight so miserable, and frightening, too," the full effect of "miserable" is achieved when it is given the support of the underlying iambic accents, so that three feet are represented in "A miserable sight." The entire passage, contrasting so strongly against Warren's angry words, is technically constructed to accentuate the pathos of the scene and the woman's compassionate pity.

Here we may conclude our detailed analysis. Some readers may object that such dissection implies an impossible degree of deliberate technical tinkering on the part of the poet, in order to produce certain effects. That is probably true. Even Frost could not be sure of the proportion of lines fashioned with cunning and the proportion fashioned instinctively or even accidentally. But does that make any difference? When these deliberate or accidental modulations continue to accumulate over a period of fifty years, the manner of their creation is less important than the fact of their existence. The reader's pleasure is derived from the discovery of these technical virtues, regardless of how they happened to occur in the poetry. Of one fact, however, we are certain. Robert Frost has said enough to convince us of his long-standing delight in those technical aspects of poetry which involve meter and speech rhythms. And fortunately he hasn't been wasting his time!

Even if we must forgo the pleasure of detailed analysis, it is imperative that the reader be made aware of the poet's versatility in adapting various kinds of metrical patterns to his subject matter. In blank verse alone, his accomplishment has not been restricted to dramatic dialogues and narratives. Those who care to study his progress in this verse form will wish to start with his earliest use of it in *A Boy's Will*. "Waiting; Afield at Dusk" is a meditative and descriptive lyric written in a blank verse which is quite stiff and imitative. How many other trials he made in blank verse before he went on to discover his own idiom, nobody knows. Nevertheless, his collected works now contain at least forty-three separate pieces in blank verse, out of a total of more than 250 poems. Several of these, including "Birches," "The Census-Taker," "The Wood-Pile," and "The Old Barn at the Bottom of the Fogs," combine his original qualities of dramatic and descriptive and reflective lyrics. Other shorter poems in blank verse are satirical fables or parables; for example, "The White-tailed Hornet" and "At Woodward's Gardens." Several of his longer pieces, including "New Hampshire" and "Build Soil" are direct blank verse satires in monologue and dialogue. In examining these, the reader may go much further than I have gone to discover the subtle variations and adaptations which the poet's skill and cunning achieve through blank verse to make it suitable for a surprising range of thought and emotion.

Before we leave blank verse, a single variant deserves our attention. Reference has been made to the extrametrical addition of a syllable, so that a regular iambic line of blank verse is thus made to contain eleven syllables. In one of his poems, "For Once, Then, Something," Frost reveals his familiarity with classical versification by using his extrametrical syllable consistently throughout. The verse form thus becomes a popular variant on the Phalaecean hendecasyllabic, with the basic metrical rhythm trochaic. The poem is ingeniously patterned after this classical form, which was a favorite with Martial, Petronius, Statius, and Catullus. It would be hard to find a more successful example in English. "For Once, Then, Something" is quoted entire in a later chapter.

Heroic Couplets

Out of 131 poems written by Robert Frost in five-stress verse, 24 are in heroic couplets, 16 are sonnets, and 46 are stanzaic pieces variously rhymed. Those in heroic couplets illustrate the growth of the poet's technical skill and may be found well scattered throughout his works, from *A Boy's Will* to *A Witness Tree*. The earliest example, "The Tuft of Flowers," is by no means imitative. Nevertheless, it is quite stiff in metrical regularity, and develops a jerkiness from the predominance of end-stopped couplets. A distinct advance may be found in his next use of it as a suitable medium for the mildly satirical fable, "The Cow in Apple Time." Here the poet's use of enjambment, or run-on lines, is so comfortable and successful as to indicate that his practice in blank verse had taught him much concerning the possibilities of iambic pentameter, even in couplets. Furthermore, the substitution of trochaic and anapaestic feet, together with feminine rhymes, enables the poet to avoid the monotony of regular lines and to make full use of speech rhythms. A comparison of these two poems is sufficient to reveal the poet's development in his mastery of couplets.

Heroic couplets are used with nice modulation in several descriptive and reflective lyrics, such as "The Valley's Singing Day," "Our Singing Strength," and "Once by the Pacific." Perhaps "Once by the Pacific" offers in this class the best example of dramatic adaptation for the elaboration of a mood:

> The shattered water made a misty din.
> Great waves looked over others coming in,
> And thought of doing something to the shore
> That water never did to land before.
> The clouds were low and hairy in the skies,
> Like locks blown forward in the gleam of eyes.
> You could not tell, and yet it looked as if
> The shore was lucky in being backed by cliff,
> The cliff in being backed by continent;
> It looked as if a night of dark intent
> Was coming, and not only a night, an age.
> Someone had better be prepared for rage.
> There would be more than ocean-water broken
> Before God's last *Put out the Light* was spoken.

Foreboding is the mood felt in the poet and conveyed to the reader through the images of late-afternoon surf hammering away at cliff-beaches beneath a lowering sky. The rhymes, so gracefully fitted to the natural sequence of the spoken phrases, appropriately supplement the rhythmical recurrence of the accents and corroborate the sense of the words. The couplets are varied nicely with end-stopped sentences, and enjambment which speeds up the motion of the poem at the beginning of the second half. Then all is slowed with ominous dignity by the one-line sentence which rounds out the next-to-last couplet and prepares the way for the final couplet. The basic metrical rhythm is successfully varied with occasional trochaic feet and caesuras. And throughout, the arrangement of the vowels, particularly the recurrence of a's and o's, is combined with the accumulation of rumbling consonants, m's and n's, to heighten the onomatopoeic effect.

Occasionally, Frost has developed heroic couplets in such a manner as to justify their arrangement into quatrains. In *A Boy's Will*, for example, "A Prayer in Spring" contains four couplet-quatrains; yet each stanza is given a unity and the poem as a whole has its dramatic progression of images and thoughts. Again, in *New Hampshire*, "The Onset" is a dramatic lyric in couplets, divided into two stanzas of uneven lengths. In that poem the division is justified by the transition from the indirect narrative to the meditative elaboration of the incident. The first half of "The Onset," built around a mood of despair, is nicely balanced against the second half, built around a theme of philosophic optimism.

Like many other poets, Frost has found the heroic couplet well suited to the purposes of satire. Reference has already been made to the mildly satirical fable about the headstrong cow. Quite different use is made of couplets in several other fables, such as "The Bear" and "A Considerable Speck." Certain poems which might be considered as parables, because they contain implied narratives told not merely for the sake of the narratives, also make use of heroics; as for example, "The Figure in the Doorway," "The Armful," and (with double couplets) the exceptionally fine "Lost Follower." Some of the epigrammatic verses depend in part on the couplets for compression and emphasis. Among these are "The Cocoon," "Dust in the Eyes," "Riders," "The Span of Life," "Waspish," "One Guess," and "What Fifty Said." Not all of these, however, are satirical in tone or implication. "Moon Compasses," epigrammatic in its brevity, is unique among Frost's couplet verses because it builds to a conclusive connotation which deliberately projects the reader beyond the final rhyme, almost as though the reticence of the poet kept him from completing the fragment:

> I stole forth dimly in the dripping pause
> Between two downpours to see what there was.
> And a masked moon had spread down compass rays
> To a cone mountain in the midnight haze,

As if the final estimate were hers,
And as it measured in her calipers,
The mountain stood exalted in its place.
So love will take between the hands a face . . .

The effect of the poem might have been stronger if the final line had ended with a period instead of the three dots, for the extensions are sufficient. Technically, the poem takes great freedom with the couplets, after the first two lines, not only in the matter of enjambment but also in matters of trochaic and anapaestic substitutions. One may recognize here the relationship between the poet's mature handling of the couplets and of blank verse, in so far as the conflict between metrical precision and speech rhythm has been reconciled through mutual consideration.

Sonnets

Before we examine the extent of five-stress verse in miscellaneous poems, its use in the sonnets deserves special attention. Of the sixteen sonnets in the collected poems, none of them could be called strictly regular in following either the Italian or the Shakespearean rhyme scheme. Nevertheless, they all represent in a new manner the poet's pleasure in showing deference to established forms, even when he takes bold liberties with metrical patterns or rhyme.

"A Dream Pang" may have been one of his early sonnets, for it shows traces of padding which would have been avoided later. The octave follows the Italian pattern, while the sestet is Shakespearean. It shows nothing exceptionally good in performance; comes off tolerably well and that is, technically, the most that may be said for it. Another early sonnet, "The Vantage Point," continues the use of the Italian form for the octave, then concludes the sestet with a quatrain (rhyming c-d-d-c) followed by a couplet. The handling of the phrases is much more graceful and adept, however; thoroughly in the manner of Frost's more mature poems in *A Boy's Will*. "Into my Own" follows the Shakespearean division of thought into three quatrains and a summary couplet, although the rhyme-scheme falls into seven couplets. Internally, this couplet-sonnet reveals an even greater technical advance in permitting the sound of sense to fight it out with the iambics. Nevertheless, the predominance of monosyllabic words permits the basic metrical pattern to assert itself with almost too much strength.

By far the most advanced and original sonnet in *A Boy's Will* is "Mowing," so thoroughly irregular as to seem at first glance to lack any pattern of rhyme. Actually the scheme reveals a shrewd economy of rhymes: exactly the number found in a Shakespearean sonnet, yet different at every point: a-b-c-a-b-d, e-c-d-f-e-g, f-g. Thus the natural divisions fall into two sestets and an unrhymed couplet, although the cumulative development of a single meditative incident is more nearly in the manner of the unified Miltonic sonnet. While these strongly conversational phrases and sentences lend themselves to the established metrical pattern, not one single line has the correct number of syllables for strict iambic pentameter, and the accents deliberately avoid metrical precision. Many lines are crowded with substitutions and extrametrical syllables which are so nicely reconciled with the iambic pattern that no difficulty occurs when it is read aloud:

> There was never a sound beside the wood but one,
> And that was my long scythe whispering to the ground.
> What was it it whispered? I knew not well myself;
> Perhaps it was something about the heat of the sun,
> Something, perhaps, about the lack of sound—
> And that was why it whispered and did not speak.
> It was no dream of the gift of idle hours,
> Or easy gold at the hand of fay or elf:
> Anything more than the truth would have seemed too weak
> To the earnest love that laid the swale in rows,
> Not without feeble-pointed spikes of flowers
> (Pale orchises), and scared a bright green snake.
> The fact is the sweetest dream that labor knows.
> My long scythe whispered and left the hay to make.

Although the iambics dominate, the persistent recurrence of substituted anapaestic feet contributes much to the richness of unstressed syllables whispering against the basic rhythm. And the discreet use of trochees and spondees gives added flexibility.

Notice that the most nearly regular line occurs exactly when the sententious quality of the thought can make best use of the metrical corroboration: "The fact is the sweetest dream that labor knows." The substance of this sonnet will be considered in a later chapter.

In *Mountain Interval*, a restrained love poem is cast in the sonnet form: "Meeting and Passing." The octave follows the Italian pattern, while the sestet is Shakespearean. But the connotations, developed from the memory of that moment when first the lovers met, follows the thought structure of the Miltonic form. Perhaps more interesting than the metrical substitutions and the highly successful enjambments is the careful use of the caesura to accentuate the thought. In this sonnet, the reader must hear the tone of conversational voice in order to understand the summary couplet which rounds out this picture of the two lovers who recall how they stopped to talk before continuing on their way:

> Afterward I went past what you had passed
> Before we met and you what I had passed.

The lack of punctuation, to set off the phrase "before we met" is characteristic of the poet's reliance on the tone and manner of the spoken phrase to clarify the meaning. This same restricted use of unnecessary punctuation is carried out boldly in *A Witness Tree*. Frost has often said that he hears every phrase and sentence of his poem as though they were spoken aloud, before he writes them down on paper. The implication for the reader is that each poem requires an audience (as opposed to spectators) before it can be fully understood and appreciated.

Certain irregularities in later sonnets are indicative of Frost's successful continuation of his experiments. "Hyla Brook" (a companion-piece for "Meeting and Passing," in that it celebrates the importance of a memory) starts out in the Italian manner, then seems to run wild in its rhyme scheme: a-b-b-a-c-c-a-d-d-e-e-f-g-f-g. Again a single image is elaborated with cumulative implications through fourteen lines; but most unconventionally, a sententious fifteenth line is added to cap the thought: "We love the things we love for what they are." Without the rest of the poem, the line may seem more mysterious than it actually is. And if the extra line seems unconventional, the separate sentence for summary was employed successfully in Milton's memorable last line to the "Sonnet on his Blindness." Lest anyone should complain of the generosity of the extra line in "Hyla Brook," Frost puts near it another irregular sonnet which has only thirteen lines! Much in the same pattern of the same period is "The Oven Bird." With these in *Mountain Interval* occurs, however, a sonnet entitled "Range-Finding," which is almost perfectly Italian in its rhyme scheme. All of these show the poet's technical adaptation of verse form, rhyme, and meter to the peculiar needs of the images and thoughts.

There are no sonnets in *New Hampshire*. When Frost returned to this form in later books, he seemed to have returned to the pleasurable restrictions of rhyme schemes which varied the established forms only slightly. "Acceptance," "On a Tree Fallen Across the Road," "The Investment," "The Silken Tent" are Shakespearean in the pattern of rhymes, and follow exactly (or roughly) the threefold progression of thought before the tie-off knot in the couplet. "The Line-Gang" and "Design," on the other hand, are almost perfectly Italian in rhymes. "On a Bird Singing in Its Sleep" again returns to the old experiment of couplets throughout, although the inclusion of this as a sonnet (as opposed to the arbitrarily excluded "Once by the Pacific") may be justified because of its careful transition and elaboration of thought, after the poem moves from the octave into the sestet.

The meditative quality of these sonnets is not always dominant. Several of them are dramatic incidents which develop a brief narrative for metaphorical or ironic effect. Some of them, like "Design" and "On a Bird Singing in Its Sleep" (companion sonnets) are fables-in-little. In all of them, the poet has demonstrated his fondness not only for the dramatic situations but also for the dramatic postures of voice-ways.

Five-stress Verse

Iambic pentameter, aside from sonnets, couplets, or blank verse, is used variously by Frost in almost fifty separate poems. They may be found in the quatrains and sestets of his epigrams; in the tercets, quatrains, and sestets of his dramatic lyrics or his reflective lyrics, in his parables, fables, and satires. At times the regularity of the metrical pattern is not matched by the rhyme; at other times the irregular rhymes are supported by irregular metrical variations. Let us examine briefly the extent of forms which have been developed within this single group.

The alternating rhymes of quatrains, as they occur in the Shakespearean sonnets, immediately suggest possibilities for poems longer or shorter than the sonnet. Such an epigram as "Immigrants" is made from a single quatrain rhyming a-b-a-b. Similarly, three or four quatrains with alternating rhymes are used in such dramatic and reflective lyrics as "Lost in Heaven," "The Strong Are Saying Nothing," and "Not Quite Social." Occasionally, in a pair of quatrains, the rhymes are permitted to interlock the two stanzas. "Blue-Butterfly Days" has only two stanzas which rhyme thus: a-b-a-b, a-c-a-c. Still another variation (a-b-b-a, c-b-b-c) occurs in "Fragmentary Blue":

> Why make so much of fragmentary blue
> In here and there a bird, or butterfly,
> Or flower, or wearing-stone, or open eye,
> When heaven presents in sheets the solid hue?
>
> Since earth is earth, perhaps, not heaven (as yet)—
> Though some savants make earth include the sky;
> And blue so far above us comes so high,
> It only gives our wish for blue a whet.

Such a rhyme scheme is merely a slight variation on the octave of the Italian sonnet. Certain of Frost's shorter poems might be considered as variations on the sestet of the Shakespearean sonnet. "The Freedom of the Moon," for example, is fashioned into a pair of sestets rhyming thus: a-b-a-b-c-c, d-e-d-e-f-f. The poet seems to take pleasure in letting the first stanza set the pattern for the rhyme, in these shorter poems, and then of requiring that the second stanza shall carry out the established pattern. This arrangement of a sestet from a quatrain and a couplet combined is prettily reversed in the familiar and charmingly graceful "Spring Pools," rhyming a-a-b-c-b-c, d-d(almost)-e-f-e-f.

Another pattern for rhyming sestets may be found when a pair of tercets, or triplets, is combined, as in two of Frost's epigrams entitled "Atmosphere" and "Fireflies in the Garden." The tercets are also employed in longer poems such as "A Star in a Stone-Boat." And at least once, Frost uses the difficult *terza rima*, capped with a couplet, to form a reflective lyric, "Acquainted With the Night," with two planes of metaphorical reference so nicely balanced in denotation and connotation as to make the symbolism highly successful:

> I have been one acquainted with the night. A
> I have walked out in rain—and back in rain. b
> I have outwalked the furthest city light. A
>
> I have looked down the saddest city lane. b
> I have passed by the watchman on his beat c
> And dropped my eyes, unwilling to explain. b
>
> I have stood still and stopped the sound of feet c
> When far away an interrupted cry d
> Came over houses from another street, c
>
> But not to call me back or say good-bye; d
> And further still at an unearthly height, A
> One luminary clock against the sky d
>
> Proclaimed the time was neither wrong nor right. A
> I have been one acquainted with the night. A

Another kind of "third rhyme" may be found in certain five-line stanzas. In *A Witness Tree*, for example, the reflective serenity of the lyric entitled "I Could Give All to Time" is made of three quintets rhyming a-b-a-b-a, and continuing the pattern throughout. "There Are Roughly Zones" might seem to have started out as a possible quartet of five-line stanzas, but it took another direction, and the poet gave the animal its head until it developed a curiously complicated and thoroughly satisfying structure of irregular rhymes.

Several of the longer poems in iambic pentameter are not divided into stanzas and are thus permitted to discover their own irregular system of rhyme as they progress. Occasionally they seem to begin with blank verse; but the poet loves to accept the responsibilities of rhyme. Some of the most interesting patterns of irregularity may be found in "The Exposed Nest," "Loneliness," "An Encounter," "The Grindstone," and "The Runaway." One example, from the poem entitled "On Looking Up By Chance at the Constellations" may be given because of its curious tendency to approximate some regularity: a-b-c-a-b-c-d-e-d-f-f-e-g-g-h-h. Occasionally, when the thought and mood and meaning of the poem can utilize irregularity in the meter as well as the rhyme, the poet breaks the pentameters deliberately, as in "Storm Fear" and "After Apple-Picking." The appearance of these lines on the page suggests blank verse; but the twofold difference may be found in the persistent rhyme and in the persistent return of the meter to the five-stress iambics.

Four-stress Verse

Robert Frost has played almost as many variations on the four-stress line as on the iambic pentameter. Well over sixty of his poems may be found to make pleasurable use of octosyllabics, in one form or another. Again, the subject matter in this classification spreads all the way from the trivial to the tragic; from slight epigrams, parables, and short lyrics to the longer dramatic narratives and ballads. The stanzaic forms employed for the four-stress lines begin with couplets, continue with tercets, quatrains, cinquains, sestets, and octaves, and end with longer arrangements in irregular verses.

The epigrams alone contain a nice spread of tetrameters. No finer example of compression in two lines could be found than

Frost's summary of his philosophic skepticism in my favorite couplet of eight-syllable lines:

> We dance round in a ring and suppose,
> But the Secret sits in the middle and knows.

Even in such a limited space, the connotations are emphasized by the four anapaestic substitutions. Couplets are combined to make a single poem out of a quatrain, in the carefully modulated epigrams entitled "Plowmen" and "Devotion." In the first of these, the clipped precision of the meter serves to accentuate the terse irony of the thought; in the latter, the regular addition of extrametrical syllables in the rhymes and the feminine rhyme in the final couplet are nicely suited to the subtly equivocal meaning. Tenacity, in a different sense, is achieved through the feminine rhymes in the first couplet of the epigram entitled, "In Divés' Dive," where three couplets are combined to make the brief unit. Still epigrammatic in tone, "A Peck of Gold" makes use of the same meter and the same couplets although the verse is arranged into three quatrains in which certain variations are played on a chorus-couplet which is repeated in each quatrain. "In Neglect" uses a single five-line stanza for epigrammatic effect, although the rhymes follow a ballad pattern. "Revelation" is also essentially an epigram, with the three quatrains tied up with alternating rhymes.

In the longer poems, Frost has used the octosyllabic couplet for many different moods and subjects. Several of the dramatic and descriptive lyrics, such as "House Fear," "A Passing Glimpse," "A Minor Bird," "A Winter Eden," and "The Birthplace" belong in this group, regardless of their possible arrangement into stanzas of two or four lines. If one studies these in the order of their progression, it will be seen that there is a definite advance in technical modulations and adaptations. In the later poems, so much variety has been gained as to make the reader overlook the basic metrical pattern. "Leaves Compared with Flowers," for example, seems to permit the conversational voice to dominate the four-stress iambics in the lines, while the rhymes fall comfortably into place. Nevertheless, the underlying metrical regularity contributes much to the poem. Again, a new tune is played on the four-stress lines by varying the couplet-rhymes so that a break occurs in the ending of the third line. "Desert Places" offers a good example:

> They cannot scare me with their empty spaces
> Between stars—on stars where no human race is.
> I have it in me so much nearer home
> To scare myself with my own desert places.

There is only one rhyme in this stanza, the third line remaining unrhymed throughout the poem. In "Stopping by Woods on a Snowy Evening," the third line is put to better use by permitting it to predicate the three sounds which are to be repeated in the next stanza, thus interlocking stanza with stanza. Such an ingenious pattern outrhymes the difficult *terza rima*.

Several dramatic and reflective lyrics make use of the octosyllabic quatrains, with alternate rhymes. "Going for Water" is an early example which may be contrasted with another narrative-reflective lyric in a later manner, "Trespass." The same quatrain form is used for dramatic narrative in "Brown's Descent" and with a strikingly different effect in the double quatrains of "The Trial by Existence," which first appeared in *A Boy's Will*. Unless one looked twice at the four-stress octaves of "The Trial by Existence" and of a later example, "Two Tramps in Mud Time," there would seem to be no close similarity. Here is an illustrative stanza from the first of these:

> Even the bravest that are slain
>   Shall not dissemble their surprise
> On waking to find valor reign,
>   Even as on earth, in paradise;
> And where they sought without the sword
>   Wide fields of asphodel fore'er,
> To find that the utmost reward
>   Of daring should be still to dare.

The iambics in these lines are permitted to continue with very few substitutions, and the regularity sustains the sententious tone of thought. Consider, however, the far more flexible handling of the same verse form in the later poem, "Two Tramps," from which one verse may be chosen:

> The sun was warm but the wind was chill.
> You know how it is with an April day
> When the sun is out and the wind is still,
> You're one month on in the middle of May.
> But if you so much as dare to speak,
> A cloud comes over the sunlit arch,
> A wind comes off a frozen peak,
> And you're two months back in the middle of March.

The difference in rhythm, as illustrated by these two passages, is the difference between declamation and conversation. The substance of the first requires a certain dignified arrangement of periods, while the weather-talk of the second can make good use of the impetuous by racy sentences, aided by the anapaestic substitutions.

According to Frost's implied attitude toward loose iambics, there is nothing to hinder him from permitting his iambics to become so persistently loose that the anapaests dominate a line. Several of his earliest poems, which seem to have been done before the poet's theory about strict and loose iambics had asserted itself, are built of four-stress lines which are basically anapaestic throughout. "The Demiurge's Laugh" in *A Boy's Will* is written in six-line tetrameters, rhyming in the ballad pattern, a-b-a-b-c-c—quite similar to the stanza form of Wordsworth's familiar "I Wandered Lonely as a Cloud." The dominance of the anapaests, however, gives an entirely different effect:

> It was far in the sameness of the wood;
>   I was running with joy on the Demon's trail,
> Though I knew what I hunted was no true god.
>   It was just as the light was beginning to fail
> That I suddenly heard—all I needed to hear:
> It has lasted me many and many a year.

It will be noticed that the pleasurable variety of these lines is obtained by the substitution of an iambic foot at the end of the second line and of a spondee so well suited to the accented thought at the end of the third line, together with the hovering accent in the middle of the irregular first line. A distinctly different flexibility is achieved in the anapaestic couplets of the dramatic monologue entitled "Blueberries," from which one passage may be quoted:

> "Why, there hasn't been time for the bushes to grow.
> That's always the way with the blueberries, though:
> There may not have been the ghost of a sign
> Of them anywhere under the shade of the pine,
> But get the pine out of the way, you may burn
> The pasture all over until not a fern
> Or grass-blade is left, not to mention a stick,
> And presto, they're up all around you as thick
> And hard to explain as a conjuror's trick."

In this conversational passage, monotony is so successfully avoided that only the fourth line is regular, while the second line, beginning with a spondee, is followed by the third line with two iambic substitutions and continues to develop a consistent irregularity of initial iambs in each first foot of the last five lines. This latter variation is also employed to give variety to the anapaestic tetrameter in "Good-Bye and Keep Cold."

An entirely different modification occurs when the four-stress lines are used in certain forms which are related to the ballad: the five-line stanzas, the six-line stanzas, or the combined five-and-three-stress lines. One pattern of rhyme is established in the single stanza of the five-line epigrammatic "In Neglect," thus: a-b-a-a-b; it is used again in "My November Guest," "In a Vale," "All Revelation," and "The Road Not Taken." Quite different is the scheme of the five-line "Pan With Us," in which a single-rhyming tercet is combined with a rhyming couplet: a-a-a-b-b. In "Ghost House" the couplet rhyme is placed within the pattern of the dominant rhyme, thus: a-a-b-b-a. In a six-line stanza such as that of "To a Young Wretch," the scheme is equivalent to the rhyme of the Shakespearean sonnet-sestet: a-b-a-b-c-c. To be sure, there is nothing to hinder the poet from experimenting with a four-stress sonnet, as in "Unharvested" (rhyming thus: a-b-a-c-b-c-d-a-d-e-e-d-f-f) and "A Trial Run" (rhyming a-a-b-c-c-a-b-d-c-f-f-c-d-f) — although these are so irregular in structure as well as in rhyme

[86]

that they may be considered merely as fourteen-line variations on the four-stress poems.

Irregularity of rhyme in the tetrameter is found in poems from the earliest to the latest. One of the earliest is the prayerlike "October," while the later ones include the dramatic-narrative-reflective poems, "A Lone Striker," "A Missive Missile," as well as the satirical poems, "To a Thinker" and "A Considerable Speck." Always the principle illustrated in these poems seems to be that Frost wants to have his cake of rhyme and ignore it too, for he manages to make his rhymes fall with the ease of accidental discovery. And in all these poems, the variations of the rhyme combine with the variations of the metrical rhythm and the tones of the spoken words. His own five-stress epigram, "In a Poem," pleasantly tells us how it is with him:

> The sentencing goes lightly on its way,
> And takes the playfully objected rhyme
> As surely as it keeps the stroke and time
> In having its undeviable say.

Ballad Verse

Ballads have always demonstrated the instinctive poetic tendency to establish a reconciliation between metrical rhythms and speech rhythms. Frost has used certain ballad verses for his lyrics, as has already been suggested. But some of his most successful metrical irregularities in this class remain to be considered. Ballads and hymns frequently alternate lines of different lengths, particularly the four-stress lines and the three-stress lines. In *A Boy's Will* there are several ballad variants. "A Line-Storm Song" is constructed in octaves which might be considered double quatrains with alternating rhymes and alternating four-and-three-stress lines. In characteristic ballad fashion, the basic iambic pattern is generously modified with trochees, spondees, and anapaests. Another early poem which shows conscious technical structure is "Now Close the Windows," with its four-stress quatrains curiously modified, by permitting the third line of each stanza to have five stresses, nicely filled out by the phrase of the sentence; then a fourth line of three stresses, in each stanza. The first two lines of each are dominantly anapaestic, the third line of each is dominantly iambic, while the fourth lines are irregular. With all these changes, the poem may be read aloud with a sense of highly rhythmical symmetry. In *Mountain Interval*, "A Patch of Old Snow" has only two quatrains, seemingly alternating four-three lines. On closer examination, however, it is noticed that the first three lines of each quatrain have three stresses each, while the last line of each has only two. Again, as in "Now Close the Windows," the substitutions are ingeniously arranged to give a richness of unaccented syllables which round out the piece. When the four-three alternating stresses are actually established in "The Oft-Repeated Dream," the substitutions again find their reconciliation with the iambics, although there seems to be as much pleasure in the irregular foot as in the regular. As an example of considerate technical modulation this psychological lyric of fear will reward anyone who examines it closely:

> She had no saying dark enough
>   For the dark pine that kept
> Forever trying the window-latch
>   Of the room where they slept.
>
> The tireless but ineffectual hands
>   That with every futile pass
> Made the great tree seem as a little bird
>   Before the mystery of glass!
>
> It never had been inside the room,
>   And only one of the two
> Was afraid in an oft-repeated dream
>   Of what the tree might do.

The rhyme scheme here is a familiar one in hymns and ballads: x-a-x-a. The same pattern may be found in "A Leaf Treader," although the alternating four-three lines are there combined to make long seven-stress lines which support the sense of weariness and fatigue. Another complicated lyric which belongs with these is "After-flakes," an irregular five-line trio of ballad stanzas rhyming a-b-c-c-b, while the stresses in the corresponding lines arrange themselves 3-3-5-4-3, with substitutions enough to make the iambics dizzy! Nevertheless, the performance of this dramatic-reflective lyric is excellent. Occasionally, the four-three quatrains may require, from the contemplative nature of the meaning, a more nearly regular faithfulness to the iambic pattern. "The Peaceful Shepherd" offers an appropriate illustration of such metrical regularity:

> If heaven were to do again,
> And on the pasture bars,
> I leaned to line the figures in
> Between the dotted stars,
>
> I should be tempted to forget,
> I fear, the Crown of Rule,
> The Scales of Trade, the Cross of Faith.
> As hardly worth renewal.
>
> For these have governed in our lives,
> And see how men have warred.
> The Cross, the Crown, the Scales may all
> As well have been the Sword.

Herein the restrained and sadly ironic posture of the words is best satisfied by the balanced behavior of the underlying meter.

Three-stress Verse

The same ballad effect of uneven lines may often be achieved by anapaestic enrichment which gives the illusion of different accents in different lines. "Reluctance," in *A Boy's Will*, is a six-line stanza, rhyming a-b-c-b-d-b, with three-stress lines throughout, except for the last lines in each stanza. When "Reluctance" is read aloud, the listener seems to feel that the accents in the second and fourth lines are at least one more than in the first, third, and fifth lines. The effect depends on the accumulation of a greater number of anapaestic substitutions and the persistence of the unaccented extrametrical syllables, interlocked with feminine rhymes. Here is the first verse:

> Out through the fields and the woods
> And over the walls I have wended;
> I have climbed the hills of view

And looked at the world, and descended;
I have come by the highway home,
And lo, it is ended.

Different effects are achieved through the same devices, in the three-stress double quatrains of "Rose Pogonias" and "Flower-Gathering"; also in five-line stanzas of "Bond and Free." Occasionally, as in "To Earthward," the three-stress stanzas are modified to good advantage by a two-stress line at the end of each stanza. Another method of giving this illusion of variety is achieved in a poem such as "The Last Mowing," where (as in "Reluctance") masculine and feminine endings are alternated.

Of the thirty-four poems written by Frost in three-stress lines many are quite regular in accent. The crisp quality of these short lines lends itself nicely to epigrammatic and satirical thrusts. Among such shorter pieces may be found "Lodged," "Nothing Gold Can Stay," "Triple Bronze," "Not All There," "Voice Ways," "Neither Out Far Nor in Deep," and "Evil Tendencies Cancel." Among the longer satirical poems in this class are the couplet-rhymed fables entitled "Departmental" and "A Drumlin Woodchuck."

Two-stress Verse

One may easily see how the brevity of dimeter lines lends itself to little poetic flashes such as the epigrammatic couplet entitled "Assertive," the tenderly playful "The Rose Family" and the gemlike "Dust of Snow." Frost has also used this metrical pattern for dramatic lyrics such as "Gathering Leaves," "Canis Major," and "Happiness." Perhaps one of the most unusual of these shorter dramatic lyrics is a symbolic incident which makes good use of the nervous little lines. In *A Witness Tree*, it is entitled "The Rabbit Hunter":

Careless and still
The hunter lurks
With gun depressed,
Facing alone
The alder swamps

[90]

> Ghastly snow-white.
> And his hound works
> In the offing there
> Like one possessed,
> And yelps delight
> And sings and romps,
> Bringing him on
> The shadowy hare
> For him to rend
> And deal a death
> That he nor it
> (Nor I) have wit
> To comprehend.

The severely restricted economy of syllables necessary to the stark metrical pattern, here, is a corroboration of the breathless tension implied by the ironic meaning.

Another kind of breathlessness, caused by an attempt to hear and perceive distant sounds and sights, physical and spiritual, is also supported by the two-accent lines in "I will Sing You One-O," which appeared in *New Hampshire*. In that poem, however, the sentences are given a variety of rhythmical changes through the introduction of trochees, spondees, dactyls, and anapaests. The poem, which develops monistic connotations out of the one-o'clock stroke of the village bell, begins thus:

> It was long I lay
> Awake that night
> Wishing the tower
> Would name the hour
> And tell me whether
> To call it day
> (Though not yet light)
> And give up sleep.

Thus the two-stress lines round out the picture of Frost's experiments and accomplishments in bringing endless possibilities of permutation and combination to his poetry. It would be difficult to say that he has used one form better than another, for each has been adapted to the needs of the moods and the meanings and the material. Suffice it to say that he has developed an extraordinary range in metrical and stanzaic modification; that he has demonstrated an exceptionally fine understanding and mastery of technical possibilities.

The most exciting movement in nature is not progress,
advance, but expansion and contraction, the opening and
shutting of the eye, the hand, the heart, the mind. We throw
our arms wide with a gesture of religion to the universe; we
close them around a person. We explore and adventure for a
while and then we draw in to consolidate our gains. The
breathless swing is between subject matter and form.[16]

EARLY LYRICS

UNLIKE most first books, *A Boy's Will* was published when
the poet was almost forty years old. He had not turned tardily to
the writing of poetry; back of him were many years of persistent
and compelling devotion to his art. His first poem to be published
in a periodical had appeared in 1890 and was followed by at least
a score of others during the apprentice years. His own most severe
critic, Frost carefully winnowed out so many of these early poems
that his first book was made up largely of his latest accomplishments before 1913, although it contained a few that had been
written more than twenty years earlier.

The perceptive reader may find in *A Boy's Will* an epitome of
growth. In spite of his later protests against the exalted tone and
diction of nineteenth century poetry, some of his earliest pleasure
grew out of his response to the ballads, odes, and lyrics of Coleridge, Wordsworth, Keats, and Shelley. The disparity between
his earlier prejudices and his later convictions may be suggested
by his particular fondness for one line of Shelley's which stayed
long in his mind as an indirect definition of poetry: "Where music
and moonlight and feeling are one." Like the romantics, he first
found in poetry a reflection of various moods which blended the
sense impressions of sight, sound, and touch. Even in *A Boy's
Will* there remain evidences to corroborate that first response.
The archaic words, rich vowel sounds, alliteration, conventional
rhythms, and ornate phrases of certain early verses are bouquets
from the literary fields which appealed to the young poet when he

began to botanize for words. They remain to represent the period when he explored and adventured widely before he drew in to consolidate his gains. Frost has given us his own apt metaphor to describe the poetic development:

"No one given to looking underground in spring can have failed to notice how a bean starts its growth from the seed. Now the manner of a poet's germination is less like that of a bean in the ground than of a water-spout at sea. He has to begin as a cloud of all the other poets he ever read. That can't be helped. And first the cloud reaches down toward the water from above and then the water reaches up toward the cloud from below and finally cloud and water join together to roll as one pillar between heaven and earth. The base of water he picks up from below is of course all the life he ever lived outside of books. . . ."[17]

The surprising discovery about Frost is that he has so completely assimilated and absorbed his own indebtedness to an extremely large "cloud of all the other poets he ever read." If any influence may have dominated, however, it is found in later poems where his own mastery yet permits him to hint at long friendships with certain lasting favorites, from Browning, Emerson, and Wordsworth back to Herrick and Jonson, from Jonson directly back to the classical poets, Horace and Catullus, Vergil, Theocritus, Martial, and those represented in the *Greek Anthology*. In the later poems, as we shall see, Frost shows that he absorbed and assimilated the spirit of the classical lyric, the classical epigram, the bucolic and pastoral poetry, even of the Greek and Latin eclogues and satires. Instead of imitating them, he has created in his own American sentences a variety of poetry as thoroughly original as any written by his friends among poets ancient or modern.

Nevertheless, the spell of the romantics such as Keats and Shelley was strong enough to leave its mark on a few of his early poems. One example of Frost's tribute to such poets may be found in "My Butterfly, An Elegy," first published in the *Independent* for November 8, 1894, and subsequently included in *A Boy's Will*. It was written while Frost was a freshman at Dartmouth College in the fall of 1892. Here are the first twenty-one lines:

> Thine emulous fond flowers are dead, too,
> And the daft sun-assaulter, he
> That frighted thee so oft, is fled or dead:
> Save only me
> (Nor is it sad to thee!)
> Save only me
> There is none left to mourn thee in the fields.
>
> The gray grass is scarce dappled with the snow;
> Its two banks have not shut upon the river;
> But it is long ago—
> It seems forever—
> Since first I saw thee glance,
> With all thy dazzling other ones,
> In airy dalliance,
> Precipitate in love,
> Tossed, tangled, whirled and whirled above,
> Like a limp rose-wreath in a fairy dance.
>
> When that was, the soft mist
> Of my regret hung not on all the land,
> And I was glad for thee,
> And glad for me, I wist.

There is no value in worrying out possible sources for the hyphenated words and phrases which sound like echoes. Obviously, the period was brief in which Frost made use of those poetic trappings which remind us of others who looked back to Spenser as the poet's poet. The alliteration, internal rhyme, and almost cloying richness of vowel sounds, together with diction so distinctly "poetical," are all at variance with the theory and practice of Frost's better known poems. Nevertheless, many lines in "My Butterfly" deserve more than passing consideration, as for example the entire sequence beginning "The gray grass is scarce dappled with the snow." In that passage is a blend of nice prosodic contrivance, imagery, and vowel sounds to give fitting expression to the poet's innate and spontaneous impulse. The passage reflects a sense of wonder and lament: something of the splendor to be found in an intricate butterfly wing; something of the yearning after such wild flight; something of the tenderness inspired by such a fragile thing; something of the sorrow love feels at losing that which is too strange to be comprehended. The diction does not conceal the magic of genuine poetry here.

The direction of Frost's growth is suggested by an incident which occurred when "My Butterfly" was accepted by William Hayes Ward, editor of the *Independent*. Ward wrote a letter calculated to be helpful. He also sent Frost a copy of Lanier's *Poems*, containing a "Memorial" which Ward had written for the edition, and suggested that if the young author could devote some time to studying Lanier's *Science of English Verse*, he might smooth out metrical immaturities. If Ward had known his contributor, he would never have written such advice. Frost came from a proud and headstrong line of forebears. Like his rebellious father, he was willing to trust his luck with a minority if inclination led that way. What others might think was of no immediate concern.

It is easy to imagine that Frost's examination of Lanier's pseudo-scholarly *Science* may have hastened the New Englander to self-discovery. True, Lanier belonged to the followers of Edgar Allan Poe, and Poe in turn had been inspired to express his own critical kinship with Coleridge and Shelley. But Frost's kinship with the romantics in "the cloud of other poets" was becoming of less importance even while it seemed to be asserting itself in such a poem as "My Butterfly."

An entirely different poem which suggests a close relationship to Frost's apprentice period is "Waiting; Afield at Dusk." In blank verse, it draws on the antique diction which reminds us of James Thompson's descriptive passages, or the similar imagery of Gray, Collins, and Akenside. There is a literary flavor in the details concerning "night-hawks peopling heaven" and plunging downward "with fierce twang afar"; concerning "the bat's mute antics" as he "pirouettes" and seeks "with purblind haste."

Among the lyrical ballads, "Wind and Window Flower" may also be examined as an illustration of early writing. Also, one

little ballad, "In a Vale," has literary borrowings that remind us
of the poet's early indebtedness to Longfellow for more than the
title of his first book. Yet "In a Vale" displays the poet's ability
to recapture with tenderness that mysterious sense of wonder and
terror which comes to a child lying awake in the stillness of
night, listening to voices, hearing strange answers to strange
questions. The happy blend of cadence and rhymes and thoughts
creates the atmosphere of childhood sensitivity and imagination.
This ability to catch atmosphere, to merge inner feeling with outer
feeling, was turned to excellent advantage with much variety in
several more mature lyrics in *A Boy's Will*.

An example of a transitional poem, written in the early years,
may be the love lyric, "Flower-Gathering." The somewhat heightened and melodic cadence of the rhythm, almost too regular, is
somehow saved by the blending of conversational tones of voice
within which are strongly emotional implications. The little
setting for this dramatic lyric is suggested by the lines: the lover
returns and greets his beloved, after a day of botanizing:

> I left you in the morning,
> And in the morning glow,
> You walked a way beside me
> To make me sad to go.
> Do you know me in the gloaming,
> Gaunt and dusty grey with roaming?
> Are you dumb because you know me not,
> Or dumb because you know?
>
> All for me? And not a question
> For the faded flowers gay
> That could take me from beside you
> For the ages of a day?
> They are yours, and be the measure
> Of their worth for you to treasure,
> The measure of the little while
> That I've been long away.

Technically, the speech rhythms have not asserted enough influence on the iambics. The words themselves are simple and, with
the exception of the gloaming-roaming pair, do not seem par-

ticularly poetical, in the unfortunate sense of the word. The thought has the power to contribute a restrained emotional tension which is highly successful, as it hinges around the girl's silent rebuke which expresses her apprehension and fear for the safety of her lover so "long away." The verse form is nicely balanced, while the octaves are made of two distinctly different quatrains. And the variety gained through the introduction of the couplet rhyme following the alternating rhymes is in part responsible for the richness of sound. All in all, the lyric has a great deal of merit. Other love lyrics in *A Boy's Will*, more subtle and more advanced, are "Reluctance," "A Line-Storm Song," "A Dream Pang," "Rose Pogonias," "Going for Water," and "A Late Walk."

It is easy to imagine the gradual shaping of Frost's belief that some of the best poetry is the simplest. His honesty toward the humble experiences of his own clouded childhood taught him an admiration for the plain and unaffected. In whatever he read he must have watched for evidence to support his own convictions. Probably his reaction against the rich fabric of exalted poetic diction occurred during his brief months at Dartmouth in the fall of 1892. The followers of Lanier were cluttering the magazines of the day with namby-pamby productions; he would turn his back on them. Wordsworth, whose "Prefaces" had considerable influence on him, had taught him (as he later confessed) not only to keep his eye on the object but also to keep his ear against himself. In heart and mind were the deepest musical sounds, and these made the outer sounds trivial and superficial by contrast. Before he left Dartmouth he wrote two quatrains which suggest that he had decided not only on withdrawal into himself but also on a simple and direct poetic diction:

> Now close the windows and hush all the fields:
> If the trees must, let them silently toss;
> No bird is singing now, and if there is,
> Be it my loss.

> It will be long ere the marshes resume,
> It will be long ere the earliest bird:
> So close the windows and not hear the wind,
> But see all wind-stirred.

Without any difficulty, one might read "Now Close the Windows" as a lyric symbol of Frost's moving into his own for poetic gain; a shutting out of sound and mere imitation of sound in nature poetry until the time should come when new perceptions could give new meanings to nature. Perhaps with this poem he began a new period of writing which brought him by slow degrees to his maturity.

Naturally, one who was willing to go his own way in open defiance of contemporary fashion would be taken to task by well meaning friends. One of them, after reading some of his poems in manuscript, confessed that the language and tone seemed a little too ordinary and prosaic; more like conversation than poetry. Very good! The tones of voice carried the overtones of human experience. Listening to his own words with a newly sensitized ear, he continued to write. Twenty years later, when he was ready to gather his poems into a book, he arranged them in such a way that they might indicate to the discerning a spiritual and artistic autobiography of mental and emotional change during the long, long thoughts of youth. Lest any should miss the purpose of this arrangement he added in the table of contents a series of glosses, or "program notes," which bound the poems each to each in a somewhat unnatural piety. His seriousness in jotting down these explanatory notes was mingled with a teasing spirit of banter aimed partly at himself, partly at the reader. Here, for example, are a few of the glosses which appeared under certain titles in the table of contents:

INTO MY OWN
The youth is persuaded that he will be rather more than less himself for having forsworn the world.

GHOST HOUSE
He is happy in society of his own choosing.

MY NOVEMBER GUEST
He is in love with being misunderstood.

IN NEGLECT
He is scornful of folk his scorn cannot reach.

THE VANTAGE POINT
And again scornful, but there is no hurt.

REVELATION
He resolves to become intelligible, at least
to himself, since there is no help else.

Artistically, the use of these glosses failed to satisfy him in later years, and he discarded them when the poems in *A Boy's Will* were first collected with those in his later books. Perhaps his reticence made him regret the unnecessary self-revelation of the almost disdainful and haughty sentences. Perhaps he discarded them because, while they made one new poem out of the book as a whole, they restricted the implicit meanings.

Having examined a few of the earliest lyrics and two transitional poems in *A Boy's Will*, we may round out the picture by analyzing a few of the more mature and finished pieces in this first book. Taken as a whole, there is a nice variety of thought, mood, stanzaic structure, and rhyme. Although the ballad meters and ballad stanzas dominate, several of the lyrics achieve an individuality through the skillful modulations and substitutions in the basic metrical pattern. "Ghost House," for example, takes on a pleasing flexibility because the anapaestic variants in the iambic basis help to stretch the octosyllabics. The same method is employed with even finer effect in "Love and a Question," "Pan With Us," "The Demiurge's Laugh," "Reluctance," and others. Furthermore, the rhyme schemes reveal another kind of pleasure in technical differentiation. These combined modulations are used with interesting results in the various sonnets of *A Boy's Will*, as we have seen in an earlier chapter.

But more important to the poem than the technical aspects are the ways in which the poet captures specific moods and thoughts in these early lyrics. "Stars," which is marred with certain immaturities of padding, successfully combines a delineation of images and thought to express outer mood and inner mood. Implied in the second stanza is the suggestion of living in a world of transience. The contrast between the apparent stability above and the tumultuous mobility below is balanced against the possible heavenly concern for earthly woes—and the probable heavenly disregard. This paradoxical balance of elements continues to develop as a structural favorite with Frost.

In "My November Guest" there is a playfulness which adds wistful intensity to the somber loveliness of autumn. Although the outer mood of sadness reflects the inner mood, there is a blend of paradoxical elements: humor in grief, pleasure in sadness, brightness in darkness. And the images unfold the thought in each verse with additional elaborations, like new petals on a late fall flower.

Atmosphere on two separate planes is achieved in a different way in another lyric, "Storm Fear." The basic meter is iambic pentameter, although the phrases are permitted to take a kind of free-verse structure which violates the metrical rhythm deliberately in order to emphasize the thought and the mood. This irregular lyric thus catches the uneasy apprehension and loneliness familiar to any who have felt a small and isolated house shake beneath the impact of a winter blizzard. The broken lines accentuate the nervousness of those within the house on this winter night, while the quick rhymes come with the shock of snow gusts against the windowpane. Subject matter has completely dictated the form.

The gradual unfolding of the thought in "Mowing" again depends upon a structural balance of images which denote outer action and connote inner thoughts and emotions. The central theme is built around this blending of the earnest love which derives satisfaction from the activities of the immediate moment. The extensions of the imagery suggest a much deeper emotional perception than that derived from a mere statement of the essential meaning. Objects and sounds, the grass, the woods, the mower, the steadily whispering swish of the scythe cutting the hay, the sunlight, the snake, the flowers—all these combine to accentuate the intense pleasure within the mower himself. Again there is the paradox, the contrast, between the apparent and the actual pleasure. Does the mower dream of what will happen, when the work is finished? Of the possible wealth from his industry? No, the love grows entirely from the doing, and the sweetest dream is the fact; that which is being done. The mower's delight does not depend on whispered secrets and promises about the future; it springs from his consciousness that his inherent earth-passion makes meaning and pleasure from the immediate work of his hands. This knowledge in turn gives a cumulative meaning to life itself. Thus the poet gives poetic form to his belief in the superlative importance of the momentary act of individual human consciousness. The sweetest dream that occurs to the mower is that love and work combine to give form and purpose and satisfaction to experience. Years later, in "Two Tramps," the poet gave a more blunt statement to this theme:

> My object in living is to unite
> My avocation and my vocation
> As my two eyes make one in sight.
> Only where love and need are one,
> And the work is play for mortal stakes,
> Is the deed ever really done
> For Heaven and the future's sakes.

The blending of opposites often depends on mildly ironic situations, in these dramatic lyrics. In "The Demiurge's Laugh" the pursuer, hot on the trail of one who is "no true god," is stopped by the sound of laughter from the lips of the pursued— and the laughter is behind the pursuer! Ashamed, the pursuer pretends not to care and sits down against a tree without bothering to continue the chase. The metaphor is so tight-locked in this dramatic lyric as to become a miniature parable. Any reader who explores the allusive extensions will find enough connotations to permit interpretation on two or three related planes. The skeptical pursuit may be a quest for knowledge in one form or another. The one word "demiurge," considered in the classical denotation as a subordinate god who created the world, suggests the connotation of creative evolution. The speaker seems to have been attracted by this false god until the ironic illusion was dispelled. Ashamed for having deceived himself, the speaker tells us that he gave up his hot pursuit. Such an interpretation, supported by the images of the poem, brings into sharper focus the reference to the laughter *behind* the pursuer. It suggests the nineteenth century faith in a scientific explanation of a creative force always advancing; the basis for the nineteenth century delight in theories of "progress." The poet may thus be projecting into poetic form his own cautious pursuit of such a scientific myth, his delusion, and his consequent loss of interest. Nevertheless, it may be fair to doubt whether the poet's denotations in such a parable are sufficiently clear to permit the reader to be sure of the intended theme of the poem. This characteristic reticence was more successfully employed in later symbolism.

Reticence is put to a more dramatic use in the subtle lyric entitled "Reluctance." The technical cunning in this poem has already been suggested. Integrated with this, however, is the slow unfolding of the central theme. On the first plane of denotation, the stanzas employ visual images which describe the end of a journey, late in the fall. Although the mood of the title is conveyed between the lines, there is no indication of the cause for such a mood. Then comes the third stanza, with its satisfying metrical substitutions within the iambic trimeter:

> And the dead leaves lie huddled and still,
>   No longer blown hither and thither;
> The last lone aster is gone;
>   The flowers of the wich-hazel wither;
> The heart is still aching to seek,
>   But the feet question "Whither?"

In the last two lines, the words imply a sense of conflict between a yearning desire and a rational common sense. Nevertheless, the motivation of that desire does not become apparent until the last stanza, in which the pointed analogy is made between the futility of trying to revive a dead fall or a dead love. Suddenly, with the last line of the poem, a dramatic tension is created in such a way that it explains the relationship between the inner sadness over the end of summer and the inner sadness over the end of a love. Outer weather and inner weather are brought into a new kind of correspondence:

Ah, when to the heart of man
Was it ever less than a treason
To go with the drift of things,
To yield with a grace to reason,
And bow and accept the end
Of a love or a season?

Thus the cumulative meaning of the poem is built steadily, in simple allusive statement, until it reaches its climax in the conclusion. Yet the total effect is subtle in its final indirection because the reader is permitted to decide for himself whether the reluctance is intended to emphasize the loss of love or the loss of autumn. The two possibilities are permitted to coincide.

The same indirection of symbolic meaning characterizes many of the mature poems in *A Boy's Will*. "Pan With Us" is a dramatic and reflective lyric which surrenders its full meaning only when the specific images and statements are permitted to develop their full connotations. Technically, this poem is not so advanced and successful as "Reluctance," because it suffers from slight padding and from slight metrical monotony. But the words and images are fresh, homely, and appropriate to the theme of Pan-in-New-England. There is no difficulty in understanding the central theme of this poem as an expression of poetic perplexity caused by public disregard for songs built around age-old and immortal things. Many of the finished performances in this first book may best be understood as variations on the theme of the artist's problems concerning the relationship between the poet and his audience. In these poems, it will be noticed that Frost's deep-rooted faith prompted him to develop his thoughts with a puckish humor because he trusted all would come right in time. His confidence in his poems had nothing to do with whether anyone in England or America paid serious attention to his work—at any particular time. He was willing to admit that his songs were not fashionable enough to please a world so easily satisfied with pretty and startling styles in poetry. The neglect of editors and of readers never made him change his mind as to the validity of his artistic beliefs. Change with him was largely growth of conviction:

I do not see why I should e'er turn back,
Or those should not set forth upon my track
To overtake me, who should miss me here
And long to know if still I held them dear.

They would not find me changed from him they knew—
Only more sure of all I thought was true.

Everything written is as good as it is dramatic. It need not declare itself in form, but it is dramatic or nothing. A least lyric alone may have a hard time, but it can make a beginning, and lyric will be piled on lyric till all are easily heard as sung or spoken by a person in a scene—in character, in setting.[18]

DRAMATIC NARRATIVES

It would be a mistake to consider Frost's dramatic narratives without considering his relation to Browning, for such a comparison establishes differences which are as important as the similarities. Although the influence of Browning is obvious, in theory and in practice, Frost developed his own objective manner in lyrics and narratives without having passed through Browning's painful experience in the realm of subjective and confessional poetry. It is doubtful if the early Frost ever shared with the early Browning any sympathy for Shelley's theory of poetry as a confession, although *A Boy's Will* does suggest in its original form the desire to arrange poetic moods and thoughts into an autobiographical pattern. Even the early lyrics in that first book, however, foreshadow the dramatic quality which found a more objective expression in the *North of Boston* narratives.

While the dramatic methods of Browning and Frost are similar, in that each uses the analytical faculty of the intellect to gain an objectivity in isolating and delineating certain psychological crises in the lives of men and women, the result is quite different. In Browning, the dramatic monologues are really extensions of the dramatic lyrics. In Frost, the dramatic lyrics develop nicely into dramatic monologues; yet the monologues develop further into dramatic narratives, and these in turn may be elaborated into dramatic dialogues and one-act plays in miniature. Even as Browning was fond of compressing indirect narratives within a limited compass of dramatic lyrics and monologues, so Frost often compresses indirect narratives within the limit of his dramatic lyrics and monologues. Nevertheless, Frost's compressions often take the form of dramatic incidents which are neither lyrics nor monologues nor narratives, although the incident implies a narrative.

Again, in method, Frost may have learned from Browning the powerful manner of striking into the middle of an emotional or psychological crisis, the better to accentuate those aspects of the soul-study most closely related to the theme of the poem. Whereas Browning's dramatic monologues imply a listener whose presence has an effect on the speaker, Frost's dramatic narratives go beyond this single method by permitting the psychological studies to develop through the give-and-take of dialogue. Furthermore, Browning's monologues frequently become apologies for the actions, past and present, of his characters. His interest in soul-history is often the interest of a post-mortem. Frost, on the other hand, seems to find more pleasure in the step-by-step unfolding of a psychological crisis at the immediate moment, as opposed to a recapitulation and reconsideration. For example, Browning's "Porphyria's Lover" is a morning-after confessional, "Fra Lippo Lippi" is an explanation of a present paradox in terms of an autobiographical reminiscence. Dramatic as Browning's soliloquies may be, they blend with the momentary consciousness of the present an equally important consciousness of the past; a meditative and reflective tone which looks backward. This is, indeed, an important element in his virtuosity. Nevertheless, this method of soul-study differs from Frost's method of concentrating on the soul-in-present-action, if such a phrase may suggest his primary concern for the immediate nuances of development, as contrasted with the nuances of past happenings. To be sure, the past is brought to bear on the present, but always in a secondary sense.

With these differences in mind, let us examine the various types of dramatic poetry in Frost's works. The dramatic lyrics in *A Boy's Will* might be arranged from such a subjective piece as "Storm Fear" to the objective poem "Pan With Us"; yet all of them would demonstrate the poet's method of striking into a situation with varying degrees of abruptness. In *North of Boston,* a transitional poem which combines elements of the dramatic and reflective lyric with elements of the dramatic narrative and dialogue may be found in the familiar "Mending Wall." Rhyme has given way to blank verse, which is more in keeping with the relaxed tone of this laconic piece. Metaphor has given way to plain statement, which begins quite casually with a homely georgic on the wear and repair of stone walls. This little prologue leads directly into the brief reference to the arrangement for mending wall with the neighbor. Then comes the mild and playful conflict of opinions, in the course of which the neighbor is characterized by a single statement, iterated and reiterated, while the narrator's character is developed through the more spritely and whimsical banter. He quizzically asks his neighbor why they should be doing the unnecessary; then teases him for his dogmatic assertion. But the repetition of meaningless dogma, "Good fences make good neighbours," symbolizes the character of the neighbor. Balanced within the playful conversation is a seriousness which finds offhand expression immediately after the whimsical remark about elves, thus:

> I see him there
> Bringing a stone grasped firmly by the top
> In each hand, like an old-stone savage armed.
> He moves in darkness as it seems to me,
> Not of woods only and the shade of trees.
> He will not go behind his father's saying,
> And he likes having thought of it so well
> He says again, "Good fences make good neighbours."

Thus, within the brief narrative and dialogue, within this detail of a New England landscape, lies an unobtrusive commentary which represents what Frost means when he refers to poetry as "a clarification of life" or "a way of grappling with life." The little sadness comes to the mischievous farmer when he sees his neighbor moving in the darkness of a shadow which hurts the roots of life itself. In spite of its offhand development, this is the central theme of the poem.

Strictly speaking, there are several lesser dramatic narratives in Frost's later books, which are related in kind to "Mending Wall," in that they use the narrative less for the gradual unfolding of psychological delineation than for the illustration of a single central idea. Different in method, "Christmas Trees," "The Exposed Nest," and "The Bonfire" are representative of this class. Occasionally, the idea is elaborated specifically or with different metaphors at the end of the narrative. In this class "Brown's Descent," "The Gum-Gatherer," and "The Axe-Helve" may be considered by the reader.

The dramatic monologue as a psychological self-revelation of a single person, after the manner of Browning, may be found in "A Servant to Servants." The delineation here approaches a study in abnormal psychology. The wife of the ambitious farmer has been broken by cooking meals and housekeeping for her husband's hired men until she becomes "a servant to servants," caught in the endless drudgery of "doing things over and over that just won't stay done." Unlike her husband, she senses the futility of bustle and labor that gets them nowhere. Remembering the insane doom of her father's brother, she walks a taut line between sanity and insanity. And her words contain a foreshadowing of the dreadful end she fears she cannot escape.

Among the dramatic narratives which are built around psychological implications, there is a nice gradation from the obvious to the subtle. "The Code" makes use of dramatic incident for the delineation of character and is thus one of the more obvious pieces in this class. Pride-in-ability leads the farmer to assert his "code" by trying to smother his boss beneath a load of hay because the boss had needlessly urged him to work faster. Again, in "A Hundred Collars," the humorous conflict develops between a timid professor and a drunken bill collector who are obliged to share the same room during one night in a country hotel. Somewhat more subtle is the study in "The Self-Seeker," where the Broken One ironically permits himself to earn the title only because he will not be broken by bickerings with an insurance company over the price of his legs, lost in a sawmill accident.

More subtle in extensions, although quite obvious in its unfolding through dialogue is the psychological study of Estelle, the unseen actress who holds the center of attention in "The Housekeeper." Estelle and her mother live with uncomplaining patience in the home of a farmer who has taken much from them and has considered his obligations completed so long as he acts the part of the good husband to Estelle, who has drifted in back-country fashion from housekeeper to common-law wife. But Estelle broods proudly over the unintentional insult of the man's "free love" attitude toward marriage, until she is able to salve the wound by running off with another man who will marry her. Proud and self-contained, she never told the first man the inner hurt he should have seen. Not out of prudishness, but because she had given herself and her property to the man she loved and had vainly hoped in return only for what honor his twisted thinking denied, she finally left without a word.

The situation in "The Fear" is almost a continuation of "The Housekeeper," for the woman who is afraid has left one man and has been living with another for some time on a lonely farm. The abrupt beginning of this dramatic narrative brings the attention to focus so sharply on the crucial scene that the deepest cause of the fear is not immediately apparent: the ever-present apprehension that the other man will find the woman. When the moment seems to have come, the fearing woman is self-dependent and bold. Returning in the dark, one night, to the empty farm where she is living with her lover, the woman sees in the gleam of the wagon-light a face beside the road. She will know the worst and advances alone to challenge the unknown visitor. He turns out to be a passing stranger, taking an evening stroll with his son. Surprised at her challenge, he frankly reveals himself in the light of her uplifted lantern. After her apologies, the relieved woman almost faints, while the lantern drops from her hand to the ground. Amy Lowell, who had a peculiar gift for misunderstanding Frost's purpose and method, tried to make melodrama out of this psychological study. "Does he kill her, or does she merely think that he is going to do so?" she wrote, in 1917. "Which one is crazed, he or she? Either way, Nature has taken her toll." Obviously, Amy was also left in the darkness when that lantern went out!

Perhaps the most poignant study of a woman in *North of Boston* occurs in "Home Burial." The conflict develops between wife and husband over the woman's way and the man's way of bearing the painful sorrow caused by the death of their first-born. Each has been hurt seriously by the tragedy. While the man tries to cover grief with daily tasks and commonplace remarks about the weather, the woman carries her sorrow openly, as if she held the unburied child in her arms. The narrative begins with the final open conflict in which the woman accuses her husband of brutal insensitivity because he could bury the child with his own hands. He tries vainly to understand her, to make her understand him. She refuses:

> "You *couldn't* care! The nearest friends can go
> With anyone to death, comes so far short
> They might as well not try to go at all.
> No, from the time when one is sick to death,
> One is alone, and he dies more alone.
> Friends make pretence of following to the grave,
> But before one is in it, their minds are turned
> And making the best of their way back to life
> And living people, and things they understand.
> But the world's evil. I won't have grief so
> If I can change it. Oh, I won't. I won't!"

The tragic situation is heightened because each is partly right. But the woman's stubborn and unbalanced perseverance in turning her back on the yearning love of the man heightens the sense of tragedy.

Tragedy and sorrow move slowly through many of Frost's dramatic poems, although the poet shows no trace of sentimentality in his handling of it. In spite of Amy Lowell's insistence, there is nothing degenerate about these people and their situations —nothing any more destructive to character than life brings to people at any time and in any place. The bitterness of hopes unrealized, the longing for the unfulfilled, the making the best of what is at hand—these have more to do with the will to live than with the will to die. Back-country New England may be dotted with lonely farmhouses which shelter grief, deserted homes storm-beaten and gray with changing seasons, fields that have gone quietly back to weeds, apple orchards that miss the hand of the pruner. But Robert Frost's poems touch these only because

the concern of poetry is primarily with sorrows and joys large
and small. His poems are blended with light and darkness, for
he knows from long experience that strong men and women still
work out a life that is good in that stubborn contest with rocky
soil and short summers.

Furthermore, as a New Hampshire farmer himself in the early
years, Frost lived with neighbors of all classes, many of them his
superiors in their ability to make a simple but sufficient living out
of a little. He has never forgotten his respect and admiration for
the courage and self-dependence he saw about him during those
years. The rigorous trial by existence in rural communities
requires ability and cunning if life is to go on. The struggle has
in it a reward that may not be recognized by up-and-coming city
people who ask larger returns on smaller investments. But the soil
has its own peculiar virtue for those who have been hurt and
healed by the accidents of choice and circumstances. And Frost
has given expression in his poems to that inner strength and satisfaction which comes from living close to the soil.

An unsuspected subtlety reveals itself in one of the most
familiar dramatic narratives, "The Death of the Hired Man." The
central theme of the poem is the transformation of the husband's
stubborn and impatient prejudice, through the deliberate and
gentle persuasiveness of the wife. Of only secondary importance
to the poem is the return and death of the hired man. The psychological implications of the poem become apparent only when one
recognizes the gradual ascendancy of the wife's latent pity and
kindliness until it dominates the husband's outspoken intolerance
and anger. That the poet intended this gradual development to
hold the center of attention, one may appreciate by examining a
brief descriptive interlude:

> She put out her hand
> Among the harp-like morning-glory strings,
> Taut with the dew from garden bed to eaves,
> As if she played unheard some tenderness
> That wrought on him beside her in the night.

"*As if* she played unheard some tenderness." We are back into the
poet's favorite game of analogies. Thus the poem is brought to

focus on Warren's gradual conversion to pity and mercy for one who had never earned a right to pity. At the beginning of the narrative, Mary wants to protect the old man from the abrupt dismissal he may receive at the hands of her husband, irked by the memory of past disloyalties. So she breaks the news and quietly waits while her husband protests, rehearses the case, and states his arguments. Mary answers with a touching description of the old man's feeble condition. Unconvinced, Warren bitterly challenges her to admit that the hired man has repeated to her the same threadbare promises about his desire to prove his worth. After quiet reproof, Mary continues her description of the old fellow's amusing but pathetic conversation. Then she reminds Warren indirectly of ways in which Silas has been valuable in days past; through simple crafts like finding water underground with a hazel prong, his knack for building a load of hay. Warren admits that, and even forgets his anger long enough to praise this last accomplishment. The advantage gained, Mary moves quietly to her intended assertion that Silas will never desert them again:

"Warren," she said, "he has come home to die:
You needn't be afraid he'll leave you this time."

When Warren answers, the anger has gone out of his voice; but he mocks her gently and challenges Silas' right to call their farm his home. Why should he have more claim on them than on his rich brother? Mary's intuitive grasp, contrasting throughout with Warren's slow searchings, goes to the heart of that trouble: Silas is "just the kind that kinsfolk can't abide." Before he realizes it, Warren is cautiously defending Silas against the rich brother's unspoken hostility. When he has been so far won over that he is willing to go in and talk to the old man, Mary sends him in alone —to find Silas dead.

Ironic fulfillment and a rounding off of the dramatic conflict marks the simple tone of the ending. There is no surprise, for the reader has been prepared by the title and has expected the ultimate outcome. Thus the attention is drawn directly to the characterization, to the dramatic give-and-take between husband and wife, to the epigrammatic and sententious quality of the rhythmic sen-

tences fashioned out of restrained conversation which is nevertheless strongly emotional. Unforgettable lines are here:

> "Poor Silas, so concerned for other folk,
> And nothing to look backward to with pride,
> And nothing to look forward to with hope,
> So now and never any different."

Again Mary's words:

> "After so many years he still keeps finding
> Good arguments he sees he might have used.
> I sympathise. I know just how it feels
> To think of the right thing to say too late."

Most memorable, perhaps, is the wistful banter between man and
wife over Silas coming home to them:

> "Home," he mocked gently.
>
> > "Yes, what else but home?
>
> . . . .
>
> Of course he's nothing to us, any more
> Than was the hound that came a stranger to us
> Out of the woods, worn out upon the trail."
>
> "Home is the place where, when you have to go there,
> They have to take you in."
>
> > "I should have called it
> Something you somehow haven't to deserve."

These terse and strong phrases have been enriched by the connotations of meaning and of voice-ways.

Here, as in so many of Frost's poems, the dramatic conflict
involves opposed aspects of good and good, such as differences
between lovers. Not always tragic, the situation may be tinged
only with sadness, as in one of the finest and most subtle narratives, "In the Home Stretch." The setting for this little one-act play
is a country kitchen, piled high with furniture and boxes which
are still being unloaded (as the poem begins) from a van beside
the farmhouse. Tired from their labors of moving from the city
to this lonely spot, the elderly man and wife survey the cluttered
room, the unkempt yard, and the little field visible through the

kitchen window. They have made this choice of home for their latter years only because he has wanted it—and she is glad only because he is glad. Loving him as she does, she tries her best to let herself believe she wanted it as much as he. At least, her cheerfully teasing remarks are competent to parry his gentle questions as to why they came. It touches the heart, but not with pity, for the dialogue makes clear that their love and understanding are enough.

Another wife stands out as the character most clearly delineated in "Snow," the longest dramatic narrative in *Mountain Interval*. In some ways, this poem is the most finished of all these little plays-in-verse. The setting is again a farmhouse living room, the time a blizzard-swept winter night. Brother Meserve, a somewhat fanatical lay preacher, has stopped at the Coles' farm on his way from a religious gathering. His horses, almost exhausted from their long struggle through drifts, are resting in the barn for a short time, before Meserve sets out on the last half of his six-mile journey home. Mrs. Cole, worried for his safety, urges him to spend the night, even after he has phoned to assure his wife that he is safe and starting again into the wild storm. When Meserve goes to the barn briefly to see that his horses are all right, Cole playfully chides his wife for being melodramatic about this man whom she can't abide, under ordinary circumstances. In spite of Mrs. Cole's repeated urging, however, Meserve sets out. The second scene, two hours later, discovers Cole sitting at the telephone and quietly waiting for Mrs. Meserve to continue her frantic questions about her husband, who has not yet reached home. Mrs. Cole begins her self-recriminations for letting the man go into the blizzard, but her husband lightly scolds her for being upset. Impatiently she shoulders him away from the phone, takes the receiver, and tries to make Mrs. Meserve speak. When she has no success, her husband asks:

"What do you hear?"

       "I hear an empty room—
You know—it sounds that way. And yes, I hear—
I think I hear a clock—and windows rattling.
No step though. If she's there she's sitting down."

Cole is amused. After a little banter, he says in quiet jest:

> "You can't hear whether she has left the door
> Wide open and the wind's blown out the lamp
> And the fire's died and the room's dark and cold?"

When finally a voice answers, Merserve is explaining that he is safe and that his wife had left the phone to open the barn door. Relieved, Mrs. Cole and her husband discuss their curious evening. So ends one of the most versatile and amusing of the longer narratives. Unlike some of the others, the lines sharply accentuate the characterization. Meserve's exhibitionism, his bombastic and conceited manner, grow with his every speech. Mrs. Cole's intense concern would not seem exaggerated and melodramatic if her husband's amused serenity and teasing were not there to serve as foils. The telephone adds to the humorous suspense of the scene. Not long after the publication of "Snow," the poet alluded to it in one particular:

"I have three characters speaking in one poem, and I was not satisfied with what they said until I got them to speak so true to their characters that no mistake could be made as to who was speaking. I would never put the names of the speakers in front of what they said."[19]

Subtlety in psychological analysis reaches its finest gradation in two other dramatic narratives: "The Generations of Men" and "Maple." In the first of these, the theme is an age-old favorite: the conversation of two strangers, a boy and a girl, who gradually fall in love with each other during this first meeting, although their reticence permits them merely to arrange for a second meeting. In "Maple" fresh treatment is given to another favorite theme: the unfolding of meaning which grows out of an apparently futile quest for the answer to an inscrutable secret.

Three different kinds of dramatic narrative remain to be considered. The first, " 'Out, out—' " describes a gruesome incident in which a boy accidentally cuts off his hand while taking away wood from a rotary saw; then dies from loss of blood and shock. The indirect implications of the incident are of far more importance than the incident itself. Yet it would be difficult to include the piece among the dramatic lyrics. The ironic symbolism of life unexpectedly and tragically snuffed out like a candle is the central theme which hinges on these lines:

> Then the boy saw all—
> Since he was old enough to know, big boy
> Doing a man's work, though a child at heart—
> He saw all spoiled.

The melodramatic shock of this compressed narrative is justified poetically by the terse power of the blunt statement, which avoids sentimentality.

Compression also characterizes Frost's handling of the ballad-narrative entitled "The Subverted Flower." With dramatic intensity, the poem plunges abruptly into the crucial moment of a quarrel between two young lovers. The central theme, growing from the prudish misunderstanding of the girl who finds the boy's physical yearnings repulsive, is given an ironic development through the use of the girl's unnatural and disgusted interpretation of her lover as a beast. But one passage in the middle of the poem crystallizes the theme:

> A girl could only see
> That a flower had marred a man,
> But what she could not see
> Was that the flower might be
> Other than base and fetid:
> That the flower had done but part,
> And what the flower began
> Her own too meagre heart
> Had terribly completed.

Although the development of this incident is unlike that of the other narratives, the psychological implications are by no means too subtle. And the total effect is extremely forceful.

Finally, an implied dramatic narrative is fashioned from five very short lyrics in "The Hill Wife," which first appeared in *Mountain Interval*. It stands out by implication as a miniature lyric drama in five scenes. The first scene, of twelve lines only, sets the stage for tragedy, and establishes the theme of fear-in-loneliness. The Hill Wife tries to tell her husband that something must be wrong with them to be so sad and lonely after the birds have left in the fall. The troubled heart is hers, not his. If there is any conflict between them, it is not so much misunderstanding as not understanding enough. Different as the two possibilities may be, there is little to choose between them. The second scene is even shorter than the first. In it a chorus voice describes the fear of the empty house when the Hill Wife returns with her husband at night. Again the reader gathers that the greater fear is the woman's. In the third scene, the Hill Wife describes her fear caused by the way a passing tramp smiled strangely and unfathomably at her before he walked into the woods with the bread she had given him. Fear of yet another kind shows itself in the fourth scene. Briefly the chorus voice tells how the Hill Wife is troubled by the persistent scrape of a pine branch which fumbles against her bedroom window with "tireless but ineffectual hands." The fifth scene, entitled "The Impulse," contains climax and denouement. The chorus voice tells how the Hill Wife followed her silent husband in field and wood, hoping that his nearness might relieve her fear of loneliness. Once, when she strayed off so far that she scarcely heard when he shouted to her, she hid herself instead of answering him. The conclusion is terse enough:

> He never found her, though he looked
>   Everywhere,
> And he asked at her mother's house
>   Was she there.
>
> Sudden and swift and light as that
>   The ties gave,
> And he learned of finalities—
>   Besides the grave.

In "The Hill Wife" the psychological analysis is developed entirely through implication, and hinges on the growing failure of the man to sympathize with the woman's accumulated psychosis.

Throughout the range of these dramatic poems may be found a gradual testing and trusting of Frost's poetic theories concerning speech rhythms and the sound of sense. The concern with simple and clear images expressed in plain-spoken and sometimes idiomatic phrases stripped of poetic artifice; the desire to let expressions of emotion and thought get along with a basic iambic pattern of metrical structure; the conscious interest in the posture of complete sentences; and the final pleasure in carrying off each piece with a quietly dramatic intensity—all these varied factors are managed with the confidence and sureness of maturity.

The rural New England people have furnished the stuff of poetry, while the sorrows are balanced with touches of humor, created by the characters themselves in their own words. Such a careful balance leaves no room for sentimentality, and Frost would be the last to look with pity where none is required or asked. The struggle against odds, the vicissitudes of love and labor, the preoccupation with the fact—these have in them a compensation. That they offer the poet abundant materials for symbol, he has proved well. He has brought to his art the capacity of eye and ear to pierce beneath the surface of the seemingly ordinary. If the still-flowing waters of his delineation and observation occasionally funnel and disappear beneath the lines, they may always be tapped by those who understand the delicate manipulation of metaphorical divining rods.

Eyes seeking the response of eyes
Bring out the stars, bring out the flowers,
Thus concentrating earth and skies
So none need be afraid of size.
All revelation has been ours.[20]

METAPHOR IN ACTION

THE metaphors in words and phrases are the lesser ones. The metaphors which are not mere accessories and ornaments require more careful examination if one is to appreciate their functional and organic necessity in Robert Frost's best poems. We have seen that the metaphor as analogy leads the poet to the development of the metaphor as a symbol which displaces and suggests a comparison not stated. From these two basic usages, in which poems are unified by a complete metaphor, the poet departs into a variety of permutations and combinations. And always the pleasure of aesthetic structure in the relation of part to part is blended by Frost with the pleasure of that discriminating clarification of thought and emotion which results from the refraction established by metaphor.

Beginning with the slight comparisons and analogies which are stated briefly and without elaboration, we are still on familiar ground. Numerous are the words or phrases which serve as connecting links between the specific image and the general analogy, for there are endless ways of calling attention to the analogy. Consider a poem complete in a single quatrain:

> The heart can think of no devotion
> Greater than being shore to ocean—
> Holding the curve of one position,
> Counting an endless repetition.

The devotion of love is directly compared to the loyal and yet ever-changing permanence of intimacy kept by the shore line which moves quietly inward with the urgent hunger of the rising tide and then moves quietly outward with the ebb. Here, in even such a slight comparison, there is a dramatic contrast which heightens the comparison: the serene passivity of the shore beneath the persistent and nervous activity of the ocean. The stated comparison leads to an extension of the metaphor in an accumulation of analogies which occur to the thoughtful reader.

Sometimes the initial comparison leads progressively to an elaboration by the poet himself or is supplemented by other analogies which grow out of the first one. Dramatically, the structure may lead to a deliberately anticlimactic conclusion which heightens the total effect:

> There's a patch of old snow in a corner
> That I should have guessed
> Was a blow-away paper the rain
> Had brought to rest.

> It is speckled with grime as if
> Small print overspread it,
> The news of a day I've forgotten—
> If I ever read it.

The first comparison in "Devotion" was established with the adjective "greater"; here it is established with the phrase "I should have guessed." The seemingly drab images promise little for poetry at the start. After the analogy is established between a square of dirty snow and a square of dissolving, soggy newspaper, it leads naturally to the second analogy between the speckled grime in the snow and the indistinct printing on a disintegrating newspaper. This in turn leads to a further comparison between the failure to remember the "news" which may not have been "read." Immediately these two words bring into focus the possible extensions of the metaphor. In their context, "news" and "read" are honored with a double significance. They have been stretched out of their conventional connotation. In extension, there is the contrast between the unattractiveness of this remnant of winter and the fresh appeal of newly fallen snow so compelling because of its pristine whiteness. Then comes the hint of regret for the possibly neglected chance to enjoy and con with satisfaction that fresh excitement. The theme of the poem is comparable to Emerson's familiar poem, "Days." Here is a slight metaphor, but it touches the mind and heart. It would be easy enough to demonstrate here Frost's suggestion (quoted in "The Function of Metaphor") that we need to know how far a metaphor may be carried before it breaks down. Let the reader carry the analogy of the small print and grime back to the fresh newspaper and the fresh snow, and the metaphor gives way. We know enough to stop this side of the breaking point.

Simple analogies may be more incisive if they touch on larger issues, yet may be included still within a narrow and reticent range of comparisons. Even if the vehicle is equally slight, the impact may have greater force:

> Some say the world will end with fire,
> Some say in ice.
> From what I've tasted of desire
> I hold with those who favor fire.
> But if it had to perish twice,
> I think I know enough of hate
> To say that for destruction ice
> Is also great
> And would suffice.

Structurally, such a compact unit, nicely balanced, strikes with the clean accuracy of a poised fist. The backward thrust of "fire" at the end of the fourth line seems to intensify the thought; the paired rhymes in the second half lead to such a natural pause after "great" that the octosyllabic line is permitted to break to give the seemingly internal rhyme greater force and to permit the laconic understatement of the last three words. But what of the metaphor? The analogy, here implied, establishes a comparison between the heat of love or passion and the cold of hate. Coupled with this is the hint of the destructive power of these two extremes of human passion; cataclysmic power. But there is also a further suggestion: these two extremes are made so to encompass life as to be a gathering up of all that may exist between them; all that may be swept away by them. Then the terse thrust of the last line emphasizes the smilingly sad acceptance, on the part of the poet. Such metaphorical indirection is flawless.

When the poet carries his symbolism to extremes, the metaphor seems at first glance to have no intended analogy. The images established the details of a specific incident, and there is an apparent end. Such a usage may be considered as a kind of synecdoche, wherein the incident is substituted for the generalization; the part takes the place of the whole. In this kind of displacement, the weight of the specific is supposedly equal to that of the general statement or analogy which has been crowded out. Such a method of using the metaphor is a favorite with Frost. It partakes of his characteristic New England reticence and fondness for understatement. Dangerous as the symbol may be in hiding the poet too well away, it is most effective when the connotations suggest the analogy. Carefully constructed, these symbolic poems are often Frost's finest because they contain sufficient emotional intensity to carry over to the reader the analogy which is in the poet's mind as he writes. Yet all is not left to intensity. Certain words are placed in that honorable position where the context gives them the prominence of a twofold meaning. Immediately the concentration on these key words seems to unlock the metaphor. The reader finds that the poem may be considered on two distinct planes of meaning: that outer plane of immediate incident which the words denote, and that inner plane of wider and more general meaning which the words connote. In a different context we have considered the key words, "promises," "miles," and "sleep," which unlock and reveal the inner plane of connotations in "Stopping by Woods on a Snowy Evening." The reader is not asked to choose connotations identical with those in the mind of the poet. If those identical connotations were to be conveyed, the poet would have resorted to that kind of metaphorical usage which would have permitted such a pointed analogy. The middle-ground position of the poem stands between the experience of the poet and the experience of the reader. The poet wagers that the discriminating reader's understanding of the implied analogy will not be too far distant from his own.

Even such a simple descriptive poem as Frost's lovely "Spring Pools" seems to me to have its key phrase, which is particularly appropriate to the present consideration: "Let them think twice."

This is the essence of poetic meaning which permits us to find two (or more) distinct planes of reference.

Such a homely picture as that of "The Cow in Apple Time" becomes a symbol-in-narrative. Taken on its first plane of meaning, it is a thoroughly accurate description of what happens to the rambunctious critter; the details are correct throughout. If the reader likes, he may accept it merely as a perfect little picture of an imperfect little cow. But there are metaphorical implications. Such a little fable establishes an implied analogy between the willful cow and a willful human being; the kind of human being still too immature to be interested in the meaning of restrictions made by others. The emphasis on "wall" and "wall-builders" leads one naturally to consider two planes of meaning for such words— and immediately the wall suggests a kind of hindering rule and the wall-builders suggest those who had something in mind when they set up the restrictions. The fable has its moral, but the poet is not immediately concerned with that. No conclusion is drawn from the incident, because the analogy is sufficient. One might find a comfortable companion piece for this fable in "The Runaway," a picture of a little Morgan colt frightened by his first sight of snow. By no means obviously, an implied analogy occurs when the possible explanation of the parent would again be treated as foolishness:

> I doubt if even his mother could tell him, "Sakes,
> It's only weather." He'd think she didn't know!

Carrying through this implied comparison with the headstrong child misbehaving, we may even hear the gossiping neighbors offering their uninvited criticism in the last lines.

As a symbolist or self-styled "synecdochist" Frost has developed his favorite variety of metaphorical displacement in other poems, such as "Our Singing Strength," "Acceptance," "A Winter Eden," "Acquainted With the Night," "The Armful," and "Putting in the Seed." The key words are plainly visible to anyone who watches for them. It often happens that the titles themselves have a word or phrase which suggests two planes of meaning. But the poem develops such suggestions much as a bud expands to reveal the heart of the flower.

Always there is a dramatic structure in the best of Frost's unified metaphors. Starting quite casually, the tension of the poem is increased until it frequently reaches its resolution only with the last line of the poem, and sometimes even with the last word. The dramatic intensity is frequently heightened by reversing the familiar process of elaborately unfolding the different analogies which suggest themselves. In his latest book, one of Frost's finest poems, "The Silken Tent," begins by establishing analogies between a woman and a tent. The poem is a sonnet complete in a single sentence. The octave falls evenly into two quatrains which establish two separate analogies. Then the sestet moves quietly into less obvious analogies which create a cumulative tension, and that tension reaches its climax only with the last word of the last line:

> She is as in a field a silken tent
> At midday when a sunny summer breeze
> Has dried the dew and all its ropes relent,
> So that in guys it gently sways at ease,
> And its supporting central cedar pole,
> That is its pinnacle to heavenward
> And signifies the sureness of the soul,
> Seems to owe naught to any single cord,
> But strictly held by none, is loosely bound
> By countless silken ties of love and thought
> To every thing on earth the compass round,
> And only by one's going slightly taut
> In the capriciousness of summer air,
> Is of the slightest bondage made aware.

Here the analogies in the octave prepare for the symbolism developed in the sestet. But the capricious gust of wind, testing the "bondage," immediately suggests the paradoxical contrast between the established pattern of the woman's virtuous life and the unexpectedly impulsive response to a gust of passionate desire. And the conflict brings into new consciousness the hitherto casual "bondage" of those "countless silken ties of love and thought" which sustain her. The metaphor here suggests more than Frost's persistent joy in the dramatic; it suggests his ability to carry into his lyrics that psychological preoccupation (without benefit of Freud) which asserts itself in his dramatic narratives.

Another aspect of dramatic structure in Frost's unlocked metaphors is suggested by "A Silken Tent." The poet strikes into the middle of an action, so that there is a momentary sense of lostness until the reader has derived some orientation from the context. The effect is to give the reader an initial sense of an unnecessarily obscure or oblique tendency. But closer examination will show that this deliberately dramatic method contributes to the poem a unity and compression which heightens the intensity. A good example of such a poem in the dramatic narratives is "The Fear." In the poems built around a single metaphor, "All Revelation" illustrates the abrupt beginning: "A head thrusts in as for the view." The poet refuses to risk a false emphasis by beginning with an anecdote which might lead the reader to the particular occasion when some crevice in a crystal cave afforded the spectator the chance to thrust his head into a geode so that he might carry away some impression of the visible wonder. The analogy between this specific activity of the inquiring eyes and the universal activity of the inquiring mind has ontological overtones which may be hidden too well away. So the poet caps the described incident with another metaphor of explanatory nature in the final stanza. Such a method almost always injures the unity of the poem, although this risk the poet is willing to take for the sake of clarity. Long ago he recognized the criticism of those who feared that he pointed up his comparison with too much care:

> Why will I not analogize?
> I do too much in some men's eyes.

Another metaphorical usage frequently found in these poems is that which concentrates on a unified emotional tension rather than on a rational analogy. In such poems, the reader is aware of a cumulative intensification of a single emotion. We have noticed that Frost likes to think of the metaphor as a kind of prism which breaks emotion into its component colors: the emotion is passed through an imaginative analogy and is thus brought under artistic control. In the present use, however, the process is reversed. Certain poems serve more as a lens than as a prism, so that words and images bring the attention to focus on the emotional sense which underlies and projects the poem. Here is an example:

> When the wind works against us in the dark,
> And pelts with snow
> The lower chamber window on the east,
> And whispers with a sort of stifled bark,
> The beast,
> "Come out! Come out!"—
> It costs no inward struggle not to go,
> Ah, no!
> I count our strength,
> Two and a child,
> Those of us not asleep subdued to mark
> How the cold creeps as the fire dies at length,—
> How drifts are piled,
> Dooryard and road ungraded,
> Till even the comforting barn grows far away,
> And my heart owns a doubt
> Whether 'tis in us to arise with day
> And save ourselves unaided.

The attention is projected outward from the fear to the images of the fear until a sense of that emotion is created in the reader. Taken singly, these images seem harmless. Outside in the dark the snow falls and the wind is blowing and the cold increases. The farmhouse would seem to offer enough protection. The tension grows, however, through the increased apprehension as to the continued violence of the storm. Then comes a touch of seeming overstatement which is acceptable. The attack on the house becomes a pitched battle, in which the forces of the enemy outside are so much stronger than the forces within: two and a child. It builds onward to a climax with the final doubt as to the outcome. Furthermore, the loose iambic pentameter which establishes itself in the first four lines, as the metrical pattern, is intermittently broken into nervous and jerky fragments, as though the speaker interrupted himself to hold his breath, to listen. And the structural nervousness heightens the tension of meaning.

Thus the whole poem becomes a metaphor which focuses on fear. The reader may find similarities of emotional focus by indirection in such poems as "Ghost House," "To the Thawing Wind," "Not to Keep," "Bereft," "The Need of Being Versed in Country Things," "October," and "Once by the Pacific."

Frost's poems of love may be considered as an independent group which use reticent indirection to focus on the implicit emotion which prompts the poems. Synecdochical displacement here reveals itself with a difference. In familiar love lyrics, the sentiment is revealed through direct statement: subjectively as a confession of the inner feeling, or objectively as a flattering description of the beloved. Frost's love poems never use these obvious devices. Instead, they recount a single incident which is transformed into poetry because of the heavy burden of the lover's emotion suffused through the images. And yet the word "love" is rarely used. Reticence and shyness are overcome by hints and indirections. The incident, creating a setting for the two lovers, again utilizes the dramatic method of breaking into a moment of tension and crisis. One of the simplest is a one-sided conversation between the hesitant lover and the silent girl:

> I'm going out to clean the pasture spring;
> I'll only stop to rake the leaves away
> (And wait to watch the water clear, I may):
> I sha'n't be gone long.—You come too.

> I'm going out to fetch the little calf
> That's standing by the mother. It's so young,
> It totters when she licks it with her tongue.
> I sha'n't be gone long.—You come too.

The first line supplies all the setting that is needed by giving us the background of the farm and those who care for it, in a double sense. But the invitation evokes responses which lovers delight to share: pleasure in little tasks that involve quiet beauty, and protective tenderness. The invitation gains intensity because of its compression. It could not be more moving if it were calculated rather than impulsive. The little charm of it for the reader grows from the love implicit and elicited, so that roundness is given to prosaic and homely images. Other love poems which have their own indirection are "Meeting and Passing," "Flower-Gathering," "A Dream Pang," "Going for Water," "A Late Walk," "Putting in the Seed," "The Telephone," and "A Line-Storm Song." Among the many others, "Two Look at Two" does not fit into the present category because the indirection there is of another kind, and rests on a pointed analogy.

Personification is merely another kind of metaphor. The transference of animate attributes to inanimate or spiritual concepts is an implied comparison for the sake of delineation and clarification. Frost has used this device in numerous ways. Yet such poems as "My November Guest" and "Bond and Free" illustrate the close relationship between the method of displacement and the method of personification. In "My November Guest" the guest proves to be Sorrow. Quite appropriately, Sorrow is personified as a woman dearly loved. She walks with the poet through the somber and stark beauties of a fall countryside, forever pointing out her sad pleasure in the browns and grays and blacks of nature, which fit her mood. The poet, who needed no such guidance in finding these subtle beauties, humors her tenderly because "they are better for her praise."

Personification is of course closely related to the fable and the parable already mentioned. In the fable, personification and synecdoche are combined to create a narrative picture in which there is an implicit comparison. Frequently the poet uses such personifications to delineate through metaphorical analogy the opposed aspects of problems which have no answer. Without explicit application, poems such as "Love and a Question," "The Trial by Existence," "Pan With Us," "The Demiurge's Laugh," and "The Lovely Shall Be Choosers" may be included in this group. "Love and a Question" seems at first to be merely a narrative picture of two lovers whose isolated honeymoon in a rustic cottage is interrupted at evening by the knock of a penniless wanderer who asks for a place to spend the night. The bridegroom hesitates and does not know how to answer the request. When the analogy is established by the reader's examination of the symbolism, the wanderer becomes a personification of poverty, appealing with its care and woe for relief and sustenance. The bridegroom represents those neither rich nor poor, on whose lives the poverty-stricken make constant demands. Each has his rights, his reasons for special pleading, and there is no simple answer to the question propounded. At the end of the poem stands merely the question mark.

The unanswerable question again becomes the focal point of a similarly constructed fable-personification, "Pan With Us." The incident reveals the immortal god of rural life and the lover of humble music standing indecisively on a hilltop in a New England pasture. His indecision grows out of his desire to play favorite and age-old tunes which are so completely out of fashion that nobody cares to listen. "Play? Play?—What should he play?" Thus the poem ends. Again the method is one of symbolic displacement. The implications are more than those which might occur if one were to consider Pan merely as a personification of a poet. The poet *is* Pan and Pan *is* the poet. There is a double conflict here: first, between the poet's shyness which makes him love the solitude which is his, and the poet's hunger for an audience; next, between his willingness to play for an audience and his indecision as to what could possibly satisfy his listeners. Thus the incident becomes a metaphorical projection of an autobiographical crisis. There are no tears, no hints of complaint. Back of the figurative language is only the sadness of the question without answer.

Several other objectively fashioned lyrics are best understood when considered as metaphors related to problems which confront the poet's relation to himself, to his art, to his audience. These have already been mentioned, with particular reference to the central metaphor in "West-running Brook." The hide-and-seek metaphor in "Revelation" becomes much richer in extension if it is considered in relation to the poet's problem:

> We make ourselves a place apart
>   Behind light words that tease and flout,
> But oh, the agitated heart
>   Till someone find us really out.

'Tis pity if the case require
(Or so we say) that in the end
We speak the literal to inspire
The understanding of a friend.

But so with all, from babes that play
At hide-and-seek to God afar,
So all who hide too well away
Must speak and tell us where they are.

The elaboration of the analogy at the end of this poem is characteristic of Frost's tendency, in certain cases, to develop one metaphor by progression to a second metaphor which is often more general than the first. Although no mention is here made of the poetic problem of revelation, the implied analogy in the first and second stanzas is corroborated by the additional analogy in the third stanza. There seems to be legitimate inference that the creator of poems is quite as much interested in the problem of communication as God himself.

Hiding too well away in a metaphor is often the cause for calling attention to the intended analogy. At its worst, this application of meaning becomes the moral tag so popular in the nineteenth century. "Thanks, thanks to thee, kind friend," chirps Longfellow to the Village Blacksmith, "for the lesson thou hast taught." Then he goes on with his application of the moral lesson. Such abuse of the poem is as deplorable as T. S. Eliot's footnotes. The happier establishment of analogy occurs when it is so intensely implicit in the poem as to reveal itself without assistance.

Those who have criticized Frost for weakening the structure of the poem are frequently just in their criticism. At other times they fail to recognize the way in which one metaphor is resolved into another metaphor so that the application becomes more correctly a progression. The familiar progression at the end of "Birches" is an excellent case in point. "So was I once myself a swinger of birches" begins the progression, and moves steadily into analogies which were never implicit in the first part of the poem; were never intended to be implicit. There is a striking difference between the flat application of the moral tag and the gradual unfolding of meaning through a progression of metaphors. Nevertheless, Frost's poems which use these progressions are never the equal of his poems shaped into a single self-sufficient metaphor. Occasionally, as in "To Earthward," the restrained intensity of a single thought may permit the successful use of images as steppingstones to the strong conclusion. But the completely right structure of such a poem as "Putting in the Seed" is more satisfying than the relaxed and rambling progressions which grow pleasurably but less forcefully from the initial statement.

We have examined a limited number of uses to which Frost has put the metaphor in his poetry. Such an approach is dangerous, because it concentrates on only one aspect of poetry and tends to ignore the other aspects. Such a danger may be alleviated if one remembers that the complete poem is so much more than metaphor, more than metaphor combined with "the sound of sense," more than these two parts combined with all the other parts which constitute a poem. Any restricted analysis may increase the understanding and appreciation of poetry only if we keep in mind those other parts which are held in abeyance while a specific part is under consideration. Testing the metaphor alone is comparable to playing the part of a single musical instrument in an orchestral score, an instrumental part which comes into its proper function only when combined with all the other instruments. As orchestral music is distinct from the mere sum of individual instrumentations, so is poetry distinct from the sum of its parts.

This distinct quality is analogous to the apex-point of greatest heat which occurs invisibly above the steady flame of a candle. It is not the flame itself, although it is dependent on the flame, even as the flame is dependent on the wax and wick. So the ultimate heat of a poem rides steadily above the apex of the poem, and defies the eye of the reader, although it may be perceived undeniably by the senses and the mind.

Young people have insight. They have a flash here and a flash there. It is like the stars coming out in the early evening. They have flashes of light. It is later in the dark of life that you see forms, constellations. And it is the constellations that are philosophy. The flashing is done; the coming out of the stars.[21]

LATER POEMS

I<small>N</small> the metaphorical passage quoted above, Robert Frost has given us a memorable statement of that inevitable change which comes over a poet as he passes from youth to maturity. The poems of youth, he implies, are analogous to flashes of sight and insight which occur as responses to images and incidents emotionally perceived. These symbolic flashes impel the early poet to bring the emotional experience under control through the words and phrases, the lines and stanzas, of verse. As the poet's observations are clarified through cumulative experience, these isolated flashes begin to assume patterns of larger meaning. Then the lyrics which have been emotionally impelled give way to lyrics motivated by wider intellectual perceptions.

Such a shift of emphasis, by no means exclusive, requires that the poet find for his individual thought a specific image or metaphor or incident, if he is to achieve that concentration and compression which fuses and unifies the symbol to a philosophical lyric. The central idea must be translated and resolved into symbolic connotation within the specific; but the specific must be delineated in such a manner that the underlying idea is neither hidden completely nor paraded openly. This hard assignment is a favorite with Frost. In another connection, we have already considered a good example in "For Once, Then, Something."

Frequently, the additional intensity and power of the poet's intellectual perception is able to make satisfactory amends for the decreased intensity of emotional response. In Frost's later poems, this compensation reveals itself vigorously in a number of distinct poetic types. In the lyrics, there is no clean division between the emotional pieces and the philosophical pieces, for the gradations proceed naturally through the descriptive and reflective lyrics to such an extreme as the metaphysical lyric entitled "All Revelation." So also, one may find a gradation of dramatic narratives which move slowly away from the psychological studies of character in the *North of Boston* poems and are modified in the later poems in such a way that the narrative is brought to focus on separate ideas clarified by analogy or by a progression of metaphors. Such dramatic narratives, however, may be understood as natural extensions of the shorter incidents used in Frost's dramatic lyrics. The direction of their development quite naturally leads the poet to other types, such as allegories and fables. Related, and yet quite distinct, are those poetic variations which take the form of extended satires or of compressed epigrams. And the high quality of Frost's accomplishment in these types will be considered in separate chapters.

Nevertheless, there is always the danger that ideas, as such, may prove less tractable than emotions, and may not always be tamed and controlled by the poetic process. Aesthetically, it is the poet's salvation to preserve in his poetry a nice balance between the opposed personal attributes of emotional intensity and intellectual intensity. Through artistic detachment, he strives always to keep the prism of his spirit transparent, free, uncolored by irrelevant convictions and prejudices, so that the objects and correspondences perceived in a moment of poetic insight may be refracted in verse with unblemished accuracy. Such detachment is hard to obtain, but it is even harder to preserve after youthful flashes have grouped themselves into patterns of meaning. Conscious of this pitfall, Frost has not always avoided it. At times, the specific symbol or metaphor in his philosophical lyrics is not permitted to contain the implicit connotation of the general thought. Then the generalization breaks through and asserts itself with such force as to injure the poem as a self-sufficient vehicle for the idea. At the other extreme, the compression of the analogy within the compass of a brief and dramatically symbolic incident may hide too well the intended connotation. Between these two extremes, however, Frost has created many finely wrought lyrics of ideas.

In the later poems some of the least successful, from a technical point of view, represent Frost's willful violation of principles I have expressed above. He always knows what he is up to, and is not much concerned with technical criticism. Before we examine some of these briefly, let us make an arbitrary division. For convenience, we may consider the poems in his first three books as early poems; those in the books starting with *New Hampshire* (which was published after Frost had celebrated his forty-ninth birthday) as the later poems. In brief retrospect, most of the poems in *A Boy's Will* are motivated by subjective and lyrical responses to flashes of sight and insight. In *North of Boston*, the dramatic narratives are primarily objective delineations of character and situation. In *Mountain Interval*, these two forms are interspersed throughout the book. Nevertheless, the bold and dangerous tendency of later poems is foreshadowed by certain mannerisms in *Mountain Interval*. With stubborn assertiveness, generalized thoughts and ideas crop out of certain poems. They are employed as elaborations of analogies not always explicit in connotation. The incident around which "The Bonfire" is built, once established, permits the speaker to develop a somewhat farfetched analogy between the fears caused by fire and the fears caused by war. A different kind of application may be found at the end of "Brown's Descent" and "The Gum-Gatherer." In *New Hampshire*, the dramatic narratives continue to move further away from those in *North of Boston* because they are too often made to serve as vehicles for ideas which have become so firmly fixed in the poet's mind that they assert themselves with too much bluntness for poetry. "The Census-Taker" is a kind of elegy written in a country lumber camp, long since deserted; but this descriptive and reflective narration of the specific incident is not permitted to convey through connotations the poet's familiar blend of reluctance and acceptance. When the cherished thought crystallizes into prosaic statement in the last line, "It must be I want life to go on living," the phrase seems too bald for poetry. In "The Star-Splitter," the narrative is obliged to give way to the poet's deliberate pointing up of the philosophic skepticism which might have been left to connotation. Again, "The Axe-Helve" is a delightful story, with accurate characterizations and implicit symbolism which is contained by the structure of the poem. Nevertheless, the framework of that poem is almost cracked by the allusiveness of metaphors in which the teleological and epistemological implications are almost too pointed. Another dramatic narrative, "Wild Grapes," gives way at the end to an application of the analogy in the form of an unfolded metaphor.

Among the shorter poems, or grace notes, in *New Hampshire*, the constellations of thought assume philosophic groupings which are at times faulty. "An Empty Threat" plunges the reader too abruptly into the middle of a dramatic argument which continues until it has become a vehicle for defending middle-ground skepticism against the attacks and threats of the extreme agnostics. "The Onset" also represents the poet's increasing tendency to move from the specific incident to a generalization.

In *West-running Brook*, certain intellectual convictions are brought to the reader's attention not only through symbols and analogies but also through the poet's extended elaborations of these analogies. The title-poem of *West-running Brook* is an excellent example of this extended application which asserts with clarity the poet's philosophic convictions; but at the expense of that aesthetic structure which is the poem itself. This same injurious poetic method is continued deliberately by Frost in *A Further Range*. The manner in which he elaborates the central theme of "Two Tramps in Mud Time" must convince the reader that the poet does not consider such a blunt method of application and elaboration to be injurious to the poem. Occasionally he proves his point; more often he disproves it. These generalized explanations of the poem inevitably strain, crack, and break apart the delicate structure of the poem. And the poem is properly the vehicle for thoughts and ideas only in so far as it can control and contain those ideas. Frost's tendency to ask too much of the poetic structure, through his use of generalizations, reaches its height in the satirical poem entitled "The Lesson For Today."

Fortunately, most of Frost's later poems manage to reconcile thought and emotion with thoroughly satisfying results. In spite of his own statement concerning the inevitable direction toward philosophical thoughts in all poets who have passed through the period of their first fine careless rapture, Frost has continued to startle us with lyrics in which the emotional tension is accentuated with penetrating and mature thought. Even in these later lyrics, there are times when it seems certain that an emotional motivation is responsible for specific flashes of sight and insight; as though the emotional quality served as a precipitate, in a double sense, to impel and to unify. Consider, for example, the crystal clarity of certain dramatic and reflective lyrics which belong to the later period and are some of the poet's finest. Among these may be included "Spring Pools," "To Earthward," "Stopping by Woods on a Snowy Evening," "Once by the Pacific," "Acquainted With the Night," "Desert Places," and "Come In."

Certain technical aspects of the later poems remain to be suggested. Although Frost seemed to lose his interest in his theory concerning the sound of sense, the principle has continued to assert itself with fine effect in the dramatic quality of the later poems. Speech rhythms continue to play against the basic metrical patterns. In *New Hampshire*, many phrases and sentences make use of idiomatic structures drawn from New England speech—and these have continued to appear sparingly in lyrics and narratives. The title-poem in *New Hampshire* is more thoroughly relaxed and conversational in tone than any of the earlier poems. Yet the tone is admirably suited to the laconic irony of such a satirical piece. In the same book, "The Axe-Helve" ventures briefly into a French-Canadian dialect which is an exception to Frost's general avoidance of all dialect. Colloquialisms, which are occasionally suited to the tone of certain pieces such as "The Star-Splitter" and "The Witch of Coös," are used with restraint and accuracy in a few of the later lyrics. Related to these are the characteristic compressions of phrase which give an elliptical quality to certain of Frost's later pieces. Almost always, however, the preliminary obscurity of such passages is removed when the tones of voice are permitted to clarify the intended sense.

In rhyme scheme and in verse form, the later poems continue

to play variations on the patterns already established in the poet's early books. Enjoying the limiting requirements of meter and rhyme, he has frequently ridiculed his free-verse contemporaries by saying that he would no sooner give up the restrictions of meter and rhyme than he would play tennis with the net down! Once, however, he turned to the use of free verse in the writing of one of the later poems entitled, "The Lovely Shall Be Choosers." This poem, built around a theme which might be considered as an ironic allegory of conflict between free will and predestination, falls naturally into irregular lines which are terminated by the length of the different phrases.

These brief suggestions as to the character of the later poems are here limited because of the manner in which they are examined more broadly in the chapters which follow.

The style is the man. Rather say the style is the way the man takes himself; and to be at all charming or even bearable, the way is almost rigidly prescribed. If it is with outer seriousness, it must be with inner humor. If it is with outer humor, it must be with inner seriousness. Neither one alone without the other under it will do.[22]

THE SENSE OF HUMOR

In Robert Frost's verse, humor is an integral part of the emotional texture and the intellectual definition. It is fused and blended with the whole in such a way that it often hides between the words. Occasionally it appears openly in playfulness or malice, then vanishes and reveals itself only in soft tones like faraway laughter. Some readers may enjoy the most obvious flashes; yet they may pass too hastily over poems in which the subtle presence of humor is related to the finished whole as an indispensable catalytic agent.

When Frost said, in one of his poems, that the way of understanding is partly mirth, he implied much that is not immediately apparent. Humor is the happiest basis for developing that critical attitude which saves the poet from taking himself or his poetry too seriously. Few people have been able to play in poetry with the same comic-seriousness employed by Frost. Sacred as his muse may be, she must adapt herself to the poet's profane moments when he wishes to cut loose with rhymed devil-may-care fun which still has beneath it a serious implication. Faultfinding critics look askance at these larks as unworthy of one who takes poetry as a high calling. Unperturbed, Frost continues to mingle the trivial and the weighty. Although his most flippant verses remain unpublished, one may find examples of penetrating foolery in the couplets and quatrains which make up "Ten Mills" or in the longer fables such as "Departmental" and "A Considerable Speck."

The humorous spirit is a two-edged blade which cuts outward

and inward at the same moment. It is the bright weapon of Frost's philosophic skepticism and it flashes with witty seriousness in many of his poems. Again, his capacity for perspective and all-inclusiveness is less like a double cutting edge and more like the tender gesture of two arms which reach out to end a lover's quarrel by enfolding opposites and reconciling them to oneness. With the gesture of love, Frost's humor brings together in his poetry the opposed attitudes of sadness and gladness, the pitiful and the absurd, the too-just and the too-merciful. Such a flexible grasp is of primary value to the total accomplishment of the poet.

Although our considerations here are essentially artistic, they cannot be isolated from the poet's attitude toward life. The integration of artist and not-artist in Frost plays a vital part in giving strength to his verse. If the way of understanding is partly mirth with him, this does not make it true for so-called humorists in general. A man may be funny without having any exceptional grasp of the human mystery. With Frost, however, the sense of the comic in life goes hand in hand with the sense of the tragic. These two viewpoints, not necessarily antagonistic, permit and protect each other. In such a close relationship, mirth is not merely an attempt to belittle and forget the tragic, because each has its own peculiar reality. But Frost's sense of humor is able to accept with calmness the sense of tragedy forever present in any inclusive attitude toward life.

This inextricable bond uniting Frost's mirth with his sadness must be recognized if we are to understand his humor. It illuminates the quality of smiling tenderness with which his poems extol and amplify the somber loveliness of images which persist in the face of death; life which survives against "the stream of everything that runs away." The poet's metaphors drawn from nature are best interpreted when this blend of smiling acceptance and sorrowful reluctance is kept in mind. With the gentle shyness of understatement, he delineates the peculiar charm of those things cherished with added zest because they are so closely bound to life's disappearances. The seasons, with their twilights of sad departure and their mornings of joyous renewal, become symbols which the poet uses to unfold and elaborate his belief that one has to be "versed in country things" to understand "what to make of a diminishing thing." If spring suffuses through his poems the greatest intensity of excitement, autumn becomes the best symbol of his confident pleasure in so many neglected images which survive with sober charm, against any change; of dormant life which has in it the power of renewal and of continuance in spite of all that vanishes and is lost. Renewal becomes the theme of many poems, beginning with such early ones as "A Line-Storm Song" and "In Hardwood Groves." In a broader sense, it finds expression through such poems as "The Onset" and "In Time of Cloudburst."

Even when pitched in a minor key, the subtle tones of voice are able to make the reader aware of that humor which is the all-pervading leaven. The yearning and reluctance of the fall-poem entitled "October" is nevertheless pervaded with wistful playfulness:

> O hushed October morning mild,
> Thy leaves have ripened to the fall;
> To-morrow's wind, if it be wild,
> Should waste them all.
> The crows above the forest call;
> To-morrow they may form and go.
> O hushed October morning mild,
> Begin the hours of this day slow.
> Make the day seem to us less brief.
> Hearts not averse to being beguiled,
> Beguile us in the way you know.
> Release one leaf at break of day;
> At noon release another leaf;
> One from our trees, one far away.
> Retard the sun with gentle mist;
> Enchant the land with amethyst.
> Slow, slow!
> For the grapes' sake, if they were all,
> Whose leaves already are burnt with frost,
> Whose clustered fruit must else be lost—
> For the grapes' sake along the wall.

In this prayerful lament is humor which takes two forms of beguiling: that which the poet invites October to impose on him, and that which the poet tries to impose on October, by shifting the argument from his own desire to the need of the unripened grapes! The wistful tones of regret suggest the analogy between the immediate transience of summer and the inevitable transience of human life: "Make the day seem to us less brief." The same minor key, alleviated with humorous acceptance, may be heard in the music of almost all the lyrics. The balance has been kept from the earliest to the latest; sadness never dominates the joy of cherishing and of love. The optimism which asserts itself with slowly increasing vigor in the later lyrics is never understood correctly, however, if it is separated from the underlying obbligato of sadness and tragic realization.

Our concern here is with only the more subtle manifestations of Frost's sense of humor. In the creative method, the nice arrangement of thought and meaning in words and sentences becomes a guide to the tones of voice. But the fine gradations of humor can be appreciated only when the tones of voice translate them into the sounds of sense, to use Frost's phrase again. Diverse as these gradations may be, they seem to permit an arbitrary division into two main categories. First, phrases and sentences indicate tones of voice which convey the poet's tolerant, sympathetic, and smiling consideration of human yearnings, sorrows, prejudices, and foibles. The quality of humor in the suggested tones of voice goes into the nature of the words, phrases, and sentences and amplifies their denotation with overtones of connotation which are not initially obvious. The calculated poetic arrangement enables the poet to give voice-ways to his own emotions and thoughts and meanings. Second, phrases and sentences achieve intended tones through a different manner of objectivity: when the characters in dramatic monologues and dialogues assert their own terse and laconic individuality through homely and idiomatic phrases which are amusingly self-revealing. The quality of humor thus removed from the immediate presence of the poet seems to come out of the nature of these casual and offhand sentences. Such a distinction, plainly theoretical, is of value only if it helps to clarify different aspects of that humor so important to the poetic process.

Returning to the first of these arbitrary distinctions, we may find that the range of Frost's self-revealing humor includes a wide spread of voice-ways. At one extreme is the smiling tenderness of the love lyrics; at the other extreme is the scornful raillery of the satires. The dominant note in them all, however, is a mischievous tone of teasing. It may be found differently if we start with the delicate shades in "October" and "The Rose Family," move on to the quizzical banter of the speaker in "Mending Wall," and conclude with the more critical jesting in "A Roadside Stand" and "To a Thinker." These "light words that tease and flout" seem to unify the detached criticism, whether it is aimed at self or at others. The precise quality of this humor needs to be thrust back into the nature of the words and sentences by means of the speaking tones of voice.

The second of these arbitrary distinctions brings into focus a separate aspect of the poet's quest for permanence in disappearances. Frost seems to be fond of searching out and finding vitality in the crabbed and twisted lives of people toughened by that very shrinking which has reduced them to somber dignity and integrity. In this sad pleasure, Frost and Robinson shared similar aims, although they wore their rue with a difference, from the earliest days. Frost's characters, artistically projected, reveal themselves in their own conversations with so much success that we are always able to smile or laugh with them; occasionally at them. Furthermore, the humor of their conversation is blended with the humor of the dramatic and ironic situations created through the slight conflicts between the actors themselves. In "Snow," for example, there is humor in the husband's teasing questions as to what his wife hears over the telephone, and that humor depends on his questions. But there is also another kind of humor which appears when the wife's emergent solicitude almost eclipses her distaste for Meserve, because her emotional and melodramatic tendencies are aroused by the situation. Again, the situation brings out the amusing qualities of exhibitionism and egotism in the evangelical visitor who rants and raves pleasantly before he plunges gaily back into the storm. In "The Code," these two separate elements of humor are apparent not only because of the laconic manner in which the hired man tells his story but also because the situation develops from amusing differences of character and temperament. Here, as in all the dramatic narratives, the poet handles his characterizations with so much love and understanding that they never become caricatures. And the psychological allusiveness, which arises from the delineation of their peculiarities, leads the reader to believe that the foibles of the characters do not overbalance their self-sufficiency and their integrity.

This brief sketch of certain limited aspects are intended to suggest the extent to which Frost's humor increases the richness of his poems. In its pervasiveness, acuteness, and spontaneity, colored by laconic Yankee shrewdness and terse variety, such a sense of humor might be compared profitably with the humor which becomes an integral part of the poetic process in the verse of other American writers. Oliver Wendell Holmes stands out as one who had more ability to display humor in occasional verse than to display anything more than occasional flashes of genuine poetry. James Russell Lowell turned to humor largely for the limited purposes of satire and caricature. Emerson and Whitman, particularly the latter, were obviously deficient in this trait which might have cultivated in them a much-needed self-critical aid to artistry. Perhaps the feminine spontaneity of Emily Dickinson's humor, so different from Frost's, might be found most nearly analogous to his in its all-pervasiveness and in its essential importance to the poetic process. In their separate ways, each manages to entangle with words and phrases a sense of the wistful, the whimsical, the comic, the sadly happy, the ironic. Of the two, however, Emily's range is the more limited. I can think of no American poet who has been so successful as Frost in combining such variety of humor with so many other poetic merits. This variety may become more apparent as we examine separate manifestations, in the following chapters.

Don't let the things I say against myself
Betray you into taking sides against me,
Or it may get you into trouble with me.[23]

IRONY AND SATIRE

THE ironic perception of paradox is motivated largely by the
sense of the humorous and the comic, even when the implications
of such paradox are tragic. Although these perceptions, expressed
in poetry, may crop out indirectly from the allusive connotations
of lyrics, they may also be brought to focus so pointedly on human
foibles as to create satires. If the satirical method is delicate and
subtle, the reader who is not alert may be caught napping by the
poet's intention. And Frost, constantly aware of life's persistent
ironies, takes pleasure in combining symbolism with satire so that
he offers us those sly and twofold equivocations which imply more
than, or the opposite of, that which is stated. At such times, it is
well for us to remember his warning: "Don't let the things I say
against myself betray you into taking sides against me, or it may
get you into trouble with me." We may also find it of value to
remember his favorite viewpoint, which brings the paradoxes of
life into ironic perspective. Whenever he describes or suggests
a contrast between the apparent and the actual, as he sees it or as
others see it, he clarifies his own common-sense position in the
Golden Mean, from which he delights to satirize those extremes
and absolutes, those pretensions and obsessions, which appear in a
humorous light to the poet as relativist.

Satire, as a criticism of life, does not necessarily assert itself as
didacticism and preaching. In poetry, the satirical method is best
utilized when it is restricted by the aesthetic limitations of the
form-giving medium. Here again, the poet's first concern must be
with his art, not with his ideas and prejudices, as such. Hence the
difference between the satire of the preacher and that of the poet.
The goal of the serious preacher is conversion; the goal of the
amused and satirical poet is accurate and pleasurable delineation.
As a middle-ground skeptic, Frost would deplore the possibility

) of extreme and deadly seriousness about even his own position. He therefore offers his satirical commentaries as critical definitions and clarifications, with an amused gesture of casual deprecation. Whether the poems take the form of crafty and ironic indirection or of obvious satirical teasing, the reader is always conscious of Frost's mischievous and affectionate laughter. The sadly playful tones of his voice, conveyed through the skillful artistry of restraint and equivocation, are intended to remind us that the goal of this satirist is not conversion!

As satirists, Robert Frost and Horace seem to share a spiritual kinship which would afford considerations more detailed than I am competent to make. Each is content to consider himself no better than his neighbors and is happy to live on good terms with those whom he satirizes. Each is always glad to remain so near to people that he may set out frequently to tease the wistfulness of idealistic dreamers who want too much from life or ridicule the smugness of greedy sit-fast conservatives who want too little from life, or the wrong things. Each agrees that the most pleasant position in society may be symbolized by life on a little Sabine farm, from which one may earn a living, develop a self-sufficient integrity, accept the obligations of neighborliness, and send out occasionally, as gifts and sales, the produce from the enriched soil and the enriched mind. Obviously, each has the same dry humor which permits him to develop little parables of laughter and love, as opposed to the withering Juvenalian invectives of laughter and hate.

Although the Latin poets certainly offered to Frost some suggestions as to how bucolic and pastoral poetry might lend itself to satire, he seems to have stumbled almost accidentally on his own poetic forms. Perhaps he found inspiration nearer home. If there were precedents for dramatic monologue and dialogue in English poetry from Chaucer to Browning and beyond, there were also precedents for satirical monologue and dialogue, from Chaucer to Byron and beyond. Nevertheless, Frost's tendency to give objective expression to his own ironic view of life, through directly satirical pieces, seems to have grown quite casually from tentative beginnings in his *North of Boston* poems. One of them, "The

Black Cottage," begins in a manner so much like the others as to permit the reader to suppose the actor on that little stage before the cottage door is building a psychological study out of his recollections concerning the dear old lady who used to live there. Her character is important to the poem, but chiefly as a point of departure for ideas which go beyond her to generalities that lead to a curiously ironic Utopia on a desert island. The theme of the poem revolves around a puzzling question raised by the naïve faith of the old lady concerning the purpose of the Civil War: When is truth true? The liberal country preacher who recognizes the welter of answers to such an ancient conundrum seems to be playing when he tosses off these gently ironic lines:

> What are you going to do with such a person?
> Strange how such innocence gets its own way.
> I shouldn't be surprised if in this world
> It were the force that would at last prevail.
>
> .   .   .   .
>
> For, dear me, why abandon a belief
> Merely because it ceases to be true.
> Cling to it long enough, and not a doubt
> It will turn true again, for so it goes.
> Most of the change we think we see in life
> Is due to truths being in and out of favour.
> As I sit here, and oftentimes, I wish
> I could be monarch of a desert land
> I could devote and dedicate forever
> To the truths we keep coming back and back to.

One virtue in the equivocation of such a commentary on the difference between the apparent and the actual is that this argument may be used by either side as the final answer to the opposition!

In Frost's next book, *Mountain Interval*, direct irony did not find a continued development toward a truly satirical verse form, although irony does occur through varied indirections. The objective self-teasing appears in "The Road Not Taken," when the poet knows he will tell "with a sigh" the old story of a choice which "made all the difference." Again irony flashes in those familiar lines of "Birches" where it is hoped that the wish to get away from earth may not be granted too soon and too completely. It also becomes the focal point of the war poem, "Range-Finding," when the spider whose web has been disturbed by the death-dealing bullet finds it to be of no importance. With sadness and pleasantry, irony threads its way through *Mountain Interval*, as it had done in *A Boy's Will*, without becoming aggressive enough to be considered satire.

In *New Hampshire*, however, the title poem is different from any Frost had written before. There for the first time he pays homage to the method and manner of the Latin *satura* and *sermones* which had been developed by Horace beyond the manner of Lucilius. Because satire has taken on such a different connotation today, it may be helpful to recall that Horace created his satires or discourses in the form of good-natured and friendly conversations with himself and others; that he loved to distribute his kindly attacks on human follies through a potpourri of anecdotes and symbols, snatches of dialogue, touches of self-appraisal and self-disparagement, homely details and proverbs. Frequently Horace seems to take special pleasure in bringing a satire to an end with a light jest. Obviously, this literary form deserved to be called a "mixture" of things, as is the Latin connotation of the word "satura" from which our word "satire" is derived. In the same Horatian sense, but after the laconic manner of the Yankee, Frost constructed "New Hampshire" as a satire which seems at first reading to be held too loosely, if at all, by a slight central theme. A closer examination reveals a deliberately informal and familiar structure of anecdotes, dialogues, self-revelation, parables, good-natured attacks on literary and commercial friends, epigrammatic sentences, and even the light jest for an ending. With teasing irony, he begins his poem by pretending to glorify a stupid boast:

> I met a lady from the South who said
> (You won't believe she said it, but she said it):
> "None of my family ever worked, or had
> A thing to sell." I don't suppose the work
> Much matters. You may work for all of me.

I've seen the time I've had to work myself.
The having anything to sell is what
Is the disgrace in man or state or nation.

There would seem to be some doubt as to whether the poet could
go on with his ironic glorification. As soon as the reader feels the
looseness of these run-on lines in a thoroughly appropriate adaptation of blank verse, he is prepared for the further development of
the fun already started so casually. (Somebody is going to be
caught off guard by the persistent equivocation and double talk.
The poet is at the old game of saying one thing and meaning
another—and somebody has to lose!) Three anecdotes are added
to support his apparent distaste for anything commercial, be they
diamonds, climate, or propaganda. Then the theme is established
as an apparently logical conclusion: "It never could have happened in New Hampshire." The seeming digression which follows is merely an exception to prove the poet's generalization
before he elaborates the theme:

> Just specimens is all New Hampshire has,
> One each of everything as in a show-case
> Which naturally she doesn't care to sell.

Now the game has taken a pleasant turn: whatever shortcomings New Hampshire may have in a commercial sense are translated by the poet into virtues. Let others ridicule; the poet stands
ready to defend such a charming showcase of "specimens." Then
follows some boasting about a few unique pieces which are actually doubtful subjects for boasting: one President of the United
States, one Daniel Webster, one claim to a family of precolonial
people who were not Indians, one real reformer, one egregious
hen fancier, one small gold mine. When the poet comes to mention
the old-style New Hampshire witch, he digresses long enough to
establish her superiority by tucking in a satirical sketch of a
new-style witch he had met recently at a cut-glass dinner in Boston.
Quite naturally the main theme is brought deftly around to
farming and writing in such a manner that the poet may defend
himself and his New Hampshire characters against the critics of
New Hampshire, from Emerson to Amy Lowell. Some modern

novelists would seem to find fault with a state in which life isn't tragic enough to be hell or perfect enough to be heaven; but if the poet could choose any permanent modification for New Hampshire, he would be content merely to have her mountains higher! This matter of choices suggests another satirical anecdote on a related subject:

> Lately in converse with a New York alec
> About the new school of the pseudo-phallic,
> I found myself in a close corner where
> I had to make an almost funny choice.
> "Choose you which you will be—a prude, or puke,
> Mewling and puking in the public arms."

Then follows a pleasant conglomeration of equivocal arguments as to ways in which an individual may assert his extreme of prudish rejection, in so far as nature and human nature are concerned, or his extreme of infantile dependence on human nature, as it becomes organized into a socialized and communistic society. But, asks the poet, wouldn't there be a possibility of finding room here for a third choice, perhaps a classical moderation in the Golden Mean, after the fashion of the ancients:

> It seems a narrow choice the age insists on.
> How about being a good Greek, for instance?
> That course, they tell me, isn't offered this year.
> "Come, but this isn't choosing—puke or prude?"

Thus seemingly bullied and buffeted into a position of embarrassment, the poet find a symbolic answer with which to bring this bundle of ironies to a conclusion:

> Well, if I have to choose one or the other,
> I choose to be a plain New Hampshire farmer
> With an income in cash of say a thousand
> (From say a publisher in New York City).
> It's restful to arrive at a decision,
> And restful just to think about New Hampshire.
> At present I am living in Vermont.

Here is a faithful use of the Horatian pattern which nevertheless permits Frost to create a thoroughly American satire, replete with Yankee turns of thought and phrase. Implicit in "New Hampshire" is the irony of inversion (in a double sense!), of anticlimax, understatement, and overstatement, together with a laconic voice-way which the phrases so accurately suggest. The Yankee terseness has found a perfect medium for satire which can make such good use of idiomatic New England speech.

Frost's understanding of the spirit of Greek and Latin poetry asserts itself at once as a confession of his delight and as an assertion of his individuality. Once the bond of kinship between him and Horace is suggested, it leads naturally to further thoughts as to the way in which Frost has paid his respects to those forms of classical poetry which are even more specifically bucolic: the Idylls of Theocritus, the Eclogues and Georgics of Vergil, as well as the Odes, Songs, and Satires of Horace. It may not be out of place to recall here that Frost decided to return to college, following his first rebellion, because of his desire to read more widely in the original texts of classical literature. His desultory reading in that field has continued and has been a vital stimulus to his own writing, although the effect is not at all obvious. Perhaps no American poet has ever brought to his own art such a wide acquaintance with classical literature with such a slight suggestion of it in details of direct reference or of slavish imitation.

The Horatian manner of handling the ode for satirical purposes may seem far removed from Frost's poetry. Consider, however, that political satire indited some years ago to President Roosevelt in particular and to the "Brain Trust" in general under the first title, "To a Thinker in Office." Horace turned critic of the state because his love of country and of common sense made him rebel humorously against political bungling; similarly, Frost's octosyllabic couplets in this poem combine banter and seriousness, as may be observed in the following passage:

> Just now you're off democracy
> (With a polite regret to be),
> And leaning on dictatorship;
> But if you will accept the tip,
> In less than no time, tongue and pen,
> You'll be a democrat again.

A reasoner and good as such,
Don't let it bother you too much
If it makes you look helpless please
And a temptation to the tease.
Suppose you've no direction in you,
I don't see but you must continue
To use the gift you do possess,
And sway with reason more or less.

. . . . . .

So if you find you must repent
From side to side in argument,
At least don't use your mind too hard,
But trust my instinct—I'm a bard.

In a quite different sense, Frost uses the manner of the ode for a
mild touch of indirect philosophic satire, in his poem entitled, "To
a Young Wretch." After taking to task a boy who has cut down
a Christmas tree from his woods, the poet considers the conflict
of good and good, not of good and evil, in this minor tragedy.
True, the boy has stolen a tree, but there may be consolation to be
found in Boethius's doctrine:

It is your Christmases against my woods.
But even where thus opposing interests kill,
They are to be thought of as opposing goods
Oftener than as conflicting good and ill;
Which makes the war god seem no special dunce
For always fighting on both sides at once.

Thus a slight incident, viewed with ironic objectivity, is turned
gracefully into a barbed epigram before the poem continues.

Vergil seems to have furnished some inspirations for our New
England poet, in satires and pastorals. Frost's handling of themes
which might lend themselves to American georgics is never strictly
Vergilian, although many details of farming and husbandry in
his poems are elaborate and accurate. He shares with Vergil, however, a desire to subordinate to the uses of poetry the practical
expositions of his georgic passages. His use of rural details is
rarely satisfied until a human being appears in the foreground.
For example, the very precise reference to correct procedure in

building a load of hay, which may be found in "The Death of the Hired Man," is introduced to amplify the characterization of the hired man and the reluctant admiration of his boss. That other description of the best way to load and unload hay, in "The Code," serves not only to develop the little plot but also to characterize another hired man. Again, although the poet's purposes are metaphorical, apple-growers would have difficulty in finding any fault with pomological details in such poems as "Good-Bye and Keep Cold," "The Gold Hesperidee," and "After Apple-Picking." Other poems which make metaphorical use of precise information of the georgic variety may be discovered by the reader, and they will certainly include "Blueberries," "The Axe-Helve," "The Grindstone," and "Mending Wall." But this digression into variations on georgic themes has taken us away from satire, to which we may return without leaving Vergil's influence.

The pastoral poetry of Vergil and Theocritus has given rise to a long tradition in English literature, although much of it has been artificial and lifeless. Frost, like Theocritus, does not treat his farmers and rural people, his hills and vales, as conventions, ideals, or types. Each of them takes everything as he finds it and lets characters converse with terse simplicity. Twice, however, Frost's bucolics have been modeled after the Vergilian pattern which permits the poet to disguise his own personality and treat in satirical allegory the circumstances of his own age. The first of these, "Build Soil," is a political eclogue delivered by Frost at Columbia University, shortly before the celebrated Republican and Democratic conventions in the election year 1932. The air was full of party promises as to the Golden Age which should rise out of the depression shambles. The situation might have reminded Frost of Vergil's familiar Fourth Eclogue, in which he prophesied another kind of Golden Age. It would seem, at least, that Frost recalled Vergil's First Eclogue, which is a dialogue between a farmer, Meliboeus, and a farm-loving poet, Tityrus (Vergil himself, no less), who happen to meet and share with each other their observations, hopes, and fears. Frost's "Political Pastoral" is also a dialogue between a farmer, Meliboeus, and a farm-loving poet Tityrus (Frost himself, no less), who share with each other their allegorical observations about the sad condition of the nation in particular and the world in general. The poem begins in the manner of a Vergilian parody, for Frost's farmer has also been forced to give up his farm. He also has to give up any serious part he may have wished to have in the dialogue, for Tityrus monopolizes it. The theme of the one-sided conversation begins with "bad times" and is followed by some weighing as to just how bad the times really are. The discussion moves on to an ironic consideration of the manner in which government might be able to establish the greatest good for the greatest number. Having lost his farm, Meliboeus is inclined to think that socialism might do the trick and give us back at least four or five freedoms. But Tityrus makes fun of any social revolution which promises to bring about a Golden Age through an unselfish plan whereby we all take care of each other. He is skeptical enough to wonder whether individuals are sufficiently developed to be ready for such heavy responsibility. If so, well and good; if not, let's start by improving individuals. After making a private agreement to try out a five-year plan of self-improvement, the farmer and the poet part, and the poem ends. The satire in the poem includes a variety of specifics which are aimed particularly at the political Utopians who promise to perfect a humanitarian brotherhood of man before the individuals have managed to perfect a mere brotherhood of brothers.

Bad times and the Golden Age is the theme of another satirical dialogue in Frost's latest book, *A Witness Tree*. This time, Horace furnishes the fitting model, in his satirical discourses, or *sermones*. As if Frost would scorn the inevitable taunts of those who accuse him of didacticism, the satire is ironically entitled, "The Lesson For Today." Such a title reminds us of the poet's self-ridicule in "Build Soil":

> "Let me preach to you, will you, Meliboeus?"
> "Preach on. I thought you were already preaching.
> But preach and see if I can tell the difference."

So "The Lesson For Today" becomes a pointed Horatian satire, aimed at the doleful pessimists who have decided the world has pretty much gone to hell. Probably not, the poet says, but if it has, let us as individuals go back to the Latins and gain inspiration for beginning again with a rebirth of thought and art and humanity. Then, through an imagined dialogue with the learned scholar, Alcuin, the poet weighs the question as to which age could be considered worse, this one or the age of Charlemagne. The comparison permits a wide range of ironic statements which make fun of the absolute certainties of scholars, philosophers, and divines. Finally the argument is summarized when Alcuin is told:

> One age is like another for the soul.
> I'm telling you. You haven't said a thing,
> Unless I put it in your mouth to say.
> I'm having the whole argument my way—
> But in your favor—please to tell your King—
> In having granted you all ages shine
> With equal darkness, yours as dark as mine.

Bad times, and a scientific patent-medicine recipe for bringing about another kind of Golden Age is the theme of another satirical dialogue in *A Witness Tree*. The butt of the jests is the twentieth century worship of science as the ultimate cure-all and savior. The poem entitled "The Literate Farmer and the Planet Venus," makes allegorical use of starlight and electric lights as symbols of the old faith and the new faith. After listening to the literate farmer's explanation as to how science will soon solve all the woes of the world, the poet gives his reasons for wanting the alternations of darkness to remain:

> Here come more stars to character the skies,
> And they in the estimation of the wise
> Are more divine than any bulb or arc,
> Because their purpose is to flash and spark,
> But not to take away the precious dark.
> We need the interruption of the night
> To ease attention off when overtight,
> To break our logic in too long a flight,
> And ask us if our premises are right.

With Frost, satire offers another method of finding metaphors. Through them he gives further definition to his acceptance of the mixed good and evil, together with all the perennial and salutary conflicts of such a precious mixture. The poet seems willing to exult in his discovery that his own conflicts are doubled because of the onslaught from two sides at once, in the Golden Mean! In his poems, he frequently turns to deal satirically with one side, then turns to deal satirically with the other side. This rejection of either extreme is a cause of confusion to some readers, who insist that he should be in one corner or the other.

From the viewpoint of poetic evaluation, much may be said in praise of certain passages in these satirical poems. The Yankee modification of classical forms is ingenious and thoroughly original. The knack of introducing symbols and metaphors is a skillful one. There are also innumerable aphorisms and epigrams which take their places fittingly as crystallizations of thought in the longer passages. Nevertheless, it must be recognized that none of these satirical poems is a thoroughly successful accomplishment. Perhaps the best of them all is "New Hampshire." Frost is never so completely the master of these longer satires as he is master of the finely compressed and unified metaphors which take shape under his hand as intricately wrought and graceful lyrics, or as he is the master of those equally dexterous and successful dramas-in-miniature. The greatest value of the satirical poems is their richness of thought and ideas which have grown out of the poet's life and experience. A more happy form of satire, as Frost has developed it to fit his own idiom, will be found in his fables.

Of animals, the human kind
Are to excess the most inclined.
On low and high we make the charge,
Indeed, upon the race at large.
　　　　　—LA FONTAINE

FABLES

THE fable is merely a specialized adaptation of metaphorical language in such a manner as to imply or state certain analogies between the behavior of animals and the behavior of human beings. This kind of comparison seems to be as old as human thought. Primitive folklore in all parts of the world is found to contain such analogies. Compressed to the smallest compass, these comparisons became metaphorical animal names which epitomized character. Our Indians, for example, honored a brave for his craftiness by calling him Fox; for stealth by calling him Panther; for keen eyes by calling him Eagle. In its most ancient literary form, however, the suggestion of analogies between animals and men frequently illustrated the faults and weaknesses of human passions, hopes, and fears. Those fables which have come down the centuries to us, under the shadowy ownership of a Greek slave named Aesop, are little bundles of entertaining animal stories designed to convey a criticism of persistent human foibles. Such a simple literary device became a popular and precious heritage because it afforded infinite variations and uses in the hands of storytellers, poets, teachers, philosophers, and preachers. Perhaps none has more frequently abused the fable, however, than the satirists from Phaedrus and Horace across the years and miles to Swift and Gay in the eighteenth century. La Fontaine, who fortunately saved the fable from itself in the seventeenth century, revealed the finer possibilities when he developed it as a flexible drama-in-miniature which could be handled with great variety through endless modifications. His thoroughly fresh treatment offered the fable as a simple narrative, with animals as speakers or with no speakers at all; as a concise descriptive recital, in which human beings intermingled their conversations with those of the animals; as dramatic tales into which the author himself might step casually as a chorus-actor whose opinions might not seem out of place. Thus the form was given new impetus, although it has again fallen out of popularity among modern poets.

Robert Frost's fondness for the implications of an extended metaphor led him quite naturally to the writing of parables and fables. Like La Fontaine, he experimented with a variety of forms until he found those best suited to his own manner. In several of his poems he has kept the spirit of La Fontaine by giving us little dramatic glimpses of animals whose actions remind us of human beings, dramatic scenes in which men and animals intermingle. Also like La Fontaine, he has experimented with different verse forms suited to the fresh and natural simplicity of his fables. None can doubt the exceptional degree of his accomplishment in this form, for his animal fables are at once varied, idiomatic, and pithy.

In a general sense, almost all tales are fables. Many of Frost's dramatic pieces, particularly the shorter ones, have certain characteristics which suggest the fable. If we limit ourselves, however, strictly to those which make use of the manners, thoughts, and conversations of animals and such lowly creatures, we may determine the specific range of Frost's accomplishment in giving to this literary form a renewed vitality that is without equal in modern poetry. The furred and feathered beings in his fables are so closely related to New England farm life that they share with their human neighbors certain thoroughly Yankee mannerisms. Yet they appear in poems which are quite distinct from the few fables successfully written in verse by Emerson. Frost's farm fables contain a wider extension of ironic and satirical delineations which give another kind of expression to his detached and objective commentary on things and people.

Many English poets abused the fable by warping it too harshly to their limitations or predispositions. Goldsmith's remark to Dr. Johnson, on the subject of the doctor's little fishes which would have to talk like whales, is a justly famous commentary. Swift confessed to Gay that he always looked about for a moral, then for a fable to illustrate it. Frost starts with animal incidents which are entertaining in themselves, and is not concerned to discover where the dramatic sketch will lead him. Sometimes the incidents suggest analogies which are implicit; sometimes they suggest analogies which are elaborated by the poet in a modified variant on the standard "application" or "moral" of the fable. Perhaps the little drama is presented with such restraint that the analogy is not even apparent to the reader. This directness of approach to the fable, as it is developed by Frost, heightens the sense of verisimilitude and avoids the unpleasant sense of artificiality.

Let us take an example. We have already considered "The Cow in Apple Time" from the viewpoint of metaphorical structure. It takes on further interest when considered more carefully as a fable:

> Something inspires the only cow of late
> To make no more of a wall than an open gate,
> And think no more of wall-builders than fools.
> Her face is flecked with pomace and she drools
> A cider syrup. Having tasted fruit,
> She scorns a pasture withering to the root.
> She runs from tree to tree where lie and sweeten
> The windfalls spiked with stubble and worm-eaten.
> She leaves them bitten when she has to fly.
> She bellows on a knoll against the sky.
> Her udder shrivels and the milk goes dry.

Although the cow does not talk in typical fable fashion, certain thoughts are induced and guessed from her actions: from the way she behaves, it would seem that she puts wall-builders and fools in the same category. It would also seem that she had some reason for scorning "a pasture withering to the roots" when she can get at forbidden fruit, albeit "windfalls spiked with stubble and worm-eaten." The final observation is accurate in farm lore: "Her udder shrivels and the milk goes dry." Taken on the single plane of denotation, this farm scene (truly dramatic for those who have tried to bring such a cow either to her senses or to her stall) gives us a little picture which is enough to make a complete poem. So like a cow, so *very* like a cow! Is it a fable? Is there sufficient analogy to a human being? Certain extensions occur when the poem is read on the plane of cause-and-effect. If the action of the cow should suggest the action of a spoiled child, a second reading brings us with delight to the discovery that this is an "only" child thus permitted to misbehave until her wildness proves harmful. The fabulist has given us hints; but he prefers to let us decide whether or not we care to make the application for the fable.

We have also considered another spoiled child in another locked metaphor, "The Runaway." That fable also is constructed in the form of a perfect New England farm scene. Although the colt does not talk, he acts in a manner that naturally leads the poet to suppose he would scorn any advice which might be given by his mother: "he'd think she didn't know." Again the analogy between the behavior of the colt and the behavior of a headstrong youngster is suggested so mildly that the reader may decide for himself whether he will have "The Runaway" as a fable or merely as a rural vignette. The reticence of the poet keeps him from pointing up the possible analogy. The charm of the poem is derived in part from the very reticence of understatement.

A more dramatic variant on the traditional form of the fable occurs in the poem entitled "A Drumlin Woodchuck." The entire situation is revealed by permitting the woodchuck to carry on a one-sided conversation, a dramatic monologue, while his wife patiently listens and admires. When the actor appears on his mounded stage in front of his burrow door, he begins abruptly with an account of that secret which has made his life a success: the cunning fashion in which he has built a safe little home to protect him from the dangers of life. Modestly smug about his snugness, he concludes his remarks in a tone of downright boastfulness. Yet there is no stated analogy between the animal and a human being. Perhaps a hint of satirical criticism may be found in the woodchuck's superior deprecation of that "loss of common sense" demonstrated by hunters so warlike as to threaten all animal life. Nevertheless, the entire tone of these ingeniously constructed octosyllabic couplets is thoroughly satirical, in the best spirit of the fable. The woodchuck seems to be talking in the clipped manner of a true Vermont farmer; Calvin Coolidge, per-

haps. A second reading brings out all kinds of analogies between
the shrewd caution of the woodchuck and of any thoroughbred
Yankee:

> My own strategic retreat
> Is where two rocks almost meet,
> And still more secure and snug,
> A two-door burrow I dug.
>
> With those in mind at my back
> I can sit forth exposed to attack
> As one who shrewdly pretends
> That he and the world are friends.
>
> All we who prefer to live
> Have a little whistle we give,
> And flash, at the least alarm
> We dive down under the farm.
>
> We allow some time for guile
> And don't come out for a while
> Either to eat or drink.
> We take occasion to think.

The fable becomes much more interesting when it is thus read
as a symbolic expression of human smugness, whether that smugness be justifiable or not. The poet isn't taking sides, or if he is,
he is taking both sides at once: these are commendable vices
which the woodchuck displays! Before the creature is through, he
even happens to display a commendable trust in the greater wisdom of his instinct for cramped safety as contrasted with the more
elaborate, but less practical, wistfulness of the Platonists. Such
analogies are suggested with restraint but with sufficient clarity
to be perceived and enjoyed. Satirical as this fable may be, the
implicit thrusts at human foibles never develop into the unpleasant
application or moral tag so familiar to the tradition of the fable.

Sometimes the fable is constructed in such a manner that the
poet is able to employ a different kind of statement to express the
imagined thoughts of animals. "At Woodward's Gardens" is a
dramatic episode in which two monkeys outwit a pestering

youngster and then confront the boy with dry and scornful silence. Their very manner of expression suggests to the poet thoughts which might be in their minds, and these imagined remarks become the conclusion or summary of the fable.

Another kind of fable is developed in a thoroughly satirical poem, "Departmental," which is nevertheless delightfully mild and humorous in tone. Human foibles are gently burlesqued in an extended series of metaphors which permit the reader to come home to roost by analogy, and to draw independent conclusions. The poem begins with an incident:

> An ant on the table cloth
> Ran into a dormant moth
> Of many times his size.
> He showed not the least surprise.
> His business wasn't with such.
> He gave it scarcely a touch,
> And was off on his duty run.

Again, these newly varied octosyllabic couplets suggest the spirit of archness and satirical teasing so well suited to the nature of the poetic material. The first incident concerning the ant and the moth affords a metaphorical jest at those ant-philosophers who have taken upon themselves the pretentious function of exploring and explaining infinite mysteries—such as moths. Then a new anecdote is added:

> Ants are a curious race;
> One crossing with hurried tread
> The body of one of their dead
> Isn't given a moment's arrest—
> Seems not even impressed.
> But he no doubt reports to any
> With whom he crosses antennae,
> And they no doubt report
> To the higher up at court.
>
> .   .   .   .   .   .
>
> No one stands round to stare.
> It is nobody else's affair.

It couldn't be called ungentle.
But how thoroughly departmental.

The last couplet stands in the place of the aphorism so familiar
as the moralizing summation in poetic fables. It is the reflection
which caps the observation. Yet who could consider such an
equivocal comment as a moral, in any sense of the word. To be
effective, a moral must be unequivocal; but the ironic manner of
Frost is better satisfied with equivocation. So the reader again
makes his own application on the basis of the final couplet. Perhaps the fable is most easily considered as a burlesque of governmental bureaucracy (lettered and numbered)—or of academic
specializations in the structure of colleges and universities. Certainly these are two forms of organization so highly departmen-
talized as to preclude the possibility of having the left hands know
—or care—what the right hands are doing! The poet's casual
diffidence in such a fable establishes a mood of amused indiffer-
ence. The very tone of the final comment is thoroughly charming
and delightful because it eschews any concern for critical efficacy
and does not propose any known remedy for such human shortcomings. If these are viewed as faults, they are smiled upon without asperity. The amused poet has no passion for correction or
even for scolding.

The same manner of detached amusement underlies still
another kind of fable, "A Considerable Speck." Although the
structure of the narrative is entirely different, the center of attention is again brought to focus on an insect. The author, describing
a "microscopic item" which timidly crawls across his manuscript
like an animated speck of dust, immediately establishes a contrast
between the living mite and himself as a Gulliver whose enormous size heightens the sense of the ludicrous. The tiny insect
performs in conscious fear before the gigantic spectator, and the
nervous actions seem like those of a frightened human being
terrified by the sudden appearance of a mysterious god. Having
run a little gamut of seemingly human acts and emotions, the little
creature seems finally ready to

Cower down in desperation to accept
Whatever I accorded it of fate.

So much for the observation concerning the action of the speck. Prompted by the performance, the poet develops his own reflections. Immediately, the satirical tones take a new direction: an offhand thrust is made at sentimental idealism and socialized humanitarianism:

> I have none of the tenderer-than-thou
> Collectivistic regimenting love
> With which the modern world is being swept.
> But this poor microscopic item now!
> Since it was nothing I knew evil of
> I let it lie there till I hope it slept.
>
> I have a mind myself and recognize
> Mind when I meet with it in any guise.
> No one can know how glad I am to find
> On any sheet the least display of mind.

Thus we have the fabulist's application again worn with a difference! Beneath the laughter is a barbed point, concealed with sufficient humor to protect any reader from being hurt. And the tone of badinage makes us enjoy the dry conclusion as quite in keeping with the sportive and playful details of the anecdote itself.

There are times when Frost's animal fables develop into extended and explicit analogies, as in "The Bear." The poem begins with a brief description of a wild bear enjoying her freedom in woods and fields. Then come the extended comparisons:

> The world has room to make a bear feel free;
> The universe seems cramped to you and me.
> Man acts more like the poor bear in a cage
> That all day fights a nervous inward rage,
> His mood rejecting all his mind suggests.
> He paces back and forth and never rests
> The toe-nail click and shuffle of his feet,
> The telescope at one end of his beat,
> And at the other end the microscope,
> Two instruments of nearly equal hope,
> And in conjunction giving quite a spread.

The analogies which continue at some length furnish abundant chance for ironic and satirical jesting, both subtle and obvious. Perhaps the tone here is more thoroughly scornful than in the gentle and more detached fables already considered. In the other fables, the sting is more gentle and kindly; here it is quite ruthless. The extended analogies also fail to establish the nice unification derived from a single focus. Nevertheless, the comparisons in these progressive couplets are stated with such terse force as to give the poem a bitterly humorous power.

More in keeping with Frost's diffidence is the way in which the fable of "The White-tailed Hornet" lends itself to shrewd yet kindly application. The dramatic incident, already described in an earlier chapter, is brought to focus on the failure of the hornet's instinct, and leads directly into the analogy:

> Won't this whole instinct matter bear revision?
> Won't almost any theory bear revision?
> To err is human, not to, animal.
> Or so we pay the compliment to instinct,
> Only too liberal of our compliment
> That really takes away instead of gives.
> Our worship, humor, conscientiousness
> Went long since to the dogs under the table.
> And served us right for having instituted
> Downward comparisons. As long on earth
> As our comparisons were stoutly upward
> With gods and angels, we were men at least,
> But little lower than the gods and angels.
> But once comparisons were yielded downward,
> Once we began to see our images
> Reflected in the mud and even dust,
> 'Twas disillusion upon disillusion.
> We were lost piecemeal to the animals,
> Like people thrown out to delay the wolves.
> Nothing but fallibility was left us,
> And this day's work made even that seem doubtful.

Thoroughly in keeping with the fable, as developed by La Fontaine, is the informal and idiomatic turns of phrase employed here by the poet. The application grows naturally from the sudden possibility that animal instincts aren't quite so infallible as modern education would have us think. The unfolding of this single thought is done with tight-packed lines of ironic ridicule. The poet somehow softens the blow and protects us by keeping himself inside the range of his own criticism, through his use of the first person plural. Finally, at the end, his twist of his logical major premise ("To err is human, not to, animal") is a beautifully backhanded compliment that rounds off all in laughter.

If the burlesque in "The White-tailed Hornet" includes the teachings of Freud and the tenets of progressive education, it also touches on the danger of making a monometaphor out of our favorite theory of evolution. We have considered Frost's conviction as to the need of being educated by poetry until we know how far we may depend on those favorite metaphors by which we live; so that we may recognize in them the ultimate ironies which may betray us. Long ago he made passing reference to this particular one: "Another metaphor that has interested us in our time and has done all our thinking for us is the metaphor of evolution. . . . It is a very brilliant metaphor, I acknowledge, though I myself get too tired of [hearing it said that] everything is evolution. I emancipate myself by simply saying that I didn't get up the metaphor and so am not much interested in it."

But this fable of the white-tailed hornet also demonstrates Frost's pleasure in adapting familiar phrases to his own poetic uses by giving slight twists to their meaning. Several such phrases occur in the passage quoted above. The rearranged reference to those things which have gone to the dogs enables him to keep the connotation and at the same time to suggest that those very attributes we supposedly share so proudly with animals are not always found to exist with purity in animals! Again, the familiar passage from the Psalms is adapted nicely to the poet's ironic purpose. This use is a far cry from mere quotation; the important modifications enrich the allusiveness. "The People, Yes," says Sandburg; then he makes a fat anthology of familiar phrases in daily speech and calls it a book of poetry. Frost's use of these familiar phrases always lifts them to a higher level of poetic significance in the context which he gives them. This metaphorical play on words and phrases might be called a dignified form of punning.

In the limited number of nicely varied fables which we have examined, satire is given a distinct and frequently subtle form. The predominant foibles so pleasantly brushed over may be brought together as different aspects of one weakness: human pretentiousness. We have observed the radical independence of the cow, the unnecessary wildness of the runaway colt, the astringent specialization of the ants, the smugness of the wood-chuck, the cockiness of the faulty wasp, the impatient concern of the caged bear for those regions beyond his reach. Frost's mildly deprecatory criticism and satirical comment on human nature in the form of these fables again springs from his central position. Aware of the not-too-little in life, he hints at the not-too-much of his own cautious and common-sense aspiration.

We dance round in a ring and suppose,
But the Secret sits in the middle and knows.[24]

EPIGRAMS

IRONY may find expression in word and phrase, in extended ode or dialogue, in parables and fables. At times, however, it crystallizes into compact and jewel-hard statement to form an epigram. And it would be a mistake to turn from irony without looking at a few of those sparks and flashes thrown off from the flint and steel of Frost's thought.

Conflicting schools of poets and scholars, who have tried to establish precise definitions for the epigram as a form of poetry, have succeeded only in demonstrating the wide range of possibilities. Certain fundamentals are plain and important. The inscriptional origin of the epigram from the stone-cut epitaphs undoubtedly bequeathed those inevitable requirements of nice compression and polished precision. The charm of the epigram has always depended in part on the success with which a penetrating observation may be accommodated within a brief compass of words. So much for the form. The subjects suitable for epigrams obviously began with laments and praise for the beloved dead and then continued to run such a miscellaneous gamut as to arrive at the opposite extreme. Some have claimed that the epigram is correctly used only when the verses ("short, simple, pointed, keen, and bright") are made to end with a saucy and stinging thrust at a living opponent. There is room for these two extremes in the form. Even the poets of the *Greek Anthology* employed epigrams which were at times loving, at times uncomplimentary; even Martial did not restrict his usages to satirical shadowboxing with his enemies.

In the matter of method, however, wit has always been indispensable to the epigram. It may be merely a mental cunning which achieves the required compression in polished phrases. Again, wit may assert itself in the epigram through felicitous juxtaposition of ideas and words not usually related to each other. Thus the effect

may be a delightful surprise which depends on mental response to
ingenious and unexpected turns of phrase.

The epigrammatic quality of Frost's poetry depends not only
on felicitous and unexpected relationship of words but also of
thoughts. Such relationships, frequently ironic, require verbal
agility to give a sense of allusiveness that is often heightened by the
terse understatement of the lines. If the irony of wordplay is combined with an irony of underlying thought, the result is a richly
textured piece of subtlety. Let us examine such an epigram:

> Nature's first green is gold,
> Her hardest hue to hold.
> Her early leaf's a flower;
> But only so an hour.
> Then leaf subsides to leaf.
> So Eden sank to grief,
> So dawn goes down to day.
> Nothing gold can stay.

Here is no sting in the tail. Each word is important in its cumulative significance. Starting with an observation, the poet moves
on to his analogies of change: nothing gold can stay, be that gold
the first coloring of spring, the perfection in the Garden of Eden,
or the glory of sky in early morning. This graceful lament seems
quite simple and sad. But there are ironic implications beneath
the first allusions of words and thoughts. Perhaps the key to these
ironies may be found in one line, "So dawn *goes down* to day."
Almost ready to accept the analogy, we may notice that this is a
curious usage opposed to our familiar references to the way in
which dawn goes up to day and day goes down to night. Is this
quibbling? Shall we allow the poet his license? Perhaps dawn may
be said to go down; perhaps Eden sank, perhaps the almost invisible flower subsides to the elaborate leaf. But might there be an
opposite implied here? Dawn is the harbinger of sunrise; Eden is
the harbinger of the rising human race; the first gold of spring
is the harbinger of summer. Each leads onward to fulfillment.
Then we cannot feel too sad in our sense of loss. The poet has
treated his lament with an ironic subtlety which suggests the
mingled sorrow-and-joy in the acceptance of loss-in-gain. The

theme is one of his favorites. The terse epigram is shrewdly fashioned with cunning juxtapositions of word and thought to present to the reader's mind arguments on both sides of the subject!

The goal of Frost's wit in his epigrams is often the revelation of ironic balance. Such an epigram as "Fire and Ice" makes the same use of a twofold consideration as does also "A Patch of Old Snow," already considered. The ironic twist occurs more obviously in the epigram which describes two lovers whose friends have left them "In Neglect":

> They leave us so to the way we took,
>   As two in whom they were proved mistaken,
> That we sit sometimes in the wayside nook,
> With mischievous, vagrant, seraphic look,
>   And *try* if we cannot feel forsaken.

Still more obviously, "Plowmen" establishes a double irony through unexpected associations: two uses of the single word "plow." A discouraged farmer might claim equal chances of success from planting seed in snow or in rocky mountain soil:

> A plow, they say, to plow the snow.
> They cannot mean to plant it, though—
> Unless in bitterness to mock
> At having cultivated rock.

The thrust of the last line is felt merely as heightened tension, for it has no sting in it. There are times, however, when Frost uses irony in the epigram for thoroughly satirical effect, as in "Not All There." In two quatrains, two opposed viewpoints are offered, although the wit unbalances them in favor of the jest, at the conclusion. The first quatrain summarizes an egotistical conceit, then the second satirizes the conceit through reversal:

> I turned to speak to God
> About the world's despair;
> But to make bad matters worse
> I found God wasn't there.
>
> God turned to speak to me
> (Don't anybody laugh)

God found I wasn't there—
At least not over half.

The sting in the tail of this epigram is by no means subtle. But the success of it again depends on an amusing surprise created by the unexpected association of familiar words and phrases first used in simple statement and then repeated with malicious implications. The poet again speaks from his middle-ground position. Any attempt to assert the nature of, or to deny the existence of, that which lies beyond human knowledge is grist for his epigrams. The same viewpoint crops out at the end of one poem thus:

There may be little or much beyond the grave,
But the strong are saying nothing till they see.

Again, at the end of another:

Heaven gives its glimpses only to those
Not in position to look too close.

Still again, with wordplay that risks the dangers of the pun, Frost turns an epigrammatic jest at the expense of philosophic idealism in his latest book:

I love to toy with the Platonic notion
That wisdom need not be of Athens Attic,
But well may be Laconic, even Boeotian,
At least I will not have it systematic.

Simple and bright and pointed as these are, none of them can equal the finely compressed summary of the poet's skepticism which crystallizes into the two-line epigram quoted at the head of this chapter.

New variety is given in another epigram entitled, "What Fifty Said." A pleasant balance of opposites is achieved, line for line, until the result becomes a successful and mildly ironic *tour de force*:

When I was young my teachers were the old.
I gave up fire for form till I was cold.
I suffered like a metal being cast.
I went to school to age to learn the past.

Now I am old my teachers are the young.
What can't be moulded must be cracked and sprung.
I strain at lessons fit to start a suture.
I go to school to youth to learn the future.

The last rhyme suggests the possibilities of humorous addition thus afforded. The deliberate arrangement of these stanzas into eight separate sentences suggests the sententious and aphoristic quality so familiar and important not only in Frost's epigrams but also in all his poetry. Phrase after phrase takes on the simple and straightforward dignity of a maxim, or suggests the gnomic character of the poet's mature thought. Inevitably, such lines are passing over into the realm of familiar quotation:

"The best way out is always through."
"Pressed into service means pressed out of shape."
"The fact is the sweetest dream that labor knows."
"We love the things we love for what they are."
"It's knowing what to do with things that counts."

The aphoristic and epigrammatic quality in Frost's poems grows naturally from his detached and objective view of things and people. It is another form of definition and clarification. And a very large proportion of Frost's shorter poems are related to the category of the epigram. "Trial by Existence," for example, is a parable; not strictly a lyric. It might be considered a kind of fable. Yet it is begun and concluded with epigrammatic stanzas which direct the attention to the central thought of the parable: "the greatest reward of daring is still to dare." A quite different poem, "In Hardwood Groves," is an epigrammatic comment on the circular pattern of human experience. The reader may find many other poems so completely motivated and elaborated from the mind, as opposed to the emotion, that they belong with the epigrams. Such discoveries will certainly include "Hyla Brook," "The Oven Bird," "On a Tree Fallen Across the Road," "On Going Unnoticed," "A Peck of Gold," "The Peaceful Shepherd," "The Flood," "Triple Bronze," and many others.

There is no clean line between poems motivated by emotion and those motivated by reason. Witty and epigrammatic lines may be found in all good poetry, even in emotional and subjective lyrics. Nowhere can this be better demonstrated than in the best of Robert Frost's verses, always enriched with gnomic touches of wisdom. It would seem that he has realized his own early longing: "I should like to have lodged a few ideas where they will stick like burrs."

ATTITUDE TOWARD LIFE

Some may know what they seek in school and church,
And why they seek it there; for what I search
I must go measuring stone walls, perch on perch.[25]

SKEPTICISM

ROBERT FROST's consistent beliefs have never been given any
integrated expression, save in his own life. It has been said that
the illumination may sometime strike through in an unexpected
flash, but that wisdom is the clear light of steady living. And the
artistic career of Frost may be divided into those two categories:
the flashes of insight, which have found expression in his poetry;
the deeper wisdom, which has found expression in his life as a
human being.

We have already considered the discrepancy between artistic
truth and moral truth; the impossibility of finding or expecting
that isolated poems, flashes of insight, should relate themselves
into a singleness of attitude toward life. They may or they may
not. Although separate poems may help to explain each other,
they may also contradict each other. The immediate mood of the
poet, at the moment of poetic creation, determines the viewpoint
and perspective of the poem. Thus we may find that such a poem
as "Sitting by a Bush in Broad Sunlight" is motivated by a strong
religious faith, while such a poem as "Stars" (at cold midnight) is
motivated by an equally strong religious agnosticism. These
opposed viewpoints, artistically valid, tell us nothing about those
beliefs by which the poet shapes the course of his nonaesthetic, or
moral, life.

A large group of one man's poems will furnish guides, however,
because the poems are never completely isolated from the moral
viewpoint of the man, as contrasted with the artist. The cumulative expression of a consistent perspective inevitably asserts itself
above the inconsistencies during a period of years. And if growth
has made the poet only more sure of all he thought was true, the
problem is even further simplified. In Frost's case there is still

another series of guideposts: his prose prefaces and lectures, which have been published in various books and periodicals.

Before we examine the beliefs which Frost has found in his spiritual prospecting, we may find help in considering his equipment and his region of exploration. My purpose here is for the moment general. Any poet begins his quest with that specialized sensory equipment peculiar to the poet: delicate powers of perception which react with intensity beneath the impact of touch and sight and sound. His strong emotions may or may not be balanced with strong powers of reason. But with or without this balance, his intense feelings reflect a growing sense of wonder at the mystery of things. Rapidly the "region of exploration" for him changes from that surface world perceived by the casual or the callous individuals; changes to a deeper level of concern with inner and underlying mysteries. Out of his wonder grow his searching questions. When the answers of others fail to satisfy him, he contrives his own. And the answers, fashioned from his observations, will be deeply colored by his hopes. Certain relationships become apparent. It seems to him as if . . . With that first "as if" he has begun his spiritual prospecting, his poetry—and "as if" is piled on "as if" in a profusion of similes and metaphors. This process of approach is identical for poetry, for philosophy, for religion: three different expressions of the same passionate hunger for understanding, knowledge, certainty.

Robert Frost's mental, emotional, and spiritual equipment seemed to be a blend of strongly different qualities in his parents. From his father he inherited an active and inquiring mind coupled with enough rebelliousness to carry skeptical caution to complete denial. From his Swedenborgian mother he inherited much of her strongly emotional and mystical faith. With these went a New England heritage of caution, moderation, and reticence which afforded him restraint in his search for questions and answers. But the immediate "region of exploration" available to him during his youth was clouded with peculiar hardships. Through chronic illness and suffering, family tragedy and sorrow, he discovered that the heart yet cherished the bitter-sweet of experience. At the same time, the harsh simplicity of life in his boyhood developed within him an almost desperate willingness to start with nothing, to reason calmly that he could expect nothing, that he would ask for nothing beyond that which his own courage and daring could achieve. Those lean years might have flavored his thinking with too much bitterness. But he was not resentful at finding himself in a world he never made; he did not try to blame anyone by guessing who or what was at fault. Hoping, he never hoped far ahead, and was too sensible to think that the world owed him a living. Yet his heart persisted in that irrational yearning which drove him outside self to discover self.

The hungry zest for life accentuated the shadow of death which became reality for him in the early death of his father. Like so many before him, he found a new sadness in the painful recognition of transience wherever he looked. Daylight returned and seasons returned; but what of human life which moved briefly from the apparent nothingness before birth to the apparent nothingness after death. There was the other kind of transience: the gradual spending of all energy to nothingness:

> The stream of everything that runs away.
> Some say existence like a Pirouot
> And Pirouette, forever in one place,
> Stands still and dances, but it runs away,
> It seriously, sadly, runs away
> To fill the abyss' void with emptiness.

What could one make of a diminishing thing such as life, in all its manifestations? On every hand he was confronted with the apparently tragic futility of things. And let there be no empty talk about the metaphorical analogy in the law of the conservation of energy. The cry of the heart is not answered if this individual life should be transformed into something else. Could such a scheme of creation make sense? Sense or not, it was apparent. Through the inner hurts of suffering and loss and futility, he continued to yearn for some kind of understanding which might save life and love from despair.

Strange it may seem that from despair, hope and faith may be born; that from it grows the surest kind of acceptance and optimism. The one consolation about such a position is that the only possible change is for the better. "The lamentable change is from the best; the worst returns to laughter." Edgar was right: "The worst is not, so long as we can say, 'This is the worst.' "

What answers had others found for these questions? Frost listened to the religious claims for immortality, for life after death, but impatiently rejected them because they could not be reconciled with that part of his life represented by matter-of-fact reason. He could not honestly go so far as to say that the yearning for persistence in life may lead us comfortably to believe (because we hope) that the individual has within him an immortal soul. He may well have; he may well have not! Skeptically he turned away, dissatisfied. He examined the purely rational philosophic claims for immortality, but rejected them also, because they could not be reconciled with that part of his life represented by the nonrational yearnings of his heart and body. Since Socrates, he found, the deepest thinkers had execrated those who sought to explain life in purely rational terms. Others pointed out that even those philosophers who had set out on a purely logical plane had done so, consciously or unconsciously, because they were impelled by the need to justify an inner wish or hope or conviction which was not logical. Plato had admitted as much when he described his venture into the unknown as "a glorious risk." To the skeptical mind of Frost, there was something sad about the way in which the opposed methods of faith and of reason were forever appealing to each other for consolation. Religions tried to buttress nonrational beliefs with the rational methods of philosophy; philosophy tried to encroach on the beliefs of religion. Why shouldn't they leave each other alone? Because of such tinkerings, the God of established religions had been mutilated and falsified until He failed to satisfy the desire of the poet's heart and life. Christianity, for example, had done its best to justify the nonrational yearnings of the human spirit by seeking to proselyte that dearest enemy, reason. Reason was called in to define the undefinable. The limited, finite mind of man tried to characterize and set limits to the infinite—and thus began the mutilations and the lifeless dogmas.

Independent and rebellious against all easy answers, Frost threw his skeptical criticism against any careless affirmations. Like Emerson, he made a principle out of nonconformity in his early days and declared that there was nothing more sacred than the integrity of his own heart and mind. For him no final questions were resolved by viewing the world from the position of religious or philosophic monism or dualism. He could not see why the materialist should be considered any more or less wrong than the idealist. Life still escaped them both when they tried to define it.

The tragic paradox seemed to him that life should contain in itself these two thoroughly opposed halves, reason and desire, which could not get along without each other and yet could not get along with each other. Regardless of all the wrong answers, however, there was certainty about the hunger, the yearning, the innate and persistent craving sent forth like tendrils from reason and desire.

Accepting the tragic implications of conflict between heart and mind (each yearning for permanence in a world of acknowledged transience), Frost found this conflict to be the bedrock of hard fact to which his incisive and analytical skepticism finally brought him. On this foundation he was ready to construct his attitude toward life, whatever it might become. Thus, as a poet and not as a philosopher, he began to build up metaphors which symbolized the basic conflict. And gradually, out of his isolated perceptions, out of his own hopes and searchings, grew his own belief and faith.

Anyone may challenge such a procedure in establishing a major premise on which to build. Frost was not fooling himself. The rational paring away which brought Descartes to his major premise finally stopped when the psychological reduction had reached that point where the activity of the emotional desire was stronger than the activity of the rational negation. So it was with Frost, who arrived at an arbitrary major premise which balanced for him the affirmations of the emotion and the negations of the reason. He proceeded cautiously. If his hopes urged him strongly toward faith and acceptance, his reason counteracted any precipitate tendency. His skepticism permitted the flexible reconciliation of the two parts in his nature. But the balance between them was so nice that he was never able or willing to try the sorry expedient of getting along without the one or the other, although he could see how such a sacrifice simplified the problem for others. So he held to his middle-ground position of skepticism without relinquishing faith, on the one hand, and denial, on the other hand. By limiting the claims of each he has been able to make them lie down together. It might be said that his skepticism acts as a balance wheel which controls the accelerations of faith and the decelerations of denial.

Such a middle course is thoroughly classical in its moderation. His playfully serious answer to "a New York alec" who asked him to choose between two extremes of conduct was, "How about being a good Greek?" Yet it should be recognized that Frost's middle-ground position in the Golden Mean has been shaped less by Stoicism than by his New England practicality somehow blended with that genuinely mystical instinct which seems to have been one heritage from his saintly Scotch mother. Considering this balanced position from a literary point of view, Mark Van Doren has defended it succinctly against frequent charges of timidity:

"Mr. Frost's place [in the poetical scene] is and always has been singularly central. He has had nothing to do with the extremes where most of our shouting has been heard. . . . Nor is it the consequence of compromise. There is an ignoble way of avoiding extremes. It is the way of being nobody and of saying nothing; of never, at any rate, being or saying enough to count. But there is another way which, difficult though it may be to define, is the only way worth considering. It consists in occupying or touching both extremes at once, and inhabiting all the space between. It consists in being capable of excess while actually achieving more than excess achieves. It consists in finding that golden mean which, far from signifying that the extremes have been avoided, signifies that they have been enclosed and contained."[26]

Now no joy but lacks salt
That is not dashed with pain
And weariness and fault;
I crave the stain
Of tears, the aftermark
Of almost too much love ... [27]

LOVE

Robert Frost likes the metaphor of life dangerously surviving at the confluence of two extremes, either one of which (taken singly) is strong enough to destroy life itself. As we have seen, however, he believes that the opposed extremes most elemental in the long drama of human activity are desire and reason, heart and mind. Such a belief crystallizes into his epigrammatic "Fire and Ice." From this epitome of endless struggle is derived the strength of character, or the destruction of character, in human beings. In Frost's own life, an awareness of this inner conflict led him to skepticism. And that skepticism, exercised boldly, led him to acceptance and affirmations. But the first of his affirmations grew from his faith that the inspiration for human striving against insuperable odds must be attributed to the irrational desires of the heart:

> Ah, when to the heart of man
> Was it ever less than a treason
> To go with the drift of things,
> To yield with a grace to reason ...

In a restricted sense, love thus becomes the positive force in life, while reason becomes the negative force. The paradox of human life is that it should be created with these two active halves: life-builders and life-destroyers. Containing these in himself, the individual becomes a living-dying symbol of the elemental conflict. In many of Frost's metaphors which clarify this analogy there is the persistent suggestion that the strongest expression of these two forces is that irrational love which springs from the heart:

Love has earth to which she clings
With hills and circling arms about—
Wall within wall to shut fear out.
But Thought has need of no such things,
For Thought has a pair of dauntless wings.

On snow and sand and turf, I see
Where Love has left a printed trace
With straining in the world's embrace.
And such is Love and glad to be.
But Thought has shaken his ankles free.

. . . .

His gains in heaven are what they are.
Yet some say Love by being thrall
And simply staying possesses all
In several beauty that Thought fares far
To find fused in another star.

The implied criticism here is an unasked question as to the value
of that far-searching discovery of absolute and Platonic oneness
which Thought may "find fused in another star." The first line
of the last stanza is also perhaps a bit skeptical in tone. Again and
again Frost reiterates his satisfaction that Love should predom-
inate, so long as these rivals cannot always assist each other. Such
is the conclusion of "Wild Grapes":

I had not taken the first step in knowledge;
I had not learned to let go with the hands,
As still I have not learned to with the heart,
And have no wish to with the heart—nor need,
That I can see. The mind—is not the heart.
I may yet live, as I know others live,
To wish in vain to let go with the mind—
Of cares, at night, to sleep; but nothing tells me
That I need learn to let go with the heart.

Love, then, is the theme that dominates Frost's attitude toward
life. Such a seemingly banal statement may be understood in all
its richness of meaning if we apply it at deeper and deeper levels
of human experience. "All of my poems are love poems," Frost

has said. Immediately the different levels suggest themselves: parental and filial love, the love of man and woman, the transference of such love to objects in the natural world because of our desire to assert our love. Possibly divine love, even for the skeptic? Let us see.

The gradual unfolding of love is as common and as mysterious as life itself. Like anyone else, Frost learned love from his parents, and returned it with additional pity and compassion as his own experience taught him to recognize the quiet and uncomplaining tragedy of their lives. The ironic sadness of such memory borders on bitterness in his poem, "The Lovely Shall Be Choosers." Those who knew his mother still recognize the accurate indication of her mute heroism. It is difficult to understand why pity and compassion born of sorrow should enrich love and at the same time intensify our hunger for it. The increased longing even for the pain of love is closely related to our joy in the bitter-sweet of all human experience. Frost's poem "To Earthward" is his most intense expression of this mystery. And it relates quite fittingly the close bond between human love and the transference of that love to beauty in nature:

> Love at the lips was touch
> As sweet as I could bear;
> And once that seemed too much;
> I lived on air
>
> That crossed me from sweet things,
> The flow of—was it musk
> From hidden grapevine springs
> Down hill at dusk?
>
> I had the swirl and ache
> From sprays of honeysuckle
> That when they're gathered shake
> Dew on the knuckle.
>
> I craved strong sweets, but those
> Seemed strong when I was young;
> The petal of the rose
> It was that stung.

The poem should not be quoted thus in part, but it is too long to be given complete here. None can fail to recognize the almost anguished intensity beneath this poem; this record of discovering self through venturing outside self. We need not pry into the biographical aspects of that venture outside self to love and win the love of one woman. Frost's own poems tell us all we need to know about the deepening of experience which grew from those years immediately before and after his marriage. Again there is the ancient mystery as to how and why man's sacred love for one woman may instill in him a love and worship for entirely different manifestations of life. Yet these two aspects are fused in Frost's early love poems, such as the shared experiences recorded in "Rose Pogonias," "Going for Water," "A Line-Storm Song." It is quite fitting that he should have suggested the wider relationship between this sense of sacredness in life by letting two lovers find the analogy together. "West-running Brook" takes us back to that conflict between "the drift of things" and the vital resistance against "the stream of everything that runs away." Through love, the poet seems to say, he found the answer to the question which bothered him most. Through love he found the justification for the tragic aspect of life itself. And again, the crux of the poem rests upon the aggressive action of life, the instinctive struggle up the stream:

> It flows between us, over us, and *with* us.
> And it is time, strength, tone, light, life and love—
> And even substance lapsing unsubstantial;
> The universal cataract of death
> That spends to nothingness—and unresisted,
> Save by some strange resistance in itself,
> Not just a swerving, but a throwing back,
> As if regret were in it and were sacred.
> It has this throwing backward on itself
> So that the fall of most of it is always
> Raising a little, sending up a little.
> Our life runs down in sending up the clock.
> The brook runs down in sending up our life.
> The sun runs down in sending up the brook.
> And there is something sending up the sun.
> It is this backward motion toward the source,

Against the stream, that most we see ourselves in,
The tribute of the current to the source.
It is from this in nature we are from.
It is most us.

The poet has finally answered his own questions in his analogies. "As if regret were in it and were sacred." His meaning is clear: that this regret and yearning for persistence and for permanence *is the sacred essence of life itself*. Out of the struggle, the conflict, comes all that "raises a little." And all the sacrifice, all the spending, all the transience suddenly changes from tragic meaninglessness to sacred purpose. It relates itself to an integrated scheme of the universe. "And there is something sending up the sun."

What may we make of this "source" to which the current of everything that runs away and everything that resists is paying tribute? Perhaps unconsciously Frost gradually projected that sacredness he found in his own love, in his own life, outward to the sacredness of the source. Always before, this projection has been responsible for religions and philosophies. And this projection becomes the God of Frost's religion. Religion has been defined as "the simple feeling of a relationship of dependence upon something above us and a desire to establish relations with this mysterious power." The expression of Frost's religious belief in "West-running Brook" coincides with this definition.

Having arrived at such a belief, Frost is not hindered by his skepticism from studying the relationships in life which suggest "the evident design" of the universe according to a divine plan. But his skepticism does hinder him, properly, from supposing that he can unravel the mysteries, the properties, the dimensions of the divine. We crave to probe into the mystery of the universe, Frost seems to say, but the place to probe is into the mystery of human experience on earth, rather than into the hidden mystery of that which is beyond our vision:

Wind goes from farm to farm in wave on wave,
But carries no cry of what is hoped to be.
There may be little or much beyond the grave,
But the strong are saying nothing until they see.

Does he suppose, then, that any earthly probing into earthly mysteries can give us final answers? Perhaps not final answers, but answers good enough to live by. Cautious as he may be, Frost knows enough of faith from experience to be willing to make good use of it. Faith, said Paul, is the substance of things hoped for. Frost is able to make sense out of that by reading it thus: Faith *may give substance to* things hoped for. And that substance, physical and spiritual, utilitarian and artistic, is achieved through action; through the discovery that "the greatest reward of daring is still to dare." Twice he has elaborated in prose his convictions concerning faith in action. And these utterances do much to suggest the structure of his attitude toward life. The first is closely related to his poem, "West-running Brook," although it may seem quite distinct at first glance:

". . . We people are thrust forward out of the suggestions of form in the rolling clouds of nature. In us nature reaches its height of form and through us exceeds itself. When in doubt there is always form for us to go on with. Anyone who has achieved the least form to be sure of it, is lost to the larger excruciations. I think it must stroke faith the right way. The artist, the poet, might be expected to be the most aware of such assurance. But it is really everybody's sanity to feel it and live by it. Fortunately, too, no forms are more engrossing, gratifying, comforting, staying than those lesser ones we throw off, like vortex rings of smoke, all our individual enterprise and needing nobody's cooperation: a basket, a letter, a garden, a room, an idea, a picture, a poem. For these we haven't to get a team together before we can play.

"The background is hugeness and confusion shading away from where we stand into black and utter chaos; and against the background any small man-made figure of order and concentration. What pleasanter than that this should be so? Unless we are novelists or economists we don't worry about this confusion; we look out on it with an instrument or tackle it to reduce it. It is partly because we are afraid it might prove too much for us and our blend of democratic-republican-socialist-communist-anarchist party. But it is more because we like it, we were born to it, born used to it and have practical reasons for wanting it there. To me

any little form I assert upon it is velvet, as the saying is, and to
be considered for how much more it is than nothing. If I were
a Platonist I should have to consider it, I suppose, for how much
less it is than everything."[28]

Here is life and faith in action without worrying about any
final understanding as to the mysteries of God and the universe.
It is similar in spirit to Emerson's major principle that the superlative value in life is to be found in the individual and momentary
act of consciousness; for through man's active and persistent
yearning and seeking and doing he places himself in accord with
the intended ways of God to man. The process requires mutual
collaboration. And the underlying principle is love, from man
toward God, from God to man. Frost stated his own belief in this
mutual collaboration when he wrote his early poem, "A Prayer
in Spring":

> Oh, give us pleasure in the flowers to-day;
> And give us not to think so far away
> As the uncertain harvest; keep us here
> All simply in the springing of the year.
>
> . . . .
>
> For this is love and nothing else is love,
> The which it is reserved for God above
> To sanctify to what far ends He will,
> But which it only needs that we fulfil.

The emphasis here is on the present moment, with no need to
trouble ourselves about the future, about "the uncertain harvest"
of death and what may be after death. The final emphasis in the
last stanza stressed the need for man's active fulfilment of deeds
controlled by love. Almost casually he says, in the prose passage
quoted above, that he thinks form-giving action "must stroke
faith the right way." The second prose statement concerning faith
in action comes equally close to the artist's field, but opens up
those prospects which are at the heart of life in any individual:

"The person who gets close enough to poetry is going to know
more about the word *belief* than anybody else knows, even in
religion nowadays. There are two or three places where we know
belief outside of religion. One of them is at the age of fifteen to

twenty, in our self-belief. A young man knows more about himself than he is able to prove to anyone. He has no knowledge that anybody else will accept as knowledge. In his foreknowledge he has something that is going to believe itself into fulfilment, into acceptance.

"There is another belief like that, the belief in someone else, a relationship of two that is going to be believed into fulfilment. That is what we are talking about in our novels, the belief in love. And the disillusionment that the novels are full of is simply the disillusionment from disappointment in that belief. That belief can fail, of course.

"Then there is a literary belief. Every time a poem is written, every time a short story is written, it is written not by cunning, but by belief. The beauty, the something, the little charm of the thing to be, is more felt than known.

"Now I think—I happen to think—that those three beliefs that I speak of, the self-belief, the love-belief, and the art-belief, are all closely related to the God-belief, that the belief in God is a relationship you enter into with Him to bring about the future."[29]

In the light of such faith, what has happened to skepticism? It still remains on duty to check any wishful thinking; any overly zealous attempt to penetrate beyond this life. Enough for Frost to confine his attention to the here and now. But his activity and his persistence have brought answers to the questions which grew out of his skepticism. And the answers, fresh in Frost's statement, are as old and certain as life itself. The choice is made quite casually between melancholy contemplation of "the larger excruciations" and the rewarding satisfaction in that kind of love and thought and action which does not need to wait on further understanding.

Greatest of all attempts to say one thing in terms of another is the philosophical attempt to say matter in terms of spirit, or spirit in terms of matter, to make the final unity. That is the greatest attempt that ever failed. We stop just short there. But it is the height of all poetry, the height of all thinking....[30]

RESPONSE
TO SYSTEMATIC THOUGHT

A CORRECTIVE is needed if anyone has been led to suppose that Robert Frost's faith in the power of love blinds him to the power of reason. The heart and the mind have their distinct attributes, their mutual antagonisms, their specialized functions. At times they fittingly renounce each other; but such renunciation is limited and temporary because their reliance on each other as balance wheels is greater than their antagonisms. But the bold ventures of Thought, with his "dauntless wings" and "ankles free," is as exciting to Frost as the gloriously wild risks of Love.

"I myself, since forty, have had a great leaning towards the philosophy department," Frost has said, "but you know that's just letting all my prejudices out: my admiration for philosophy." His first and perhaps his keenest interest in the history of philosophy is a poet's pleasure in metaphors: a detached delight in those various analogies invoked by thinkers who have sought to define spirit in terms of matter. But this skeptical criticism of philosophic ventures into definition of the unknown and the unknowable has led him to that mingled praise-and-blame: "the greatest attempt that ever failed." Obviously the failure should not hinder either philosophy or poetry from striving forever anew to attempt that "grazing closeness to spiritual realities," even though closeness is all that may be hoped. Because of the mutual interests of these two separate approaches to age-old and forever-unanswered questions as to how and why and wherefore, Frost has paid tribute to philosophers by making his own uses and meanings from philosophic questions and metaphors in his poems. He might say of philosophers what Emerson said about the stimulus of books in general: "I value them to make my top spin." But he is not averse to poking fun at those vain and presumptuous members

> Of the hive's enquiry squad
> Whose work is to find out God
> And the nature of time and space. . .

Out of his skepticism grows his impatience with philosophers who have reduced life to a shadow by concentrating on the ultimate realities beyond life as the only proper objects of worship. If the Christian religion taught us to think of ourselves merely as pilgrims here, traveling toward our heavenly home, Frost is willing to blame the Greeks in general and Plato in particular for passing on to the Christians such a vitiating shift of emphasis. He once gave his own malicious definition of Platonism in an amusing passage which referred to his difference from Edwin Arlington Robinson:

"I am not the Platonist Robinson was. By Platonist I mean one who believes what we have here is an imperfect copy of what is in heaven. The woman you have is an imperfect copy of some woman in heaven or in some one else's bed. Many of the world's greatest—maybe all of them—have been ranged on that romantic side. I am philosophically opposed to having one Iseult for my vocation and another for my avocation. . . . Let me not sound the least bit smug. I define a difference with proper humility. A truly gallant Platonist will remain a bachelor as Robinson did from unwillingness to reduce any woman to the condition of being used without being idealized."[31]

Let us return to Frost's general interest in the metaphors of philosophy. As one might expect, the strongest stimulus was imparted by the metaphors and ideas of nineteenth century scientists and philosophers concerning astronomy, geology, evolution, and the impact of these new scientific theories on philosophy and religion. The melancholy conflict between science and religion, still hotly waged during Frost's youth, was grist to his poetry rather than a stumbling block to his belief. That the ideas current in the last quarter of the century colored his beliefs is perfectly obvious. But the theory of evolution corroborated his own cautious reasoning concerning "the evident design" of the universe. Let us consider briefly a few of the metaphors of faith which he derived from current scientific theories. In "A Line-Storm Song" there is an analogy drawn from the geological fact of "the ancient lands" where the ocean had "left the shells before the age of the fern." And closely related to this geological phenomenon is the analogy in the optimistic poem entitled, "In Time of Cloudburst." The evolutionary aspects of astronomy also furnish him metaphors of faith in orderly design and purpose, as in the poem "On Looking Up By Chance at the Constellations." Perhaps the most strikingly balanced and rounded expression of Frost's faith-restrained-by-skepticism may be found in the progressive metaphors of "A Star in a Stone-Boat," with its constant allusions to evolutionary astronomy. In that poem the believing and doubting unbeliever develops his thoughts casually, loquaciously, and with wonder. If the "one world complete in any size" which he can comprehend is a cold meteor, such is the caution of the skeptic. If he stops to wonder about those who "may know what they seek in school and church, and why they seek it there," or is amused by the answered prayers prayed in vain, such is the rebelliousness of the noncomformist. If he can still find joy in contemplating the vast mystery of "jostling rock in interstellar space," the most lofty element in his pleasure is derived from his trustful belief that the vast process is related to the larger scheme of life in the universe. He is not troubled that the mind does not comprehend that which lies beyond human experience, for he is again content with the here and now. Let nobody talk to him about the disturbing perplexity of infinite distances:

> They cannot scare me with their empty spaces
> Between stars—on stars where no human race is.
> I have it in me so much nearer home
> To scare myself with my own desert places.

And what of his reaction to those evolutionary theories which arrive at a mechanistic interpretation of life? Once, in illustrating the way in which a metaphor carried too far would break down, Frost used this anecdote:

"Somebody said to me a little while ago, 'It is easy enough for me to think of the universe as a machine, as a mechanism.'

I said, 'You mean the universe is like a machine?'

He said, 'No. I think it is one . . . Well, it is like . . .'

'I think you mean the universe is like a machine.'

'All right. Let it go at that.'

I asked him, 'Did you ever see a machine without a pedal for the foot, or a lever for the hand, or a button for the finger?'

He said, 'No—No.'

I said, 'All right. Is the universe like that?'

And he said, 'No. I mean it is like a machine, only . . .'

'. . . it is different from a machine,' I said."[32]

His point was to show the need for understanding how to test the strength of a metaphor. The obvious conclusion from this rebuttal is that to Frost even a concept of a machinelike world still left unsettled the question as to the Prime Mover who started the machine. Frost's own attitude takes him closer to the teleological position of the vitalist doctrine that the processes of life are directed to the realization of certain normal wholes or entelechies. The passage already quoted concerning man's relating himself to an evident design by devoting himself to form-giving suggests to me, however, that Frost's thinking is not identical with the vitalist doctrine of entelechy, but is more closely related to the persistent and varying Greek doctrines of forms which actively expressed the potential character, or "virtue," of the individual. According to the Greeks, each of us has a "virtue" of which we are capable in our particular position or occupation, and the supreme goal of human effort is to discover this "virtue" through action. As to the action of form-giving, even in humble manner, Frost says, "I think it must stroke faith the right way." And this kind of self-expression seems related to the kind of "virtue" around which Aristotle built a moral system and an ideal for man. The analogy between Frost's thoughts on form-giving and Greek thoughts on "virtue" is stimulating; but the fragmentary nature of Frost's expression on this point forces us too soon into guesses if we try to develop the analogy too far. Anyone interested may care to read in this light two poems: "The Axe-Helve" and (more tantalizingly reticent) "Maple."

Returning to nineteenth century concepts which aroused metaphorical responses in Frost's poems, we may find no difficulty in understanding his attitude toward Darwinian theories of evolution. Again the first pleasure for him was the poet's response. In "Education by Poetry" he said: "Another metaphor that has interested us in our time and has done all our thinking for us is the metaphor of evolution. Never mind going into the Latin word. The metaphor is simply the metaphor of the growing plant or of the growing thing. And somebody very brilliantly, quite a while ago, said that the whole universe, the whole of everything, was like unto a growing thing. That is all. I know the metaphor will break down at some point, but it has not failed everywhere." In several of his poems he has tested it. "Sitting by a Bush in Broad Sunlight" is a poem which unfolds two metaphorical evidences for religious faith. In the middle of it occurs this pair of quatrains:

> There was one time and only the one
> When dust really took in the sun;
> And from that one intake of fire
> All creatures still warmly suspire.

> And if men have watched a long time
> And never seen sun-smitten slime
> Again come to life and crawl off,
> We must not be too ready to scoff.

Other poems, including "Design" and "On a Bird Singing in Its Sleep," make use of such evolutionary ramifications as protective coloring and hereditary instinct as analogies for hints at a larger plan. But the danger of the metaphor of evolution, Frost hints, is that it may lead us into monomania or monometaphor: the excessive fondness for explaining all aspects of life through a single analogy. Science, for all its accomplishments and discoveries and revelations, is still "no true god" to him. It seems as though his poem "The Demiurge's Laugh" is an indirect criticism of the nineteenth century tendency to fall down and worship the new metaphor of evolution as expounded by Darwin. If all did not fall down and worship, the dissenters still felt the impact of this new idea as a force strong enough to shake and threaten the structure of their own public and private metaphors by which they lived. Frost plays humorously with the presumptuousness of any scientific monomania which proposes to reduce life to rational intelligibility. In his poem entitled "The Bear" he draws his own analogy between the caged creature seeking a way out and the caged man seeking vainly to find his way beyond the limitations of his own knowledge:

> The telescope at one end of his beat,
> And at the other end the microscope,
> Two instruments of nearly equal hope,
> And in conjunction giving quite a spread.
> Or if he rests from scientific tread,
> 'Tis only to sit back and sway his head
> Through ninety odd degrees of arc, it seems,
> Between two metaphysical extremes.
> He sits back on his fundamental butt
> With lifted snout and eyes (if any) shut,
> (He almost looks religious but he's not),
> And back and forth he sways from cheek to cheek, ·
> At one extreme agreeing with one Greek,
> At the other agreeing with another Greek
> Which may be thought, but only so to speak.
> A baggy figure, equally pathetic
> When sedentary and when peripatetic.

Here the criticism is aimed not at man, as such, but at man as the victim of the old monomania: reason. Again the skeptic would restrain reason from supposing that it can pick the heart of the universal mystery. "There may be little or much beyond the grave"; but science and philosophy will always fall short of ultimate answers which can be demonstrated.

Without bothering with consistency, Frost's attitude toward life reveals a peculiar consistency. His criticism is aimed at excesses in all forms. Destructive as his faultfinding may seem, it aims to destroy only the illusions which are injurious to the full development of human life. And the faculties of the mind, glorious as they may be, are able to cope with only a limited aspect of human life.

From his critical position in the Golden Mean, Frost surveyed the utterances of nineteenth century philosophers with mingled sympathy and antipathy. From what has already been said, one may understand why he rejected to a large extent the sense of futility of human effort which occurs in Herbert Spencer almost as strongly as it occurs in Schopenhauer. Nor did Frost need to wait for Bergson and William James to help him reject Spencer's mechanistic and materialistic doctrines concerning the universe. But there were some appealing metaphors in Spencer, whose concept of dissolution as the unhappy epilogue of evolution was considerably modified by Bergson. Each used the familiar and poetic figure of the stream of everything that runs away. In Frost's poetry, as in the writings of Bergson, life is a positive force which grows through the very persistence of its desires. And it seems clear that Bergson's images and ideas influenced Frost's images and metaphors: the struggle of life against the constant stream, the undertow, of matter; the stubborn and endless fight of the spirit against the lag and slack of things toward death. We have examined Frost's use of these images in his poem "West-running Brook." Even to stand still against this stream, says Bergson, is to deny and defy the negative spending of matter. And Frost has a startlingly fine metaphor of two young lovers whose "master speed" enables life to defy the wasting stream of death:

> No speed of wind or water rushing by
> But you have speed far greater. You can climb
> Back up a stream of radiance to the sky,
> And back through history up the stream of time.
> And you were given this swiftness, not for haste,
> Nor chiefly that you may go where you will,
> But in the rush of everything to waste,
> That you may have the power of standing still—
> Off any still or moving thing you say.
> Two such as you with such a master speed
> Cannot be parted nor be swept away

From one another once you are agreed
That life is only life forevermore
Together wing to wing and oar to oar.

Frost's belief in the value of contraries in life is similar to Bergson's; but the poet's belief in the constant dissolution of matter, as alluded to in "The Master Speed" and "West-running Brook," is closer to Spencer's. Again, Frost's conviction that we live wisely and dangerously at the confluence of opposing forces (again the stream image) and that the dangers are converted through struggle into strength—these are similar to ideas expressed by Bergson. The triumph that grows from opposing forces suggests, but is distinctly different from, Hegel's metaphor of thesis, antithesis, synthesis: the belief that every condition of thought or of things leads irresistibly to its opposite and then unites with it to form a higher whole. Such a definition of progress is enough to arouse Frost's humorous faultfinding:

"Hegel saw two people marry and produce a third person. That was enough for Hegel—and Marx too, it seems. They jumped at the conclusion that so all truth was born. Out of two truths in collision today sprang the one truth to live by tomorrow. A time succession was the fallacy. Marriage, reproduction and the family with a big F have much to answer for, in misleading the analogists. Fire flashes from the flint and steel of metaphor and if caught in lint it may spread, but that is no reason why it should spread to burn the world. That is monomania or monometaphor."[33]

The poet is at his old game of watching an idea break down; of pointing out the strength and weakness of metaphor. And again the skeptic, interested in the conflict of opposites which may prompt to action, asks the question: "How soon?" Frost's interest in the relationship between contraries is not Hegel's interest. It comes closer to that of Aristotle, who said that "the knowledge of opposites is one." And we are back to the two halves of human life; to the position in the Golden Mean from which these two halves may be contemplated and utilized. There is room enough and danger enough in living between such opposites without worrying about change and growth.

But the concept of life which flourishes at the dangerous confluence of opposites was very popular in nineteenth century philosophy, and later. It is not strange that Frost should remind us of Bergson and William James when he speaks of "the shocks and changes we need to keep us sane," or when his metaphor in "Good-Bye and Keep Cold" hints at the increased vitality and excellence of living boldly within the fear of death, or when he urges that "the greatest reward of daring is still to dare." Bergson said it thus: "In a general way, in the evolution of life, just as in the evolution of human societies and of individual destinies, the greatest successes have been for those who have accepted the heaviest risks." And William James urged similarly a faith which should "offer the universe as an adventure rather than a scheme."

Such a philosophic background explains Frost's optimistic acceptance of a world which may seem too evil, too confused, too hopeless for some people. He speaks as one "acquainted with the night," and finds that the moon, as his favorite timepiece, "proclaimed the time was neither wrong nor right." He is ready to make the best of the worst because he finds that the worst lends itself to the desired and sacred struggle. There is a difference between the passive acceptance of "whatever is" and the active doing with "whatever is." There is no need to wish that the darkness and confusion and chaos might be dispelled: they lend themselves to the human process of form-giving; they test the Aristotelian "virtues" of mankind. And "resourcefulness is more than understanding!"

> Now let the night be dark for all of me.
> Let the night be too dark for me to see
> Into the future. Let what will be, be.

Out of life and death grows Frost's principle of love, out of love and reason grows Frost's acceptance. And with these walls within walls to shut fear out, Frost can laugh at the philosophic concern with epistemological problems about the extent and validity of knowledge. Again, one might collect quite a bouquet of his poems which had their roots in the poet's consciousness of the discrepancy between what man wants to know and what man is capable of knowing. The familiar skepticism sums up the paradox thus:

> They cannot look out far.
> They cannot look in deep.
> But when was that ever a bar
> To any watch they keep?

And in such poems as "Not Quite Social" and "For Once, Then, Something" he pleasantly accepts the taunt of those who belittle his refusal to be concerned with a desire to arrive at absolute philosophic truth. His acceptance of the limited powers of the mind color the lines of such poems as "Dust in the Eyes," "A Passing Glimpse," "Fragmentary Blue," and "Lost in Heaven." But he distinguishes between his skepticism here and idealism, at one extreme, or agnosticism, at the other extreme. The unlocked metaphor of "An Empty Threat" gives up its underlying meaning if it is considered in the light of the present discussion. There is no futility in life so long as there is opportunity for the simplest kind of affection and action, even within the most limited areas of existence. Reduce life to its coldest and most barren simplicity, still there remains reason for the illogical acceptance of whatever is: "I stay." If one lives there desperately, with little enough for windbreak between him and the North Pole, there may be consolation in staying, provided there is someone for the heart to cherish, something for the hands to do. And in contrast, consider the men whose eager and searching minds have made hopeless wanderers and explorers of them. The man who lived on the edge of Hudson Bay could shrug his shoulders at the empty threat about failure and futility of life in such arctic barrens; could say that his inspiration for staying in one place arose from remembering the unhappy fate of the Bay-discoverer:

> Who failed to find or force a strait
> In its two-thousand-mile coast;
> And his crew left him where he failed
> And nothing came of all he sailed.

Finally, the one who stays is able to find an answer not only for the overbold explorer but also for the overbold doubter:

"Better defeat almost
If seen clear
Than life's victories of doubt
That need endless talk talk
To make them out."

So Frost's middle position establishes itself again—this time in the Golden Mean between the extremes of philosophic concepts concerning the limitations of knowledge. It brings him back again to an acceptance of life as he finds it and as he interprets it. As he says in "Not Quite Social," he has rebelled against following the crowd, but he has never rebelled against that bondage which holds him with love and thought to the humble confines of earth.

Stop dodging the issue, the absolutist says to Frost. For heaven's sake, be consistent! And don't leave us so much in a quandary as to whether you are a monist or a dualist: choose! Frost's answer is quite simple. He says, I don't dodge any issue. Those who fail to understand my position are those who want life neatly arranged in pigeonholes of comfortable classification. Frost sympathizes with anyone, be it an absolutist like Plato, a theologian like Thomas Aquinas, or a mystic like Swedenborg, who takes the glorious risk of that irrational jump from the dualism of this world to the monism of the absolute. He has said that such a progression finds concrete analogy in the metaphor of the truncated pyramid. It seems as though one finally arrives at the shoulders of this truncated pyramid, the two shoulders which may represent the dual aspect of life; that there rises above these two shoulders the invisible and unachieved apex of the pyramid as the desired unification of life in the absolute. He admires the way in which we all can feel a sense of hopeful faith and recognition which makes us say, "I know," when a philosopher like Plato makes that final poetic lunge into the unknown.

Is it purely a dream that makes us imagine the completion of the truncated pyramid in spiritual lines to the apex? No, the evident design of the pyramid seems to call for it. So Frost can admire the courage of the risk, although he wants always to keep in mind that such a flight away from and beyond the empyrean can arrive at the conviction and the certainty only through hope and belief. He is willing to fluctuate between two positions: a dualist in his thinking, a monist in his wishing. And this for him is a tenable position. He is not willing to be consistent in any philosophic system because he constantly fluctuates between the darkness and the light of these two positions, exactly as the earth moves back and forth through day and night.

His persistent objection is to the kind of cheating to which theological discourse resorts when it tries to have its cake and eat it too. The theologian accepts in dogmatic fashion the monism of an absolute God, but then wants to put Him aside for a little while so that he may enjoy the free speculation of the philosophers. But this spoils the bold courage of the first choice: the willingness to step forth into the unknown; the heroic seeking, in the face of an apparent dualism, an equally apparent but not provable monism.

In his own fluctuations, Frost never wants to turn his eyes away from the probability. He likes the incident in *Pilgrim's Progress* where Pilgrim is asked:

"Do you see yon shining gate?"
"Yes," said he, "I *think* I do."

And all the rest is the story of Pilgrim's being willing to act on the supposition that he thought he saw the goal. So with Frost, he has his moments when he thinks he sees it. And then he slips back into the sad knowledge that only a kind of momentary inspiration can give that conviction. To him, even the religious mystics who were honest were forever moving into and out of the wildly exciting faith and conviction; but time and again they were conscious, when honest with themselves, that they had lost the vision which took them into the presence of the flamelike spirit; that most of the time they stood, like him, on the two shoulders of the truncated pyramid.

One may find in his poetry several metaphorical records of moments in the poet's life when mood and circumstance have conspired to give him those wished-for but momentary glimpses. Out of such moments grew such poems as "For Once, Then, Something," "A Soldier," "The Trial by Existence," and "Sitting by a Bush in Broad Sunlight." Perhaps the wildest and finest flight of this kind may be found in that poem with the giveaway title, "I Will Sing You One-O."

In all these approaches to systematic thought, Frost is kept from trusting dogma because it cannot encompass in rational terms the irrational and continuous flux of matter and spirit. Herein he shows his essential kinship, again, with Emerson. The symbols, the metaphors, through which he reads meanings must be held lightly so that he may be able to translate them into equivalents lest rigidity should freeze and destroy vital flexibility; lest the truths of experience escape us, and subside into dogma.

One can safely say after from six to thirty thousand years of experience that the evident design is a situation here in which it will always be about equally hard to save your soul. Whatever progress may be taken to mean, it can't mean making the world any easier a place in which to save your soul—or if you dislike hearing your soul mentioned in open meeting, say your decency, your integrity.[34]

THE INDIVIDUAL LIFE

Frost lives in a world where the odds are stacked high against the individual, where opportunity is the exception and not the rule, where forces press so hard against the individual as to make him seem destined to defeat from the start. In America the ancient Calvinistic doctrine of predestination has blossomed anew in the doctrine of naturalistic determinism; the harsh justice of a discriminating God has given way to the more harsh injustice of nature and the machine age. The confusions and evils of life overwhelm us, say the determinists. Noble and heroic as man may be in cheeping little songs about a bloody head that is unbowed, he is doomed to failure. And there remains to the anguished individual nothing but pity for himself and his poor fellow man.

"I am impatient of such talk," says Frost. "All ages of the world are bad—a great deal worse anyway than Heaven. If they weren't, the world might just as well be Heaven at once and have it over with. . . . There is at least so much good in the world that it admits of form and the making of form. And not only admits of it but calls for it."[35]

But can he prove it? In our world of blackness and chaos, wars and the rumors of wars, what form may be given to the individual life to redeem it from a tragic sense of futility and failure? The questions and the challenges have been taken up and answered by Frost in flintlike prose, in a profusion of metaphors. He begins by considering and including all the hindrances, confusions, negations, sorrows. If the individual can give any shape and meaning to his own life he must do it by finding some way of converting these liabilities into assets. It will not do to close our eyes; it will not do merely to whistle in the dark. Hope is what it is, but not enough to save life from tragedy. Only hope in action can produce results which comfort and satisfy.

Frost starts with fear and in fear. Strip life down to nothing, if you can; or since you cannot, strip it down to its essence. Then in fear proceed to see what can be done. In fear of what? In fear of disappointing that essence; in fear of failing to realize the limited potentialities of that essence. But what are the potentialities? There is the crux for the individual: the persistent desire and struggle to discover those possibilities. This basic principle in Frost's attitude is again related to the basic principle of the central idea in Greek thought: the desire to perceive the peculiar idiom of the individual which makes him different from any other individual; then to combine that idiom with those potentialities, or "virtues," which he shares with all men. Call it your soul, says Frost, or if you are embarrassed to use that word, call it your integrity: the interrelating of all your various parts to form a complete whole.

But where would one start? Where he is now, with whatever he is doing now. The artist in Frost permits him to borrow the word "form" from the Greeks and make it his own in a metaphor: start with little forms. "Fortunately, too, no forms are more engrossing, gratifying, comforting, staying than those lesser ones we throw off, like vortex rings of smoke, all our individual enterprise and needing nobody's cooperation: a basket, a letter, a garden, a room, an idea, a picture, a poem. For these we haven't to get a team together before we can play."[36] Does such a beginning seem too trivial? It has a cumulative value which will eventually combine the trivial into the larger units of experience.

Still more important, such action makes sense because it seems to be related to the larger design of the universe. "We people are thrust forward out of the suggestions of form in the rolling clouds of nature. In us nature reaches its height of form and through us exceeds itself. When in doubt there is always form for us to go on with. Anyone who has achieved the least form to be sure of it, is lost to the larger excruciations."[37] Or, to translate the negative lostness into discovery, one may discover through the relating of little details in form the outer relating of larger forms into a pattern that has meaning. The direction is toward the source of the larger meaning.

But suppose one does not find meaning? That failure may be the largest of all excruciations. The finite is still too great for our comprehension, and what shall we say of all that is beyond the finite? Frost's teasing answer to that is obvious: Why say anything? One of his poems has a giveaway subtitle: "Resourcefulness Is More Than Understanding." There is an old truth that needs renewing, to save so many from broken hearts and broken heads. The poem is a brief narrative of an episode in a zoo, a pleasant picture of how a boy teased two monkeys with a lens or burning-glass until

> They stood arms laced together at the bars,
> And exchanged troubled glances over life.
> One put a thoughtful hand up to his nose
> As if reminded—or as if perhaps
> Within a million years of an idea.

With further teasing, the boy ventured too near and "there was a sudden flash of arm" which gave possession of the burning-glass to the monkeys. After a brief series of smells and bites and tastes of this curious weapon, the monkeys calmly buried it in their bedding straw and then

> Came dryly forward to the bars again
> To answer for themselves: Who said it mattered
> What monkeys did or didn't understand?
> They might not understand a burning-glass.
> They might not understand the sun itself.
> It's knowing what to do with things that counts.

So many of Frost's poems touch on this theme of resourcefulness and doing. The purpose is not merely to keep hands busy lest Satan should find mischief still, not merely to keep so busy that the mind won't be able to cast troubled glances at the mystery.

The resourcefulness is aimed to combine thought and love into action which can make a comprehensible little world within an incomprehensibly big world. "Triple Bronze" is a pleasant group of metaphors on this theme. In his poetry, Frost frequently hints at this general formula for defense against the confusion of a confused world: studying to make the limited "snug in the limitless."

> If I can with confidence say
> That still for another day,
> Or even another year,
> I will be there for you, my dear,
>
> It will be because, though small
> As measured against the All,
> I have been so instinctively thorough
> About my crevice and burrow.

Frost has kept as old favorites two books which contain for him separate statements of the idea. They are *Walden* and *Robinson Crusoe*: records of two entirely different men placed in entirely different situations. Yet each combined resourcefulness with a love of doing. Frost stressed his pleasure in this relationship: "*Robinson Crusoe* is never quite out of my mind. I never tire of being shown how the limited can make snug in the limitless. *Walden* has something of the same fascination. Crusoe was cast away; Thoreau was self-cast away. Both found themselves sufficient. No prose writer has ever been more fortunate in subject than these two."[38]

Only a critic who fails to read these metaphors correctly could call such an attitude romantic. Frost reads the metaphor of Crusoe's experience as the story of a man who accepts his situation in life and makes the best of what is at hand, without querulousness, impatience, or bitterness. He manages to survive with a modicum of comfort and with considerable satisfaction. He was ready for something better when the opportunity came, just as Thoreau was willing to give up his hermit life after he had finished his experiment and proved his own metaphor of life.

Considering resourcefulness in doing, Frost likes to divide people into two categories: those who visualize life at its best as a perfection toward which people work; those who visualize life as being nothing more or less than whatever they find it to be, good and bad enough to permit the working of crude material into some kind of shape. The first group, to carry out the viewpoint, would have approached Robinson Crusoe's problem of building a house by saying something like this: "The best building material for the house I need here is a certain permanent material found on the other side of the world. And I can't get it. What a pity!" The second group would have accepted Crusoe's solution which was, in spirit, "Here is loose sandy rock in which I can dig a cave; here is turf for a wall and boughs for thatch. It's not the best, but it is the best available."

In such a division, the first group thinks of trying to overcome all drawbacks that hinder the attainment of perfection. Eventually they grow disappointed with their position, which they are forced to accept as a compromise. The second group never uses the word compromise because there can be no such position so long as the best use is made of whatever there is at hand. This second viewpoint has its own idealism, of course, in that it presupposes that one cares to do the best he can. If, then, compromise is made, it is a deliberate and self-imposed shortcoming.

The first group is closely related to the Platonists; the second, to the skeptics of almost any age. In youth, most of us start out to be Platonists. We believe in an ideal form of life for the individual, for society, for government, for the nations of the earth. We are willing to discard whatever is, in order to speed the establishment of the Kingdom of God on earth, as soon as we can. It seldom occurs to youth that God has any slow plan of His own under way, and the young idealist cannot see any inconsistency in growing impatient with God. Wanting short cuts to heaven, he believes his plan in execution is a divine inspiration which justifies a violence that is, in itself, contrary to natural law. Eventually the idealist achieves (or fails) and settles down to enjoy (or resent) the consequences of his action. To be sure, he will not have much sympathy in later life for anyone who comes along with divine inspiration to execute by violence of word and deed another short cut to heaven. He must then raise new questions as to what is authority; as to what is right, and when. The result is usually confusion, bitterness, and pessimism.

Such is my understanding of Robert Frost's point of view. He summed up his own attitude neatly in the sentence already quoted: "More than once I should have lost my soul to radicalism if it had been the originality it was mistaken for by its young converts." There is another recourse of the individual which is equally opposed to his desire for the initial development of resourcefulness and self-dependence in unfolding the possibilities of the individual: the appeal for help to individuals or institutions outside self. His poem entitled "Build Soil" is his own essay on self-reliance. Back of it is the realization that we begin as dependents and become conditioned to a state of dependence. Our lives take their initial forms, he has said, from "the promises our ancestors have made for us." And outside heredity there are the forms of the home, the community, institutional education, government. Nobody is able to start from scratch. We find ourselves in a definite framework and bulwark already built up by human experience against the too-great confusion of the universe. But the initial salvation of such a heritage may prove to be our ultimate ruin if we lean on it too heavily: it is a faulty substitute. Any life which throws itself too persistently into the sustaining arms of others—individuals, society, institutions—will find in this centrifuge merely a subterfuge which fails to sustain. The other extreme, the centripetal extreme, can prove equally fallacious, although few of us develop inward far enough to reveal that danger:

> We're always too much out or too much in.
> At present from a cosmical dilation
> We're so much out that the odds are against
> Our ever getting inside in again.
> But inside in is where we've got to get.
> My friends all know I'm interpersonal.
> But long before I'm interpersonal
> Away 'way down inside I'm personal.
> Just so before we're international
> We're national and act as nationals.
> The colors are kept unmixed on the palette,

> Or better on dish plates all around the room,
> So the effect when they are mixed on canvas
> May seem almost exclusively designed.
> Some minds are so confounded intermental
> They remind me of pictures on a palette:
> "Look at what happened. Surely some God pinxit.
> Come look at my significant mud pie."

"Build Soil" continues to develop the analogy between the seemingly selfish act of inner cultivation and the seemingly futile act of building and enriching the soil for the soil's sake first, without any immediate concern as to what may come of it:

> Build soil. Turn the farm in upon itself
> Until it can contain itself no more,
> But sweating-full, drips wine and oil a little.
> I will go to my run-out social mind
> And be as unsocial with it as I can.
> The thought I have, and my first impulse is
> To take to market—I will turn it under.
> The thought from that thought—I will turn it under.
> And so on to the limit of my nature.
> We are too much out, and if we won't draw in
> We shall be driven in.

Like so many other elements in Frost's attitude toward life, this doctrine of selfishness reflects the viewpoint of the artist. The virtue of selfishness is too easily overlooked by those who wish to make a fetish out of service to others before there is enough in self to serve out. But from the virtue of selfishness wells up that slow accumulation of understanding which expresses itself in art forms as doing well, in social forms as doing good. The self-discovery of selfishness determines which of these uses best expresses the character, the idiom, the "virtue" of the individual. The finding of that idiom is described in an unlocked metaphor at the heart of Frost's poem, "The Axe-Helve."

> He showed me that the lines of a good helve
> Were native to the grain before the knife
> Expressed them, and its curves were no false curves
> Put on it from without. And there its strength lay
> For the hard work.

And when the persistence of selfishness has enriched the soil of the individual, when the knife of discernment has expressed the strength of the idiom, all this is merely preparation:

> Don't let me seem to say the exchange, the encounter,
> May not be the important thing at last.
> It well may be. We meet—I don't say when—
> But must bring to the meeting the maturest,
> The longest-saved-up, raciest, localest
> We have strength in us to bring.

In Frost's attitude toward life there is a very close relationship between self-discovery and the apparently trivial form-giving. The process of finding self is a circular one, as is all reasoning. We venture outward into experience and the outer experience brings us back into a new self-knowledge. He has spoken of how the writing of a poem is akin to going to the North Pole: to see if the adventurer could get back! The writer later ventures into print, not to see if he can write but to wager that he can; and when he is recognized by others, he is back to self again. Falling in love is another kind of excursion outside self to find self. But Frost's most persistent suggestions of falling in love includes the love of labor because of a kind of sympathy that is developed between the actor, the act, and the thing acted upon. In all his metaphors of farm labor, reference to "the earnest love" and "the sweetest dream" is tied up to a broadening of perceptions. Horizons are pushed back. Through the action comes a sympathy not only for the rhythmical pattern of natural life but also for the shared experiences of human life. And gradually the doing is related to larger and larger significance. Out of the slight pleasure of doing comes the need for finding larger means of form-giving. And, on the other hand, out of the need for that which keeps body and soul together comes the pleasure in the doing. The two relate themselves until the hard work becomes play. Frost develops this same theme in his narrative of two tramps looking for work and finding the poet splitting his own wood:

> Nothing on either side was said.
> They knew they had but to stay their stay

And all their logic would fill my head:
As that I had no right to play
With what was another man's work for gain.
My right might be love but theirs was need.
And where the two exist in twain
Theirs was the better right—agreed.

But yield who will to their separation,
My object in living is to unite
My avocation and my vocation
As my two eyes make one in sight.
Only where love and need are one,
And the work is play for mortal stakes,
Is the deed ever really done
For Heaven and the future's sakes.

Out of the need for doing, pleasure; out of the pleasure of doing, the deed—and from the two in one, the thing done well and with meaning.

Fear, selfishness, action, self-dependence, self-discovery, integrity: a curious sequence. But the experiment produces results, and the results give fulfillment to experience. So many of Frost's characters in his narrative poems show their first concern for that primary virtue: integrity. The hired man in "The Code" had his own kind of integrity:

The hand that knows his business won't be told
To do work better or faster—those two things.

And different aspects of integrity are central in the characters of "The Self-Seeker," "The Servant to Servants," "The House-keeper," and "In the Home Stretch." The ultimate test of Frost's attitude toward the fate of the individual, in a situation where it will always be about equally hard to save your soul, your decency, your integrity, is a substantial heritage of vital New England Puritanism. It crops out in metaphor after metaphor. Perhaps it hides most quietly in the poem entitled, "The Old Barn at the Bottom of the Fogs." The itinerant laborer who slept in the barn found that the props to keep the barn doors closed could not be used from within to keep the barn doors locked. He drew his own analogies, and hinted that his own sense of integrity didn't permit him to live with comfort so long as there were "prop-locks" to his life. He had his bitter words for the rich whose locked houses were propped outside with mortgages. Like the old fellow in "The Death of the Hired Man," he wouldn't be beholden to anyone; didn't want to depend on that which someone else might be able to do to him with props that could "lock him in to stay."

But what of the black and evil world, with all its chaos and confusion? Again approaching the problem with the artist's viewpoint and the poet's metaphor, Frost accepts the formless as raw materials which may come in handy to him whenever he gets around to further kinds of form-giving. The crudities of life become assets. Using as inspiration the form-giving manner of nature, we apply our own modest creative cunning to the unshaped possibilities about us to make forms which have their own meaning and beauty. Let the excruciations seem unbearable to those who prefer bewildered yearning for heaven and are dissatisfied with anything less than perfection. Frost willingly accepts the mixed goodness and badness:

"I thank the Lord for crudity, which is rawness, which is raw material, which is the part of life not yet worked up into form, or at least not worked all the way up. Meet with the fallacy of the foolish: having had a glimpse of finished art, they forever pine for a life that shall be nothing but finished art. Why not a world safe for art as well as democracy? A real artist delights in roughness for what he can do to it. He's the brute who can knock the corners off the marble block and drag the unbedded beauty out of bed. The statesman (politician) is no different except he works in a protean mass of material that hardly holds the shape he gives it long enough for him to point it out and get credit for it. His material is the rolling mob. The poet's material is words that for all we may say and feel against them are more manageable than men. Get a few words alone in a study and with plenty of time on your hands you can make them say anything you please."[39]

*Saints, like John Bunyan, are all right in jail if they are sure
of their truth and sincerity. But so also are many criminals.
The great trouble is to be sure. A stuffed shirt is the opposite
of a criminal. He cares not what he thinks of himself so long
as the world continues to think well of him. The sensible and
healthy live somewhere between self-approval and the ap-
proval of society. They make their adjustment without too
much talk of compromise.*[40]

THE INDIVIDUAL AND SOCIETY

ROBERT FROST's attitude toward the individual in his relation
to society grows consistently from his initial concern for the development, first, of that inner strength and worth of the individual
which permits one to be worthy of the society in which he lives.
Two kinds of pity injure the desired integrity of the individual:
self-pity, which makes a person turn to society for assistance, and
sentimental humanitarianism, which expresses itself in social institutions—schools, relief organizations, government. The well-
meaning pity of the humanitarians encourages the abandonment
of that self-discipline and individual action which is the basic
unit of social strength.

Social consciousness grows naturally from the loving relations
of the individuals in the family. Carried one step further, these
relations express themselves in the community. And the metaphor
which represents the key to Frost's social outlook is the metaphor
of community relationship: neighborliness. The spontaneous expression of friendliness and love, the outgoing spirit of sympathy,
may be felt as the motivation for the series of narrative poems in
his "book of people." This love in action goes beyond the calculated and rational:

> We saw the risk we took in doing good,
> But dared not spare to do the best we could
> Though harm should come of it.

Nevertheless, Frost's sense of kinship and brotherliness does not tempt him into the monometaphorical idealism which has been voiced down the ages from Athens to Brook Farm and back to Moscow about the common brotherhood of man and the utopian dream. "We congregate embracing from distrust as much as love," he says. And so long as individuals have yet to learn ways of living with integrity even among those whom they are disposed to love, Frost finds all talk about an international brotherhood merely a subject for jest. For his pains in adumbrating his impatience with the cheap idealism of the believers in the get-social-quick programs, Frost was once called a "counterrevolutionary." If argument had degenerated to name-calling, Frost said, he was willing to retaliate by calling his leftist critic "a bargain-counter revolutionary," who forever wanted to pay too cheap a price. To him, all dreaming about a utopian condition in society falls under the head of that false yearning for heaven which was considered in the preceding chapter. And his critical answers on this subject are all too plainly stated in "Build Soil":

> Keep off each other and keep each other off.
> You see the beauty of my proposal is
> It needn't wait on general revolution.
> I bid you to a one-man revolution—
> The only revolution that is coming.

Frost's reaction toward social utopias and "isms" is to "steal away and stay away." It reminds one of Emerson's reaction to the Brook Farm invitation: "I have not yet conquered my own house. Shall I raise the siege of this hen-coop and march baffled away to a pretended siege of Babylon?"

Social institutions represented by schools and colleges come in for their share of criticism from Frost because they are too prone to superimpose artificial concepts on the individual instead of encouraging the student, through the genuine process of leading-out, to discover his own position and beliefs as an individual. Instead of finding in schools the truth which makes them free, students are too often loaded down with secondhand ideas and prejudices which make them the captured subjects of their teachers.

Speaking as a college professor, Frost once summed up his own hopes for teaching:

"The freedom I'd like to give is the freedom I'd like to have. That is much harder than anything else in the world to get—the freedom of my material. You might define a school boy as one who could recite to you, if you started him talking, everything he read last night, in the order in which he read it. That's just the opposite of what I mean by a free person. . . . I think what I'm after is free meditation. I don't think anybody gets to it when he's in anybody's company; only when his soul is alone. . . . I would so run a course by self-withdrawal. I would begin a course by being very present, and then slowly disappear. A sort of vanishing act. I'd rather melt away just as I stood there, and leave a fellow more and more alone, and let him feel deserted, like a baby in a room alone. Give him that terribly abandoned feeling, left to the horrors of his own thoughts and conscience."[41]

Again, in considering the social implications of government, Frost's primary concern is with that expression of governmental power which increases or diminishes the rights of the individual. Brought up a States' Rights Democrat, he had followed with reluctance the gradual centralization of more and more power in the federal government, and has preserved his wish that government itself might refuse its own advantage by refraining from centralization beyond a certain point. Obviously, he has been disappointed.

Governmental interest in its citizens as expressed through social legislation calculated to bring reliefs of various kinds is no satisfactory palliative for increased centralization. It has too often vitiated its own purpose through the vastness of programs which have been unable to show discrimination. And the result has been to focus Frost's social thinking on questions as to how far mercy should carry us into sentimentalism. Long ago, when he was still so uncertain as to the future that he depended occasionally on borrowed money, he wrote a poem entitled "Good Relief," in which he considered questions as to how far we should go in sharing the griefs and sufferings of others. Should we give all our money to the poor and suffer equally with them? Or, if we hear that children in France and China are being tortured by the results of war, should we torture ourselves equally? Where did justice come in to counterbalance mercy? On a similar theme the benign and kindly Emerson has a strong passage which reflects the spirit of Frost's social thinking:

"Society everywhere is in conspiracy against the manhood of every one of its members. Society is a joint-stock company, in which the members agree, for the better securing of his bread to each shareholder, to surrender the liberty and culture of the eater. The virtue in most request is conformity. Self-reliance is an aversion. It loves not realities and creators, but names and customs. . . . Every decent and well-spoken individual affects and sways me more than is right. I ought to go upright and vital, and speak the rude truths in all ways. If malice and vanity wear the coat of philanthropy, shall that pass? The doctrine of hatred must be preached, as the counteraction of the doctrine of love, when that pules and whines. . . . Do not tell me, as a good man did to-day, of my obligation to put all poor men in good institutions. Are they *my* poor? I tell thee, thou foolish philanthropist, that I grudge the dollar, the dime, the cent I give to such men as do not belong to me and to whom I do not belong. There is a class of persons to whom by all spiritual affinity I am bought and sold; for them I will go to prison if need be; but your miscellaneous popular charities; the education at college of fools; the building of meeting-houses to the vain end to which many now stand; alms to sots, and the thousand-fold Relief Societies;— though I confess with shame I sometimes succumb and give the dollar, it is a wicked dollar, which by and by I shall have the manhood to withhold."[42]

Such a passage may be misinterpreted by the careless thinker so that it falsely seems like an ugly and selfish example of "rugged individualism." But the individualism of Emerson and of Frost is more discriminating than that; it urges selfishness as a palliative to the kind of sentimentality which permits mercy to encroach on that which is just. And Frost has strongly criticized that kind of governmental relief which encourages professional poverty and professional "greedy good-doers." Not long after he had returned from England in 1915 he was asked to speak before a Junior League group on the poor people in his poems, and he was properly indignant. Here is his own account of that talk:

"When I meet very wealthy people, I have to face them. I remember facing once a small group, not a thousand miles from Philadelphia. I did it for a charity-working friend of mine. She told me that the girls I must speak to must be gone for: they were worth at least a million apiece, and I could be rough on them. I knew they were all helping her in her charity work, so you can see my state of mind. I felt cross to be there. I took for my text, 'Let not man bring together what God hath set asunder.' Let the rich keep away from the poor for all of me! ... It says in the Bible, you think—I don't—it says in the Bible that you always have the poor with you. That isn't what it says. It says, 'For Christ's sake, forget the poor some of the time.' There are many beautiful things in the world besides poverty."

Here is bitterness, not against the rich or poor, but against the rich or poor, *as such*; against the professional show of either for gain or for boastfulness and vanity. Frost's ironic bitterness against sentimental pity for the poor flashes in such a poem as "The Figure in the Doorway"; the unfortunate wretch who was so unfortunate as to live off in the solitude of the country!

The same balancing of sentimental sight with insight is the theme of the companion poem "On the Heart's Beginning to Cloud the Mind." The most pointed of these satirical poems is "A Roadside Stand, or, On Being Put Out of Our Misery." In the latter, the ineffectual wistfulness of those who want their roadside stand to bring in a little extra money makes the poet recall projected governmental legislation which will end all such wistfulness:

> It is in the news that all these pitiful kin
> Are to be bought out and mercifully gathered in
> To live in villages next to the theatre and store
> Where they won't have to think for themselves any more;
> While greedy good-doers, beneficent beasts of prey,
> Swarm over their lives enforcing benefits
> That are calculated to soothe them out of their wits,

And by teaching them how to sleep the sleep all day,
Destroy their sleeping at night the ancient way.

Then, after letting his own heart cloud for a moment, he concludes:

I can't help owning the great relief it would be
To put these people at one stroke out of their pain.
And then next day as I came back into the sane,
I wonder how I should like you to come to me
And offer to put me gently out of my pain.

Here Frost has tried the application of the Golden Rule on the "beneficent beasts of prey." As for passing judgments on the seriousness of another's griefs, we are quite willing; but we are secretly proud of our own pain and grief and we hope that nobody will quite take ours away from us. Such a merciful gesture would be unjust to us!

In raising the old question as to which comes first, mercy or justice, Frost recognizes the inability to find any final answer. The conflict between opposing goods is of more interest to him than the conflict between good and bad, for he finds the first actual tragedy while the second tends to melodrama, with a villain conveniently there to be blamed. He makes this point nicely in his remarks "To a Young Wretch" who has cut a Christmas tree from his woods without asking permission:

It is your Christmases against my woods.
But even where thus opposing interests kill,
They are to be thought of as opposing goods
Oftener than as conflicting good and ill;
Which makes the war god seem no special dunce
For always fighting on both sides at once.

Another approach to merciful humanitarianism amuses Frost: our eagerness to protect our right to succeed, but our refusal to protect our right to fail. If it becomes illegal to fail, it will be because sentimentality has confused the relative virtues of mercy and justice. He has his own favorite illustration:

"We are in danger, in our way of thinking that mercy comes first in the world. It comes in, but it comes in second. The thing you are most interested in is justice; all you ask for is justice in the struggle.

"I had a boy come to me with poetry the other day. (*Who* is a poor thing?) He came to me with talk about mercy on earth—everything has now gone merciful; kinder times ahead. I let him talk and have it all his own way. Finally he came out with the poetry he had brought. I said,

'You've come for mercy.'

He looked at me for a second and said,

'No, sir, I just want fairness.'

(You see, they really have more spunk than you think.) I said, 'I thought so.'

After I treated him with fairness—and he came out, as it happened, very poorly in my estimation—then I might in mercy carry him home to his mother. Mercy is there, of course. It is part of everything. But there is so much confusion about who is a poor thing, nowadays, that I can't help saying there is not much of that sort of thing around my poor people."[43]

Frost does not mean to imply that mercy has no place in the laws of organized society. He believes in the importance of laws which keep us from being too free for our own good, and recalls ironically in "Build Soil" that we have put important curbs on the freedom to be too selfish:

> Everyone asks for freedom for himself,
> The man free love, the business man free trade,
> The writer and talker free speech and free press.
> Political ambition has been taught,
> By being punished back, it is not free:
> It must at some point gracefully refrain.
> Greed has been taught a little abnegation
> And shall be more before we're done with it.
> It is just fool enough to think itself
> Self-taught. But our brute snarling and lashing taught it.

The interrelationship of individuals in society automatically requires fences to restrain the inevitable too-much of uncontrolled greed, selfishness, freedom. The ideal of democracy is to let down as many fences of restraint as may safely be let down. Frost likes to remember the Platonic thesis that in good times a democratic government can even afford to let down the bars until liberties are abused as licenses; that then the fences are put back and that in time of grave national danger we permit our liberties to be called in temporarily until fences are restraining every kind of freedom to act independently as individuals. The difficulty is always to keep fences flexible enough to meet shifting demands of circumstance and neighbors. Anyone who will not go behind his father's sayings about fences (individual or nation) forever moves in darkness, "not of woods only and the shade of trees," but rather like "an old-stone savage armed."

My proof of being not unbounded. . . .
Though by a world of doubt surrounded.

CONCLUSION:

WITNESS TREES AND REAL-ESTATE

In these dark and ominous times when we hear so much frantic talk about the dangers of inflation, many people have advised the purchase of land and property as a bulwark against chaos; a farm in Connecticut, perhaps, to which the lucky owner may retreat if the black night should descend when other helpers fail and comforts flee. Such proposals are of considerable interest to Robert Frost because he has been speculating in various kinds of real-estate for many years without any fears or hopes for inflation. His latest book of poems, *A Witness Tree*, may well be considered an artistic commentary on the general subject of personal holdings and property. With genial grace he invites any troubled investors to walk the poet's boundaries and listen to a variety of anecdotes, songs, and parables which he has made while perfecting his own valid defense against confusion.

Don't be discouraged if you aren't familiar with the uses of witness trees or if you are afraid Frost's latest book on real-estate may devote too much time to them. His first poem will set you straight. For his purpose, the title is an extremely felicitous metaphor. Those who have explored the boundaries of forest land in New England are familiar with the colonial method (still practiced) of marking the corner of a forest lot not only by pounding into the ground an official iron stake but also by cutting notches or blazes on the largest tree near the stake to bear mute witness to the location. Obscure and lost in underbrush as the little iron marker may become, the skeptical doubter who challenges the existence of the boundary may find that the notches on the witness tree stand out as bold and convincing evidence. You see that such a symbol is particularly happy for a landowning poet who takes so much pleasure in walking various boundaries and in pointing to his own modest claims.

Long ago, discerning readers noticed that Frost's poetic method frequently makes use of metaphors which are notched like witness trees to indicate the twofold direction of the poet's thoughts. In *A Witness Tree*, he has arranged his anecdotes and songs into separate groups. Poems which are notched only "one or two" times because they are built around a central metaphor compose the first group. The second consists of poems in which the progression of metaphors and images permits the reader to find each one notched "two or more" times. Then, almost as though Frost had grown tired of his own boundary search for notched trees, he calls "time out" for his third group and offers a miscellaneous array of poems which do not fit nicely into the first two categories. His last unit of poems deals largely with country people lost "over back" in isolated stretches of rural landscape. Thus the four divisions give pleasing arrangement to the poet's playfully serious converse as to the manner in which he and others have made themselves snug in a chaotic world.

Robert Frost has always been a bit sheepish about his own real-estate holdings and has often talked about them in his poems with a somewhat oblique and ironic manner of reference. To be sure, the authentic character he has always given to country images and details—barns and stone walls, brooks and mountains, woodsmen and farmers—would convince any reader that his preferences do not include city blocks and fashionable suburban developments. Yet his images arrange themselves into metaphors at once pertinent to Gotham and to the rural districts north of Boston. It would seem that he must have been writing *A Witness Tree* over a goodly number of years without expecting to give it such a timely utterance. I dare say he is going to be embarrassed when people tell him that his book about property and investments is so pertinent to the present moment.

The devil will quote his own scripture in answer. He may select the third poem to corroborate his ancient belief that the present moment has always been timely enough to satisfy him, whether that present were yesterday, today, or tomorrow. And the kind of boundaries which interest him have always offered attractive propositions to anyone with a speculative turn of mind. Don't misunderstand him: he knows how to give correct emphasis to the first syllable in real-estate. Far as his imagination may roam, his investments are not in those cheap air-castles fashioned out of despair or wishful dreamery. This sly old Yankee is a shrewd investor who never settles for anything until his preliminary questions permit him to be certain that he has a clear title. Before he began to speculate seriously in real-estate, he perfected his technique by devoting some time to swapping horses—breathe it not in Gath—and that shady period in his career undoubtedly developed an ingrained streak of caution. At present, however, he has nothing to sell; he offers you his observations with a casual and familiar take-it-or-leave-it gesture.

There is a teasing humor about this man whose language is so consistently indirect. At times he has been so equivocal and round-about that some readers have thought he was constantly making fun of systematic philosophy. Again he has infuriated others who wished he would say what he meant or that he would mean what he says. I guess it must be that horse-trading streak in him that makes him talk in riddles. But take my word for it: he is always *thinking* about property—and that's the Yankee in him. You must be on your guard all the time, for you will not get his slant on things unless you understand this consistent viewpoint. If you can't cock your head in appraisals just the way he does it, you will still enjoy his poems. But if your lack of understanding leads you into careless enthusiasms, you are likely to make the mistake of buying a piece of land on a rocky hillside pasture in New Hampshire or Vermont—and you could live to regret that.

Of course, all his books of poetry touch on the appraisal, development and twofold protection of property in one form or another. *A Witness Tree*, containing some of his finest observations, is a satisfying corroboration of all that he has said before. It is comforting to find that he never actually goes back on his word. Those who are familiar with his earlier poems will find pleasure in the new shape he gives to a point of view always growing more profound without any need for self-contradiction, on the one hand,

and without danger of dogmatic monotony, on the other. Here again is the same shrewd and patient wisdom fashioned with bright cunning into unforgettable poems.

He has told us a lot about himself, in an offhand manner. Long before the publication of his first book, however, he had become so absorbed in his real-estate games that he didn't think it important to tell us how he got started. Yet the evidence is fairly clear that in his accumulation of property he first speculated in lowlands and valleys for some time. It wasn't that he had any fear of high places or disliked the uplands; he always watched them casually from the corner of his eye. In many of his poems he implies that the best way to evaluate a piece of upland property is to get below and look up the hill at it. This slant permits one to appraise it for how much better it is than rock-bottom and to avoid any qualms as to how much worse it is than such a real-estate paradise as the Garden of Eden. This uphill slant is the secret of Frost's speculative approach.

One might expect to find in his poems touches of regret for such a timid start, but that would be a mistake. This unpromising approach enabled him to accumulate an ever-improving terrain, now rich and varied. He has never parted with those bleak and doubtful lowlands, although he added to them long ago many stretches of green intervales which hold, beneath the shifting light, depths of good soil. And those who have walked completely around his boundaries must have noticed, far back within, his own cautious hills and his own aspiring mountain peaks. It is a large estate now. But he could never have been content with property which did not include depths and sloping pastures to give definition and contrast to hills and mountains.

He says some very smart things about his method of procedure. If you start out by choosing some attractive height-of-land location, he warns, you may find that you bought only the view. Then a good winter blizzard may come along and blow you so far down into the wrong valley that you'll wish you had never been tempted by that useless vista, pretty as it may have been. Historically, Frost thinks, more men have staked their claims for views than for farm lands. He for one is willing to have a blizzard or a thunderstorm hit us all so hard that it will blast us back to farm lands. If war should do the trick, he would probably consider it worth the heavy cost. He thinks the worst real-estate agent he ever dealt with was Plato, who might have had a better influence on the profession if he had been blessed at least temporarily with a stiff case of astigmatism. Of course it is common knowledge that too many view-vending real-estate agents since Plato have done too much cribbing out of his sales-talk notebooks. Having examined those arguments long ago, Frost chuckles over them all and frequently has his ironic jokes at the expense of those who suffer from various forms of Platonic hyperopia.

When examining property, he thinks it consoling to use our two eyes for looking out and sideways at the identical moment. He has developed his own vision until he can encompass the two extremes of landscape and still focus his attention on the middle ground. He would like to do better, but he is honest about his limitations. He never pretends he can see a mountain in the far distance, even if it is visible to more imaginative eyes. Recognizing the hoax perpetrated in all seriousness by wishful people like the early Picasso, who wanted to see all sides at once, Frost is nevertheless sadly sympathetic with the desire. Contrariwise, he is amused by the painfully nearsighted who seem always unhappy about their investments and properties. They have developed such critically microscopic eyes that they can't see the forests because of the dead trees, can't see the crops because they are forever cursing the weeds.

Autobiographical as Frost's poems may be, some of his best hints to investors are always handled with the objectivity of the true artist. If one should examine such metaphorical hints in *A Witness Tree*, it would be apparent that they are grace notes which harmonize with an earlier poem, "Build Soil," which took the form of a conversation between two advanced investors who knew what land was good for, once it had been acquired. Before they had finished their conversation, each was agreed that speculators frequently spent too much time in listening to the wishes and special pleading of agents; that there was need for more individual planning. One of the characters in "Build Soil" suggested that his threefold approach to investment was first to consider honestly his own limitations and capacities, then to enrich his own property and soil until it could make the most of those limitations, and finally worry about prices and selling when he really had something worthy of market competition.

A new slant on this problem may be found in "All Revelation." Because of the poet's oblique manner of getting to the point, it would seem that his anecdote is merely built around his curiosity as to what one bold prospector is trying to find. But the poem might also be considered an indirect commentary on those who put too much stock in the false kind of sales talk forever poured on us by high-pressure agents. I suppose "All Revelation" will offend a few, particularly those who have devoted so much emotional energy to wildcat promotion schemes and have raved too lustily about the attractive features of corner lots in heaven. Fortunately the poem will baffle and confuse the wildcat speculators so much that they won't find in it any reference to themselves. Under such circumstances, Frost's riddles permit him to be very polite in his rudeness. The incident and the situation, compressed by the metaphor into a single moment, might be elaborated as an implied narrative of a prospector whose peculiar searches take him deep underground to a crystal cave where he glances appraisingly into the flashing mystery of an enormous geode. Wondering what the prospector thought and did about that strange sight (just what he had in mind, so to speak), Frost concludes that this self-dependent and exploratory method is a wise one; that no other approach to valid appraisal has ever improved on it. If the bold prospector had not been aggressive in his search, no secondhand answers would have satisfied him. Emerson elaborates the same thought in different metaphors, about halfway through his essay *Nature*. One might make an enlightening comparison between Emerson and Frost, two Yankees who have known and said many sharp things about the best ways for man to evaluate property. Each agrees that the individual is bound to be disappointed in his investments if he pays too much attention to the revelations of others, be they devils, men, or gods.

In spite of all his individualistic caution, Frost cherishes with passionate intensity that which he has acquired. With him, land frequently becomes the symbol of our most stable values. One so persistently devoted to the land might seem dangerously near to becoming its slave, or to be gloating over it with the possessive pride of the miser. But the poet's images of profits and dividends may always be reckoned most easily in terms of spiritual worth. He is the lover, not the slave. He yearns so constantly to share with the land this sense of possession that he offers his life to the land. Such a love becomes identical with the poet's deep love of his country. "The Gift Outright" is a poem written many years ago, yet its recent appearance marks it as the best war poem published since our latest enemies tried to dispute our ancient claims. At the risk of injuring the poem, I must quote a few lines from it here:

> Something we were withholding made us weak
> Until we found it was ourselves
> We were withholding from our land of living,
> And forthwith found salvation in surrender.
> Such as we were we gave ourselves outright—
> The deed of gift was many deeds of war . . .

Supporting "The Gift Outright" are three shorter poems which follow it and elaborate the viewpoint of property and possessions considered not from material angles but from spiritual ones.

An underlying sadness runs through these poems of possession. Life may be viewed tragically from mountain peaks or from valleys. It little matters that Robert Frost's tragic view was developed in the lowlands. That which does matter is his refusal to accept any invitation to "come into the dark and lament" those mortal boundaries which encroach on his instinctive and highly developed passion for possession. These mortal encroachments are able only to intensify the hunger of that pursuit which colors the poems of this fierce possessor. In his earlier books this intensity found expression in such poems as "Reluctance" and "To Earthward." In *A Witness Tree*, the theme is continued in such poems as "Carpe Diem," "The Quest of the Purple Fringed," and "Our Hold on the Planet." It also finds a different kind of expression in those many passages which offer sly answers to the pessimists and the bearers of evil tidings.

Naturally, such a book would be incomplete if it failed to consider the relation of the individual property holder to society and the state. Taxes on income and real-estate raise perennial questions which are indirectly handled in one of the finest poems. With habitual circumlocution the poet hides his remarks about possessions and taxes by giving the poem this title: "I Could Give All to Time." Don't be fooled by the metaphor. Frost finds his analogy, not through income-tax blanks and checks but through the more dramatic image of a customs officer who wants to stop us and take away from us so many of those precious things which we have accumulated through love and sagacity. The taxations of our government are not different from the periodic requirements of customs officers who challenge and charge us whenever we cross another boundary in our travels; but the poet goes further to find analogies between these charges and the insistence of Time that we pay a more serious tax, which mounts until finally we are required to surrender everything. Long ago, in "West-running Brook," he pointed out that the resistance to this forced spending is an instinctive human virtue. Instead of inflammatory hints at revolution, Frost quietly accepted the implications of that poem and urged that such resistance was at once futile and sacred. The paradox of human yearnings for permanence and the machinelike persistence of taxation, diminution, change, and loss to the individual may be found at the core of Frost's tragic sense of life. Recognizing and accepting this, the poet is not perplexed. Many of his poems have touched on the source of that paradox: heart and mind, the irrational desire and the rational knowledge contained within each human being. If we are so made, he says, the only vanity is to take too much pride in the bravery of human resistance to such change and loss; the only shameful humility is that which despairs at resistance because it seems futile. He acknowledges the sadness of giving up that which the heart has made sacred with its own cherishing. At the same time he insists that, so long as there is individual consciousness, there may be joy and a more intense pleasure in owning and being owned. Knowing these things, Frost concludes his poem with a bold assertiveness which is as intensely sincere as it is consciously ironic:

> I could give all to Time except—except
> What I myself have held. But why declare
> The things forbidden that while the Customs slept
> I have crossed to Safety with? For I am There
> And what I would not part with I have kept.

As so many have said, Frost's metaphors for these ancient problems and mysteries which touch on the individual and his relation to property are surprisingly varied. Those who have not recognized the subtlety and strength of his two-edged symbols may have missed much pleasure and understanding of our best poet. Furthermore, his fondness for the irony of paradox requires a cunning on the reader's part to match his own. A few years ago he wrote another poem in which he contrasted Time's perpetual drain of taxations with the heart's pleasure in those accumulations which make us talk wistfully of progress:

> We saw leaves go to glory,
> Then almost migratory
> Go part way down the lane,
> And then to end the story
> Get beaten down and pasted
> In one wild day of rain.
> We heard "'Tis over" roaring.
> A year of leaves was wasted.
> Oh, we make a boast of storing,
> Of saving and of keeping,
> But only by ignoring
> The waste of moments sleeping,
> The waste of pleasure weeping,
> By denying and ignoring
> The waste of nations warring.

The casual reader who comes on such a poem might conclude that Frost's outlook is a gloomy one. But he has consistently refused to be either an optimist or a pessimist about his lifelong investments in such a hopelessly wicked old world as this. In several of his new poems, and in many of the old ones, he makes pleasant use of those who have mistakenly grown dissatisfied with their investments and are forever looking wistfully backward or forward to more fortunate days. The despairing groans of his neighbors drive him frequently into happy songs which tease. Yet anyone who has examined the rocky texture of Frost's philosophic real-estate will not think of these lyrics as expressions of Pollyanna-like cheerfulness. Always there is inner humor to balance outer sadness, or outer humor to balance inner sadness. As he puts it, in "Wind and Rain":

> It were unworthy of the tongue
> To let the half of life alone
> And play the good without the ill.

Perhaps his clearest statement of his favorite position in the Golden Mean finds expression in the "Phi Beta Kappa Poem," delivered at Harvard in 1941. There he gave metrical form to ideas delightfully expressed in a prose letter on his sixtieth birthday, after the Amherst students had sent their greetings. In the letter he ridiculed the manner in which men assumed honors for themselves by deciding that they were living in the worst of all possible ages. Then he summed it up with this scornful flash of wit:

"It is immodest of a man to think of himself as going down before the worst forces ever mobilized by God."

Those who are interested in the aesthetic aspects of property will take particular pleasure in the varied felicity of the poems in *A Witness Tree*. From the beginning, Frost has never been bothered by those factions which have frequently clashed in argument as to whether poetry should give primary emphasis to manner or to matter. He has shown that good poetry always establishes a considerate relationship between being and meaning. To him, there are two distinct pleasures which the poet shares with his audience. The first is derived from happening on an idea freshly revealed. The second is derived from the delightful and appropriate images, phrases, and sentences which are combined and arranged to give a fitting weight and shape to the newly discovered idea. The thought of the poem and the form of the poem are so interdependent that neither one is artistically valid without the other. If he were required to choose one as more important to the poetic process than the other, he would probably be willing to trust in the vitality of the thought or idea to assume and acquire, in the act of finding its best statement, a genuinely poetical expression. Here again he shows his kinship with those American poets with whom he belongs in degree of accomplishment rather than in manner: Emerson, Whitman, and Emily Dickinson.

In matters of poetic theory, as in matters of real-estate, Robert Frost's breadth of vision is by no means so diffuse that he cannot bring it to focus with sharpness and clarity when occasion arises. Affable in his friendliness, he likes a good argument so much that he is always willing to define his differences. To him, the play of mind and heart is the thing, and he delights in the endless conflict. His own summary is perfect:

> And were an epitaph to be my story
> I'd have a short one ready for my own.
> I would have written of me on my stone:
> I had a lover's quarrel with the world.

NOTES

[1] From Robert Frost's prose introduction entitled "The Figure a Poem Makes," in *Collected Poems of Robert Frost*. Henry Holt and Company, New York, 1939.

[2] From Robert Frost's definitions of poetry, printed on the dust jacket of *West-running Brook*. New York, 1929.

[3] From Robert Frost's "Introduction" to Edwin Arlington Robinson's posthumous *King Jasper*. New York, 1935.

[4] From "Education by Poetry: A Meditative Monologue" given by Robert Frost at Amherst College; published in the *Amherst Graduates' Quarterly*, Vol. 20, No. 2 (February, 1931), pp. 75-85.

[5] From "The Figure a Poem Makes."

[6] *Ibid.*

[7] *Ibid.*

[8] From "The Poet's Next of Kin in a College," a talk given by Robert Frost at Princeton University on October 26, 1937; published in *Biblia*, Princeton, Vol. IX, No. 1 (February, 1938).

[9] From Emerson's essay, "The American Scholar."

[10] From Robert Frost's "Foreword" to his one-act play, *A Way Out*. New York, 1929.

[11] Quoted by W. S. Braithwaite, in "Robert Frost, New American Poet," *Boston Evening Transcript*, May 8, 1915, Part 3, p. 4.

[12] From "Education by Poetry."

[13] *Ibid.*

[14] "Dust in the Eyes," in *West-running Brook*, 1929.

[15] From "The Figure a Poem Makes."

[16] From Robert Frost's commemorative comment on "The Poetry of Amy Lowell," in the *Christian Science Monitor*, May 16, 1925.

[17] From Robert Frost's "Introduction" to *Dartmouth Verse*. Portland, 1925.

[18] From "Foreword" to *A Way Out*.

[19] Quoted by M. P. Tilley, in "Notes from Conversations with Robert Frost," in the *Inlander*, Vol. 20, No. 4 (February, 1918).

[20] Last stanza of "All Revelation," in *A Witness Tree*, 1942.

[21] From "The Poet's Next of Kin in a College."

[22] From "Introduction" to *King Jasper*.

[23] From "Build Soil," in *A Further Range*, 1935.

[24] One of the "Quantula," in *A Witness Tree*, 1942.

[25] From "A Star in a Stone-Boat," in *New Hampshire*, 1923.

[26] Mark Van Doren, "The Permanence of Robert Frost," in the *American Scholar*, Vol. 5, No. 2 (Spring, 1936).

[27] From "To Earthward," in *New Hampshire*, 1923.

[28] From Robert Frost's open letter to the *Amherst Student*; published in the *Amherst Student*, March 25, 1935. The substance of this exceptionally fine letter finds poetic expression in Frost's Phi Beta Kappa poem, "The Lesson for Today," in *A Witness Tree*, 1942.

[29] From "Education by Poetry."

[30] *Ibid.*

[31] Quoted by R. P. T. Coffin, in *New Poetry of New England*. Baltimore, 1938.

[32] From "Education by Poetry."

[33] Quoted by R. P. T. Coffin, *op. cit.*

[34] From the letter to the *Amherst Student.*

[35] *Ibid.*

[36] *Ibid.*

[37] *Ibid.*

[38] Quoted in *Books We Like—Sixty-Two Answers.* Boston, 1936.

[39] Quoted by R. P. T. Coffin, *op. cit.*

[40] From Robert Frost's "Introduction" to *The Memoirs of Stephen Burroughs.* New York, 1925.

[41] From Robert Frost's talk, "The Manumitted Student"; published in the *New Student*, Vol. VI, No. 1 (January 12, 1927).

[42] From Emerson's essay, "Self Reliance."

[43] From Robert Frost's talk, "Poverty and Poetry," given at Haverford College on October 25, 1937; published in *Biblia*, Princeton.

INDEX

INDEX

KEY TO ABBREVIATIONS

Surnames, alone, are used except when confusion may arise.

Articles are omitted from titles of poems.

Long titles are compressed.

Poems quoted *entire* are indicated thus: "quoted."

Poems quoted *in part* are indicated thus: "excerpt."

Poems analyzed briefly, or at length: "anal."